# Asian Pacific Americans
# in the Workplace

# Critical Perspectives on
# Asian Pacific Americans Series

The **Critical Perspectives on Asian Pacific Americans** series aims to educate and inform readers regarding the Asian Pacific American experience and critically examines key social, economic, psychological, cultural, and political issues facing Asian Pacific Americans. The series presents books that are theoretically engaging, comparative, and multidisciplinary, and works that reflect the contemporary concerns that are of critical importance to understanding and empowering Asian Pacific Americans.

SERIES TITLES INCLUDE

**Juanita Tamoyo Lott,** *Asian Americans: From Racial Category to Multiple Identities* (1997)
**Diana Ting Liu Wu,** *Asian Pacific Americans in the Workplace* (1997)

SUBMISSION GUIDELINES

Prospective authors of single or co-authored books and editors of anthologies should submit to us a letter of introduction, the manuscript or a four- to ten-page book proposal, a book outline, and a curriculum vitae. Please send your book manuscript/proposal packet to:

Critical Perspectives on Asian Pacific Americans Series
AltaMira Press
1630 North Main Street, Suite 367
Walnut Creek, CA 94596
(510) 938-7243

# Asian Pacific Americans in the Workplace

by

Diana Ting Liu Wu

ALTAMIRA
PRESS

*A Division of Sage Publications, Inc.*
Walnut Creek ■ London ■ New Delhi

For information address:

AltaMira Press
A Division of Sage Publications, Inc.
1630 North Main Street, Suite 367
Walnut Creek, CA 94596

SAGE Publications Ltd.
6 Bonhill Street
London EC2A 4PU
United Kingdom

SAGE Publications India Pvt. Ltd.
M-32 Market
Greater Kailash I
New Delhi 110 048 India


PRINTED IN THE UNITED STATES OF AMERICA


Library of Congress Cataloging-in-Publication Data


Wu, Diana Ting Liu.
    Asian Pacific Americans in the workplace / by Diana Ting Liu Wu.
        p.    cm. — (Critical perspectives on Asian Pacific Americans series)
    Includes bibliographical references and index.
    ISBN 0-7619-9122-0 (pbk.). — ISBN 0-7619-9121-2 (cloth)
        1. Pacific Islander Americans—Employment.  2. Asian Americans—
    Employment.  I. Title.  II. Series.
    HD8081.P33W8  1998
    331.6'3994073—dc21                                                97-33727
                                                                                   CIP


97    98    99    00    01    02    03    10    9    8    7    6    5    4    3    2    1

Editorial Management by Nicole Fountain and Joanna Ebenstein
Production Services by Andrea D. Swanson
Cover Artwork by Daniel Neh-Tsu Wu
Cover Design by Daniel Neh-Tsu Wu

# Contents

## Section II: Individual Attributes, Group Interactions, and Organization Issues

# Section III: Strategies for Change

For the Future Generations,
My Loving Family,
and
the Memories of
Robert P. S. Liu and Douglas N. Wu

# Preface

Early in 1981, a series of articles I authored about the organizational life of women in China were published in the *San Francisco Chronicle*. My mentor, Dr. Nevitt Sanford, suggested that I research the organizational life of their counterparts in the United States. I embraced this recommendation with great enthusiasm, conducted a modified pilot study, and produced a modest research report on "Immigrant Women in Professional Occupations." That work was done by interviewing a group of Asian American immigrant women who worked and excelled in historically male-dominated professions in the physical sciences and business.

The conclusion of the above report was quoted in many journals and picked up by various news media. That, in turn, sowed the seeds for an expanded research study of Asian Pacific Americans working in various levels of U.S. organizations. The full-blown study, inclusive of the aspirations and work experiences of Asian Pacific American men in the American workplace, has resulted, in part, in the current book.

Due to administrative duties as the chairperson of my department for three years and a subsequent unexpected illness from which it has taken me some time to recuperate, I was forced to accept a five-year hiatus from my work. It was not until 1993 that I began to pick up where I had left off, continuing the research process and updating my interview data by traveling from coast to coast, and to Chicago, Louisiana, Texas, and the various metropolitan areas where the majority of Asian Pacific Americans reside. The data culled from their experiences serve as the foundation of this book.

The technical framework of this book is based on principles of organization theory, using a multicultural organizational model. The study also uses principles, models, theories, and methods from other disciplines, synthesizing theory and learning from academic research with participative observation of case studies of Asian Pacific American workers. A significant amount of relevant research from various social science disciplines was reviewed, and insights were also drawn from the literature of college and university ethnic studies and Asian American studies courses. From these combined sources, practical suggestions are provided that may help Asian Pacific Americans and other minorities to gain valuable knowledge about working in American organizations and for the organizations to acquire knowledge about the Asian Pacific American experience.

My main goal was to create a different and interesting approach to exploring cultural diversity in the workplace, and the Asian Pacific American workforce in particular. At the same time, this book may contribute to a variety of intellectual disciplines, namely, the field of management and also the field of ethnic studies, which has begun to grow and develop in stature and impact in recent years.

The population groups selected for the field studies include both immigrants and U.S.-born Asian Pacific Americans. The individuals interviewed include managers, professionals, entrepreneurs, and members of the working class. Special attention is given to balancing the representatives of different Asian groups and to achieving equity in terms of harmonizing the number of male and female participants; younger versus more mature participants; well-established versus more recent immigrants; and U.S.-born Americans of Asian Pacific heritage, whether bilingual or monolingual.

Although the principal purpose of this book is to serve as a text for undergraduate students, its scope is broad enough that it also offers a major source of information for companies wishing to implement workshops or programs for more effective management of diversity. Through such resources, organizations may find the most appropriate methods of recruiting, training, coaching, and mentoring to minimize cultural differences, therefore maximizing productivity and efficiency in the workforce. Individuals can especially benefit from gaining a better understanding of organizational systems and corporate culture by comparing their own work experiences with those of the Asian Pacific American individuals discussed in the case studies.

I am a firm believer that any learning process, whether self-initiated or in a classroom situation, should be an enjoyable one. I use interview cases and vignettes to fully illustrate researched information, concepts, and theories. I am convinced that this is the most effective way to broaden the scope of readers' knowledge and for them to gain intrinsic understanding without causing them to feel overwhelmed by the volume of material presented or by many theoretical constructs and concepts that are not yet familiar to or popular with them.

One of the techniques I applied to maintain a smooth flow to the main text was to isolate highly technical information and theoretical concepts in boxed inserts in several chapters and in notes at the end of each chapter. The boxes highlight the important theoretical notions, and many of the notes provide supporting data and offer suggestions for more detailed study.

Also at the end of each chapter, discussion questions or experiential case analyses have been added to bring out the reader's own personal experiences and perceptions and allow these to serve as an extension to the intrinsic understanding of diversity issues in the workplace. I greatly enjoyed writing and formulating these questions and exercises especially for this book. I tried to provide challenges and hope that students will be stimulated by these activities. Finally, I hope that the book can help readers reeducate themselves to the principles of inclusion, mutual respect, and social justice.

I welcome your feedback on this book. Please feel free to contact me at Saint Mary's College of California, Moraga, CA 94575; e-mail dwu@stmarys-ca.edu.

Diana Ting Liu Wu, Ph.D.
*Department of Business Administration*
*Saint Mary's College of California*

# Acknowledgments

I wish to acknowledge the support, assistance, cooperation, and encouragement of the many people and organizations that helped me to accomplish this project. First of all, I owe an enormous debt to all the people who agreed to be interviewed and who provided additional information later on to bring this work to completion. Second, thanks to my editor and publisher, Larry Shinagawa and Mitch Allen of AltaMira Press, a division of Sage Publications, for their invaluable assistance in shaping this book.

I am also indebted to the Faculty Development Committee of Saint Mary's College of California for its generous support of my research; to my thousands of diligent students for asking such provocative questions; and to my colleagues at Saint Mary's for creating a wonderful, encouraging climate. In particular, I want to thank Katherine Roper, who generously shared her thoughts and publishing experience with me from the inception of this book; among the many others are Jerry Bodily, Dave Bowen, Edwin Epstein, John Thompson, Don Snyder, Wilber Chaffee, Suneel Udpa, Kusum Singh, Steve Sloane, and Ted Tsukahara, all of whom read my work at different stages and served as important sounding boards; and Norman Andreassen for his year-long, tireless efforts as my special editor to improve the clarity of the writing and for making me look good. Without his consistent good nature and superb skills, I could never have delivered this work in a timely manner.

In addition, I am grateful to my very dear friends, Joan Von Kaschnitz for imparting her proficient knowledge of English usage and style to me for decades; Drs. Ellie and Bob Fisher, for our many years of intellectual discussions and their constructive critique of my very first draft; to Chancellor Rose Y. Tseng for her confidence in me and for providing much useful information for chapter 6; to Dean H.Z. Liu, Dr. Martin Lee, Dr. Leon Chua, and Drs. Clara and B.L. Ho for reading and affirming my working proposal and providing insiders' perspectives on Asian Pacific Americans in the East Coast and midwestern regions; and to Dr. Mervin and Margie Freedman, Dr. Donald Corbin, Dr. Paul Mininger, Dr. Royal Foote, Dr. Barry Phegan, and to Minor and Rosemary Schmid for their unflagging support of me for more than two decades.

I also wish to thank the following people who have directly or indirectly inspired me to undertake this academically and intellectually challenging work or who offered me their personal encouragement throughout the duration of this project: Brother Mel Anderson, Brother Jerome West, Brother Camillus Chavez, Brother James Leahey, Brother O. De Sales Perez, Brother William Beattie, Brother Brendan Kneale, Sister Clare Wagstaffe, William Hynes, Valerie Gomez, Penelope Washbourn, Theodora Carlisle, Fred Anderson, Stephanie Bangert, Norm Bedford, Marguerite Boyd, Tom Brown, Jack Cassidy, Kristine Chase, Monica Clyde, William Halpin, Eric Kolhede, Bill Lee, Joe Lupino, Asbjorn Moseidjord, Alan Pollock, Nelson Shelton, Nobi Stienecker, Roy Allen, Mike Walter, and Stan White.

Special appreciation is extended to the following friends who have provided cheer, laughter, and emotional support during the writing of this book: Ben and Jane, Diana and Leon, Shirley and David, Linda and Peter, Celia and Larry, Angela and H. S., Beulah and C.B., Helen and John, Lily and John, Shirley and Raymond, Veve and Walter, Trudy and Joe, Linda and Fred, Louisa and Tony, Margaret and Leong, Sophie and Jack, Maryann and Bill, Jeanne and Sam, Emily and Martin, Jean and Tony; and all of their children, especially Amy, Larry, Chris, Melinda, Joyce, Serene, Norman, Linus, Mona, Judd, William, Leon, Cindy, Lily, Catherine, and Vicki, who provided me with fresh perspectives on traditional thoughts.

I owe deep gratitude to my parents, Robert P. S. and Alice Liu; my sister, Holly Wong; my brother, William Lau, and his wife Mila; and to Patrick

Fontaine, who are all globe-trotters, representing the circle of space-age business associates who transact business worldwide and travel to Asia, Europe, and many other parts of the world as frequently as I make my trips to Safeway and the ATM. Their conviction of blending world culture at the speed of light has brought me yet again the perspective that America's rising diversity is its major strength behind the new world order.

Finally, I owe more than thanks to my family: George, my husband, for his loyalty and support of my many nontraditional, nonwifely roles; Gloria, my first daughter, a television host and a creative journalist, who has given me continuous inspiration, always boosting my spirits with her wit and humanity; Greta, my second daughter, a Wharton School MBA who works on Wall Street and has brought me many insights into her fast-moving generation, helped me gather research material, and also gave me valuable suggestions for formulating the theoretical typology model; Dan, my son and youngest, a recent architecture graduate who introduced me to many aspects of youth culture and also contributed his artistic style with countless hours in the design process for the cover of this book. Without their significant contributions and prolific ideas, I would not have enjoyed the wonderful experience of producing such a book.

SECTION I

# The Emergence of Asian Pacific
# Americans in the Workforce

PART ONE

The Emergence of Asian Pacific
Americans in the Workforce

# Introduction

## The Remodeled Minority

*Important note to the reader: The scenario below is fictitious but was derived from pertinent comments taken from several actual interviews. The names of the participants (as well as the names of all of the others interviewed for this book) were changed to protect their privacy.*

Stan looks like a mild-mannered, mellow kind of guy, the sort who sits on the sidelines at these big conventions, watching his colleagues do all the networking, all of the show and tell.[1] But Stan sure does not speak like a mellow guy. He is one of those Asian Pacific Americans who has "made it" in the American scientific workforce. He, and many others who share his general background, tend to believe that their own intelligence and personal achievements have transformed the old "house boy" stereotype of Chinese Americans into a more recent, and far more positive, "model minority" image.

"You want me to be frank?" Stan asks, speaking to a small group of colleagues. "Okay, listen to this: Herrnstein and Murray[2] are 100 percent on the ball as far as intelligence is concerned. The statistics in *The Bell Curve*[3] prove that the intelligence of Asians tops all the other *Homo sapiens*. You want to know something else? Among Asians, Chinese are the smartest, just like the Jews are the brightest among Anglos. All the most significant discoveries are made by Chinese and Jews. Don't look so shocked! Aren't you Chinese? Are you Shanghainese? You had the good fortune to be born into a Shanghai family. Don't you know how the noodle-eating northern Chinese compare to the rice-eating southerners? Just think of all the most successful and famous Asians in the United States. Ninety percent of them are from the north of China, and half of them are Shanghainese. What do the southerners do? They stay in Chinatown and make fortune cookies. I tell you, it's all in the genes. Just look around at this convention. How many African Americans do you see? See all those Asians over there? They're speaking Mandarin to each other."

"You are so audacious!" interrupts C.L., one of the Asian Pacific Americans in the group to whom Stan has been speaking. "Why are you spilling your guts so loudly in public like that?"

Deep down, C.L. knows that such ethnocentric thinking is not unusual; it is actually quite common among Chinese Americans who immigrated to the U.S. during the late 1940s and early 1950s to escape the communist takeover of mainland China.

C.L. is one of the "second-wave educated Chinese" who came to the U.S. between the late 1950s and early 1970s as graduate exchange students from universities in Taiwan and Hong Kong. Unlike the earliest immigrants to the U.S. from China, who viewed themselves as sojourners in America, this "second-wave" group of immigrants came hoping to build new homes as permanent settlers, truly believing in the U.S. as a land of opportunity where their children could receive a better education and a more promising life.[4] Many, like C.L., stayed to join the American workforce and established careeers in medicine, engineering, education, and other professions. A few became university professors, entrepreneurs, local politicians, or psychologists and sociologists.

"Look around more carefully," C.L. continues. "I see people with Asian Indian ancestry, Japanese ancestry—you can't just ignore them all, Stan. And as for African Americans, how much do you really know about them? Have you studied African American history or culture? If not, perhaps I can recommend a few of Carter Goodwin Woodson's books."[5]

As it happens, C.L. has recently read through his grandchildren's ethnic studies textbooks, including chapters on African American scientists and scholars. With the material fresh in his mind, C.L. decides to chastise his colleague.

"As I recall, your wife received a blood transfusion last summer, Stan. Don't you think you should acknowledge the debt of gratitude you owe to an African American, Dr. Charles Drew?[6] And didn't you also telephone your children to let them know that their mother was recovering her health? If so, you may wish to thank Granville T. Woods, also an African American, for inventing the transmitter technology.[7] When your wife recovered, you drove her home in your air-conditioned car. Are you familiar with the name Frederick Jones, the inventor of the refrigeration system? Are you aware that Jones, too, was an African American?"[8]

Actually, C.L. knows all too well that his supposedly well-educated colleagues do not devote much of their time to reading or studying anything that lies outside of their own fields of expertise. In fact, C.L. believes that a too-narrow focus has prevented some of his friends, and even one of his own sons, from receiving promotions which might otherwise have been theirs. Remembering such disappointments, C.L. becomes more compassionate.

"You know," he says, "no one should dismiss the devastating psychological effects of having been conditioned for generations to expect no more than second-class citizenship. Many African American children grow up in an economically depressed environment and are subject to fear and oppression. How do you believe your own children and grandchildren would behave if they had to worry every day about the possibility of getting shot? If the first thing on one's mind is mere survival; getting good grades in school is probably the last thing on one's mind.

"And even so, many African Americans continue to excel. They refuse to give up on their dreams of social justice and true equality. A few have dared to use confrontation as a mechanism of social change—but soon, there will be a transition from using physical power to using knowledge-based power. I have taught college students for some years now. The number of brilliant Black scholars is increasing."

"Personally, Stan, I think you are cruel," says Ng, who has also been listening. "It is cruel to make remarks about Chinatown and the Cantonese. They are the forefathers in this country, the ones who built the foundation for us latecomers. Think of their sweat and blood, their tremendous hardships and the humiliation of enduring the White man's world, the corrosive effects of continuous exposure to the discriminating system set up over many generations by Europeans. The establishment of Chinatown sheltered many valuable souls. They provided part-time jobs in their business establishments so students like you could work and earn the money you needed to attend college. Without them, you would not have your graduate degree. You would not be at this conference today."

Ng, a Cantonese descendent, belongs to a more recent group of Chinese Americans, those who come from Hong Kong or Taiwan armed with modern business skills—and the investment capital—to stimulate California's economy and revitalize its real estate market. The BMWs and Mercedes of "investment immigrants" like Ng dot California's neighborhood landscapes.[9]

"I also think you are a little ignorant," Ng continues, "to connect *The Bell Curve* with the 'model minority' image. There are many kinds of intelligence. Even if there is some validity to the comparison of I.Q. scores, those who have a high I.Q. may not be worth a dime if they can't acquire an E.Q. along the way." By the term "E.Q.," Ng is referring to "emotional intelligence," a concept widely celebrated since Daniel Goleman demonstrated in his recent book that lack of E.Q. can cause problems in all aspects of life. It can also sabotage the intellect and ruin careers.[10] But it is not something fixed at birth; E.Q. can be nurtured and further developed in each of us.

Ng, who recently participated in a discussion group on the controversial subjects of I.Q. and E.Q., actually finds Stan's arrogance somewhat amusing. He decides to take Stan down a few more pegs. "I guess it's true there will always be a need for scientists," Ng continues, "but economic growth and American prosperity in the next century will depend on the contributions of the Asian Pacific Americans who understand more than the pure sciences or high technology. The future belongs to those of us who can combine knowledge of human potential, business, finance, and international trade. American trade with Asian and Pacific countries totals more than 300 billion dollars, more than any other region in the world.

"Look at Pacific Rim Plaza and the North Valley in San Jose, California; it's a perfect example of how one skilled in business—in this case, a group headed by Asian Pacific Americans—can transform a depressed neighborhood into a growth area, even in today's slow economy. We *are* the model minority. As President Clinton said, we represent a bridge."

"Excuse me," snaps Ann, "but I think all of you guys are missing the point. Intelligence alone, without human compassion and humanity, is monstrous." Ann is a social worker of Vietnamese ancestry. Her husband, a Korean American, is a college professor of engineering.

"You glorify this catchy but simplistic and meaningless term, 'model minority,' and yet you harbor racist attitudes toward other groups. Every week I read anti-Asian news accounts, and yet prejudice against African Americans and Latinos is more widespread among Asian immigrants than among the U.S.-born generations. Many U.S.-born children of immigrant Asians are deeply ashamed of their parents' racism.[11] So please, don't congratulate yourselves too soon for your successful contributions to the American economy and workforce as scientists, engineers, physicians, or entrepreneurs.

"How much do any of you really know about the different groups of Asian Pacific Americans on a national scale? It's a different situation for the newest immigrants in the inner city, the disadvantaged refugees—take, for example, the new Phnom Penh.[12] Sure, the most highly educated and exceptionally talented among us have built professional careers—but how many of you know any Asian Americans who have worked their way up into managerial positions? How many of your friends have broken through the "glass ceiling"?[13] How many of you can even say you truly understand the workings of American organizations? How many can say you are truly equals in the workforce?"

Neither Stan, C.L., nor Ng seem to have sufficient knowledge to respond to Ann's questions. The group disbands and they all quietly go their separate ways. Thus, our study of Asian Pacific Americans in the workforce has begun.

## The Perceptual Paradigm

The discussion between Stan, C.L., Ng, and Ann serves to illustrate aspects of the self-concepts of this small segment of the Asian Pacific American population, as well as some of their perceptions of other Asian Pacific Americans and of the world around them. The intention is to organize this information into a perceptual paradigm which will allow readers to translate the experiences of Asian Pacific Americans into experiences similar to their own, thereby gaining a greater measure of understanding of the Asian Pacific American experience. Psychologists in general have long held that each individual gives his or her own meaning to stimuli, with different individuals interpreting and processing the same situation in different ways.[14] As described by Krech, Crutchfield, and Ballachey, the cognitive process of the individual mind is not a photographic construction but rather is partially a personal construction.[15] Each perceiver selects (or ignores) objects and interprets symbols and events in light of his or her own experiences, like an artist painting a picture of the world that expresses and reflects his or her own individual view of reality.

For example, the Asian Pacific Americans in our story all enjoy professional careers and seem to have "made it" in mainstream America, despite several of them being foreign born. Collectively, individuals such as these have created the positive perception of Asian Pacific Americans known as the "model minority" paradigm. However, another perception lies behind that paradigm, one which contains an implicit political message: the U.S. remains a land of opportunity for hard-working minorities, and despite racial discrimination in American society, Asian Pacific Americans, as a "race," have become "successful." Therefore, according to the model, their actions and beliefs should be emulated by members of other races who wish to achieve similar goals. This gives a false perception of success as depending on qualitative judgments about the culture of a given ethnic group and also deemphasizes many complex social, political, and historical factors.[16]

It is important to mention here that many today interpret a "race" to be a social and political construction, as defined by Omi and Winant,[17] but a more encompassing definition would be the broader context proposed by Shinagawa and Pang; that is, a "race" is "a group of individuals who are given a set of values, beliefs, and sterotypical behavior based upon their perceived visible averaged phenotype, most especially by their skin color."[18] Using this latter definition—in which the perceptions of others are the deciding factor—it is possible for individuals who do not necessarily identify with a particular race to belong to it nonetheless. The significance of perception thus cannot be stressed highly enough. We will return to this notion later and present further examples.

According to a recent article in the *New York Times* (May 30, 1996), Asian Pacific Americans have now decisively undergone a perceptual transformation[19] in that more and more ethnic groups of Asian or Pacific Islander heritage have finally embraced the term "Asian Pacific American" as their racial identity, although this coming together has been largely for practical reasons—namely, to impact social and political equality on a larger scale. Nevertheless, on a different level, the reality remains that each ethnic subgroup still has its own distinct needs, agenda, and concerns. As the story of Stan and his colleagues demonstrates, even among Asian Pacific Americans with the same general economic standing and the same ethnicity and country of origin, there are different perceptions, priorities, and visions. This book attempts to reveal these differences by presenting individual cases and life histories of a variety of Asian Pacific Americans and their perceptions and insights regarding adaptation to the American workforce.

## Asian Pacific Americans in the Workforce:
## A Recent Manifestation?

Today, almost 10 million Americans can trace their roots to Asia and the Pacific Islands. Along with a vast array of skills, Americans of Asian and Pacific Island ancestry brought their remarkable traditions of hard work and respect for family and education to their new country. Their belief in the American Dream of equality and opportunity enabled them to face the challenges of adversity and discrimination and achieve a record of distinguished service in all fields, from academia to government, from business to military, and medicine to the arts. . . .

In recent years, newly arrived groups of Asian and Pacific Peoples have continued to enrich our proud tradition of cultural diversity and endow our Nation with energy and vision. Today, as we prepare to enter the 21st century, we must continually strive to fulfill the ideas that originally attracted so many immigrants to our shores.

U.S. President William J. Clinton
*(Proclamation of Asian Pacific Heritage Month, May 1997)*

Asian Pacific Americans have become the fastest growing minority group in the United States. Currently, half of the immigrants entering the United States arrive from Asian and Pacific nations. Furthermore, widespread news accounts and other publicity in recent years indicate that Asian Pacific Americans have become this country's most successful and affluent minority group. No doubt many Americans feel somewhat confused, or even alarmed, by the unprecedented and seemingly overwhelming number of new arrivals from Pacific Rim nations. What forces or events lie behind this change? Why is it happening now? And what are the implications for the future of the American workforce?

Part of the story is a change in U.S. immigration policy. Historically, up until the U.S. immigration law was amended in 1965, immigrants admitted to the U.S. were almost exclusively of European extraction.[20] Not surprisingly, therefore, as recently as 1965, the Asian Pacific American population was estimated at only one million people. By 1980, however, it had more than tripled, reaching 3.8 million, and by the 1990 official census, it was 7.3 million (7,273,662).[21] The number of Asian Pacific Americans was recently estimated to be 9.8 million people in 1996,[22] and is expected to reach 12.1 million by the year 2000.[23] This rate of population growth surpasses the rates for White Americans, African Americans, and Latino Americans.[24]

The new Asian Pacific Americans are not only more numerous than their predecessors, they are also a far more diverse group. The Asians who did come to the U.S. in the past were not only fewer in number, they came from fewer different countries and, in general, tended to be more alike both in terms of background and in terms of the contributions they made to American society. For example, most of the Chinese immigrants who arrived in the eighteenth century had peasant-class backgrounds, and, once in America, nearly all worked as laborers. In contrast, today's Asian Pacific Americans reflect a broader spectrum of cultural values, economic backgrounds, and social classes. Whether from the largest Asian immigrant groups, such as Filipino Americans or Chinese Americans; a midsized group such as Korean Americans, Japanese Americans, Asian Indian Americans, or Vietnamese Americans; or a small population group such as the Thai Americans and Pacific Islanders,[25] Asian Pacific American immigrants today, as a group, are likely to be highly educated.

According to a 1994 survey by the U.S. census, 41 percent of Asian Pacific Americans have four-year college degrees, compared to 22 percent for the general population. About 18 percent of Asian Pacific Americans hold doctoral or professional degrees, in comparison to only 9 percent of the general population. And 23 percent of Asian Pacific American workers are professionals: the Asian Pacific American population includes nearly 11 percent of this nation's practicing physicians and 7 percent of our scientists and engineers.[26] Additional statistics are given in chapter 2.

Based in part on compelling statistics such as those presented above, and on reports on television and the other media, Asian Pacific Americans have been dubbed America's "model minority."[27] Whether one embraces this portrait or rejects it as stereotype or myth, the fact remains that the Asian Pacific American workforce is a vital human resource too valuable for organizations to waste or underutilize. Many Asian Pacific Americans are well positioned to contribute substantially to economic development and organizational change, especially with regard to valuing diversity. They bring cutting-edge technology and a variety of skills to the American workforce that are revitalizing business communities and helping to ensure American competitiveness in global trade.

As President Clinton remarked to the Congressional Asian Pacific American Caucus (CAPAC) Institute dinner in Washington, D.C., on May 16, 1996:

> Our ticket to the future economically is in the Asian Pacific Region. It already accounts for a quarter of the world's output, growing every day. Already more than half our trade is with the nations of the Pacific, sustaining three million good American jobs.
>
> Exports to Asia have increased by 44 percent. . . . A lot of you have been in the forefront of that, and I thank you for your contributions to America. . . . Your devotion to learning, to hard work, to family, to the ideas of entrepreneurialism and the idea of engagement with the rest of the world . . . will keep America great in the 21st century.

## Focus of This Book

This book focuses on the presentation and analysis of some unique personal experiences and individual perceptions of Asian Pacific Americans of varying backgrounds and personalities. The basic framework is grounded in organization theory with a multicultural perspective and multidisciplinary approach. It is also engaged in the humanistic orientation; people's attitudes, perceptions, feelings, and goals are essential elements of this book. On a practical level, it recognizes that racism still permeates our society and the work environment. But prejudice and discrimination are not genetic traits of the White majority; they span across races, genders, and generations. Without a doubt, it is in all of our best interests, and is our common duty, to fight this common enemy. Racism cannot be accepted. But this book is not about the causes or nuances of racism. It is about how a variety of resourceful individuals used different strategies to transform themselves, develop professionally, and transcend undesired circumstances. Thus, the emphasis is on the self and the micro-environment, whereas the goal is to make a contribution to larger realms.

So far, chapter 1 has provided only a brief, general introduction to the complex subject of Asian Pacific Americans. Following this summary of the book's overall plan, the remainder of chapter 1 offers further historical information about Asian Pacific Americans—currently the fastest growing segment of the U.S. population—and a typology model for Asian Pacific Americans.

Chapter 2 supplies the reader with statistical data and basic background information on the Asian Pacific American population and its different ethnic components. Topics include the classifications and categorizations used by the U.S. government and how Asian Pacific Americans are currently perceived statistically in terms of ethnicity, community, occupation, educational attainments, and dollar earnings.

The subject of motivation theory and theories concerning role behavior in the workplace are introduced in chapter 3 to help explain the internal forces, familial predominance, and cultural influences acting upon many among the Asian Pacific American population and their performance in the workforce. Several case studies are used to help readers make continuous connections between theories and practices. Many readers will find the subjects' strong personalities and the factors that influenced the attainment of their goals especially intriguing.

Chapter 4 focuses on recent and current workplace experiences of individual Asian Pacific Americans; their self-images; and other perceptions, attitudes, and behaviors as influenced by the work environment. Five individual

cases concerning persons of different ethnicities and the historical background of their time are used to gain understanding of these individuals'
differing approaches to a career path and their reflections upon their experiences. Discussion questions centered on different ethnicities are provided at
the end of the chapter.

Chapter 5 considers the issues of generation identity and gender identity
using additional case studies. Many comments made by the "baby boomers"
will be of special interest to second- and third-generation Asian Pacific
Americans. Other cases illustrate the dilemmas and stresses felt by younger
Asian Pacific Americans in an increasingly competitive domestic economy
and globalized civilization. The viewpoints of the younger generation are
contrasted by the patient wisdom of the "silent generation" and the intense
perspectives of two young women who, by any standards, are "super achievers." The latter represent modern women living on the leading edge of the
coming twenty-first century.

Chapter 6 introduces a major issue in relation to the American work
environment—the glass ceiling—and the research conducted in this area. The
theoretical concepts and current research into decision-making and leadership
styles in relation to Asian Pacific Americans are presented and discussed.
Some possible approaches are introduced by which Asian Pacific Americans
may be able to improve their positions within organizations, along with
thoughts about future prospects for breaking through the glass ceiling.

Chapter 7 begins with a discussion of the importance of understanding
organizational culture and also considers the values of appearance and office
etiquette and the appropriate behavior for creating opportunities for promotion and career advancement. The sound advice of several management
consultants and executives is provided as a useful guide to anyone wishing to
enter the executive ranks and become a manager or administrator, whether
they are Asian Pacific American or not.

Chapter 8 returns the discussion to the importance of a harmonious balance
between the influences of external forces, such as globalization, and the needs
of individuals, their families, and the organization. Will globalization be a
force for change for the future? Can organizations make the workplace more
conducive to family needs and enable *every* individual to achieve a fuller
development of his or her human potential, at the same time accomplishing
the organization's goals? Finally, if there is a "model minority" worthy of the
respect and emulation of the rest of the world, it is suggested that such a
model can be found in the idea of a globally oriented, ethically sensitive,
inspirational organizational manager who, regardless of background, with the

support of corporate America can bring about positive changes for all individuals, families, communities, and nations.

The eight chapters in this book are also divided into three main parts. Section I provides the basic background information, theoretical constructs, and statistical data relating to Asian Pacific Americans. Section II presents cases revealing individual experiences, group interactions, and issues that relate to Asian Pacific Americans within the context of formal organizations. Section III contributes models for change, once again, for the individual, the group, and the organization.

Each chapter closes with discussion questions, a case for critical thinking, and an experiential exercise. To obtain the maximum benefit from the book, active participation in the exercises and in case discussions is strongly encouraged. There is no better approach than active involvement for enabling readers to make personal connections between their own experiences and others', consolidating the theories and concepts presented in the text. Therefore, as soon as you finish reading the text of each chapter, proceed to its end sections right away and start working through or thinking about the exercises and questions.

According to an ancient Chinese sage, the journey of a thousand miles begins with the first step. As we will see below, the first steps in the journeys of Asian Pacific Americans were taken many generations ago.

## A Typology Model:
## Three Typologies for Asian Pacific Americans

Based on research data, general observations, and in-depth interviews with individual Asian Pacific Americans, a general pattern emerged which illuminates the adaptation process of being an Asian Pacific American. It appears that the Asian Pacific American population can generally be distinguished with a typology clustered with three types of compromising pairs, each recognizable by its distinctive characteristics. How any particular individual is identified as belonging to one of the three paired types depends on the interplay of many factors, including (1) basic personality and perceptual paradigm; (2) life situation and experiences, such as whether one grew up in the U.S. or overseas before entering the country; (3) the economic, political, social, and other external forces in the environment; and (4) the availability of opportunities for interacting with others within U.S. society. All such factors may contribute to an individual's belonging to one or another category of the typology.

The construction of a typology which uses paired types was based on a deliberate decision to reflect the traditional Taoist polarities, called *Yin* and *Yang,* which set the limits of the cycles of change. The original meanings of this archetypal word pair were the sunny and shady sides of a mountain. Like the mountain, every simple, recognizable object has its two sides: *Yang,* the active and rational; and *Yin,* the passive and intuitive. The forces of *Yin* and *Yang* are opposed yet complementary and mutually dependent; taken together, they represent harmony and the balance of all things.

It is vital to emphasize that the proposed typology offered here is not meant as a tool for "rating" individuals, and that there are neither desirable nor undesirable traits per se, neither an intrinsically "good" nor a "bad" side to the polarizations.

| *Yin* | | *Yang* |
|---|---|---|
| Abnegators | ⟵——⟶ | Pragmatists |
| Assimilators | ⟵——⟶ | Autonomists |
| Progressivists | ⟵——⟶ | Altruists |

*Definition and Description*

## 1. Abnegators/Pragmatists

*Abnegate*: to deny oneself or renounce
*Pragmatist*: self-important one; one who acts only in practical matters

Asian Pacific American individuals of Abnegator/Pragmatist type are the indigent souls who may be impoverished extrinsically or intrinsically, or both. The extrinsically disadvantaged include many impecunious immigrants who arrived in the U.S. under arduous circumstances and remain in ethnic enclaves due to factors such as educational disadvantage or a language barrier that prohibits or limits their adjustment to mainstream American culture. Many such individuals have untransferable educations or professions from the old country and so are forced to live in the U.S. in substandard conditions with others in similar circumstances. Some survive on public aid programs. Others may find employment in ethnic enterprises for low wages, which further curtails assimilation. Abnegators have never developed the skills needed to socialize with people whose lives differ substantially from their own. They generally abide by their own traditions and may live their entire lives, and eventually die, within an ethnic community—almost as though they had never left their nation of origin. It is also true that many such individuals did not choose to emigrate but rather came to the U.S. under extenuating circumstances, such as refugees who were uprooted by revolution, war, or some other cataclysmic political event.

The Abnegator/Pragmatist type also includes many immigrants who are better educated but may not possess any kind of cultural literacy. They include U.S.-educated technicians and academicians, as well as investor immigrants, who may be astute business entrepreneurs and quite sophisticated in their technical skills and knowledgeable about investments. In most cases, the people who are of this second type of Abnegator/Pragmatist are highly temporal. They may feel nostalgic or express affiliation with the culture of their nation of origin, expressed by retention of native cuisine or other household traditions out of habit, but there is neither a strong feeling of devotion nor any intellectual attachment. At the same time, they feel no special loyalty to U.S. culture, whatever they perceive it to be. Instead, they often feel they owe allegiance mainly to their own agenda and to whatever project(s) they have on hand at the moment. They will tend to pick and choose from among the various elements of both U.S. mainstream culture and the culture of their nation of origin whatever they deem to be fashionable, and they will deliberately use these mixed elements, often with skill and great intelligence, in their pursuit of their own goals. For example, such individuals often maintain their traditional culture at home and speak their native language within the family, but they join in the mainstream culture from 9 to 5 in order to obtain the economic benefits which support their family. They may live in suburban America, but they socialize almost exclusively with members of their own ethnic group and invest only as much of their time and energy into the assimilation process as is required to support their workplace activities.

## 2. Assimilators/Autonomists

*Assimilate*: to take in and understand; to make similar
*Autonomist*: one who is independent in the sense of being self-contained and self-governing

Asian Pacific American individuals of the Assimilator/Autonomist type are those who have gone through the acculturation process; they can be further divided into two groups. Those in the first group have assimilated into the mainstream American culture and become distanced from their own ethnicity. Many have severed most ties with any ethnic-based family or "old country" traditions. In some cases, an Assimilator/Autonomist simply has no personal experience of the traditional Asian Pacific American culture(s) from which his or her ancestors emerged. In other cases, an Assimilator/Autonomist may, for a variety of reasons, have deliberately chosen to turn away from the "old" and embrace the "new." Many individuals of this type consider themselves "completely Americanized" and have little, if any, conscious identification with their ethnic culture of origin. They are likely to speak English at home and unlikely to teach their children more than a few words of any Asian languages they may know. This sort of "one-way street" acculturation is often the result of a lengthy process spanning multiple generations of U.S.-born family members and can include assimilation through intermarriage with White Americans or with individuals of other ethnicities who do not identify strongly with their own ethnic heritage.

Members of the second group have gone through acculturation and become assimilated through education or enterprise but have emerged as independent thinkers who are well integrated, more expansive, more complex, and have developed their own value systems. They may embrace the notion of multiculturalism or perceive themselves as being a "person of the world." Devoting their time to their own profession and the things they know best, they concentrate on making a contribution to their own field of expertise, whether this be in the arts, sciences, or humanities. They are very often creative people with innovative ideas, and they are capable of feeling at ease in any cultural or social setting.

Assimilator/Autonomists tend not to separate their workplace self-image from their at-home self-image. The people with whom they socialize will be very similar to the people with whom they work in terms of culture and values, educational attainment, economic status, social consciousness, and intellectual capacities.

### 3. Progressivists/Altruists

*Progressivist*: one who promotes reforms or changes and believes in progress
*Altruist*: one characterized by a selfless concern for others

Asian Pacific American individuals of the Progressivist/Altruist type, like the Assimilators, are typically well-versed in American culture and values, but they differ from the Assimilators/Autonomists in that they are also immersed in their Asian Pacific American traditions. They are likely to identify strongly with their ethnic heritage. Thus, like the better educated members of the Abnegator/Pragmatist group, Progressivists/Altruists make use of elements from both their own ethnic traditions and from mainstream American culture, but unlike the Abnegators/ Pragmatists, Altruists are more idealistic than pragmatic. They are more socially responsible and have greater compassion for humanity. Instead of focusing on a personal agenda, the Progressivists/Altruists will tend to focus on "the big picture" and direct their energies toward improving life not only for other Asian Pacific Americans but for the betterment of society as a whole.

Having built careers for themselves and secured comfortable homes beyond the poverty and other limits of the ethnic enclave, some Progressivists are willing to return and use their position to help members of more recently arrived immigrant groups through activities such as teaching, training, and mentoring individuals. Others remain in the mainstream and use their position as a platform from which to advocate social change and champion the cultural diversity movement. Either way, individuals of the Progressivist/Altruist type are the ones who try to change the traditional organizational culture, promote diversity in the workplace, and foster the development of human growth. They are the transformationists who hope to create a new world order for the advancement of humanity and civilization.

Table 1.1
*The APA (Asian Pacific American) Typology Model*

|  | *Abnegator/Pragmatist* | *Assimilator/Autonomist* | *Progressivist/Altruist* |
|---|---|---|---|
| Major Traits | Passive, narrow-minded, self-centered, predisposed, dislikes conflict, and tends to focus on deficiencies. Has a negative view of people. | Positive, sociable, flexible in mind: creative, independent thinker. Has considerable faith in other people. | Assertive, capable, conscientious, and committed. Often charismatic. Has compassion for other people. |
| Attitudes | Tendency to withdraw inwardly. Lacks faith in humanity as a whole. Works for extrinsic needs only. | Thorough in handling projects. Critical of those who lack appropriate world-view. Works for intrinsic rewards. | Outgoing and friendly. Strong desire to improve the conditions of human existence. Works for social causes and humanity. |
| Perceptions | Poor (low) self-esteem. Easily depressed. Lack of control and of foresight. Fatalistic. | High self-concept. Believes in the self as having the power to effect change. | High self-concept. Willing to "play the game" to transform social setting and the workplace. |

*Remarks*

The divisions between all three types are permeable, so it is possible (even normal) for individuals to move from any one type toward another. Factors such as education and training programs and constructive organizational and social policy change are powerful forces for moving individuals from left to right on Table 1.1, just as traumatic life events and negative social forces such as the glass ceiling, sexual harrassment, or a tragedy in the family can act to move individuals, at least temporarily, from right toward left.

Furthermore, individuals who are "fresh off the boat" may experience more difficulty in a new environment, but in no way does this make them inadequate or stereotypical. They may fall into any one of the three types, depending on the various internal and external factors mentioned previously.

## Summary

Asian Pacific Americans, a term used by the U.S. Census Bureau for convenience, describes a diverse group of individuals perceived in the U.S. as constituting a unique race. Since the Immigration Act of 1965 opened the door for Asian Pacific Americans, a large number of professional-class and wealthy investor immigrants have entered this country from Asia and Pacific Rim countries. This elite group, along with many highly educated U.S.-born Asian Pacific Americans, has evoked a public perception of Asian Pacific Americans as a "model minority" who, despite being perceived as members of a social underclass who experienced racial discrimination throughout U.S. history, have achieved success in American society.

This book is intended to shed light on the work experiences of Asian Pacific Americans by presenting individual case histories in the context of organization theory.[28] The technical framework of the book is founded on principles of organization theory using a multicultural perspective model while synthesizing theory and research with case studies of Asian Pacific American workers, drawing also on the contributions of such notables as Ronald Takaki, Sucheng Chan, Harry Kitano, and Roger Daniels.[29] The text is divided into three sections. Section I provides basic background information, theoretical constructs, and statistical data. Section II presents cases revealing individual experiences, group interactions, and issues that relate to Asian Pacific Americans in the context of formal organizations. Section III contributes models for change, once again, for the individual, the group, and the organization. The research methodology involves both qualitative field studies and quantitative analysis.[30] Suggestions for improving the traditional organizational culture and facilitating individual growth are also provided. Discussion questions, a case for critical thinking, and an experiential exercise appear at the end of each chapter to facilitate active participation in class discussions.

Finally, I hope that readers will not only acquire a deeper understanding of the experiences of Asian Pacific Americans workers but will also profit from new perspectives that can help individuals become more effective participants in the U.S. economic mainstream and eventually transform the workplace. The book can be a source of information for organizations wishing to implement programs for more effectively managing diversity, such as training, coaching, and mentoring to minimize cultural differences and maximize productivity and efficiency. It can also assist students and prospective managers in understanding the role of Asian Pacific Americans in the workforce as well as organization systems and traditional corporate culture.

◆ ◆ ◆ ◆ ◆

## CASE FOR CRITICAL THINKING

### *Bridging Community Differences with Cross-Cultural Understanding*

The Martin Luther King, Jr. Korean Scholarship was first presented to the City of San Francisco by the Seoul Metropolitan Government in 1993. Each year, the scholarship enables a small group of African American students to travel to Yonsei University International Graduate School in Seoul, Korea, where they undertake a seven-week course of studies in the language and culture of the Korean people. It is hoped that this exchange will not only broaden the perspectives of the individual participants but will ultimately inspire greater understanding between all members of the African American and Korean American communities, two groups which have suffered within a climate of misunderstanding and miscommunication that led to the Los Angeles riots of 1992 following the Rodney King incident.

On June 17, the 1995 Martin Luther King, Jr. Scholarships were awarded to Derek Fleming, Jimi Reed Harris, Joell Frank Jones, Brajah Norris, and Lydia Sims in a ceremony held at San Francisco's Korean Center. "We think

[this] program needs to continue," said Michael Smith, a 1994 recipient of the scholarship. "We believe in Martin Luther King, Jr.'s dream in bridging communities. We are bridging gaps between cultures, ethnicities, races, but we are also bridging gaps between people."

Commissioner Cynthia Ong of the San Francisco Redevelopment Agency congratulated the five 1995 recipients by saying, "We've forged amazing connections. We've linked the two countries of America and Korea. We've linked the two cities of Seoul and San Francisco. We've linked the two communities of African American and Korean American." Ong was one of several dignitaries and leaders in attendance from both the local Korean and African American communities.

However, while the ceremony was reported in ethnic journals such as *Asian Week*, no reporters from any of the major media appeared to be present. A 1994 recipient of the scholarship, Michael Hornsby, pronounced, "With no major media here, I must be in the right place. Major media's probably covering a young brother doing something wrong." And Hornsby's sentiment was echoed by Reverend Amos Brown in his closing remarks: "If one of them were throwing a brick or burning something down, it would make the front page of the *Chronicle* or *Examiner*."

1.  Is there any truth in the statements made by Michael Hornsby and Rev. Amos Brown?
2.  Should the merchants themselves have done more for community involvement?
3.  If you were in charge of fostering good relations among people with different ethnic backgrounds, what tactics and strategies would you institute? What types of organizations might you propose?

◆ ◆ ◆ ◆ ◆

## EXPERIENTIAL EXERCISE

*"Asian Pacific Americans are better off than they were twenty years ago."*

*Objectives*

1.  To test your understanding.
2.  To compare your understanding with that of classmates.

*Starting Exercise*

1. Each student should think of as many facts as he or she can which either support or contradict the idea that Asian Pacific Americans are better off today. Make up a "Yes" and "No" list to organize your facts.

| *YES* | *NO* |
|---|---|
| Asian Pacific Americans are paid better (on average) than they were in years past. | Asian Pacific Americans are still paid less than Whites. |
| Asian Pacific Americans have more professional degrees. | Asian Pacific Americans still can't get the top jobs. |

2. Divide into groups of five or six and compare individual lists.
3. Which individual in the group appears to be most knowledgeable?
4. Do race or cultural differences determine individual knowledge?

## NOTES

1. This book is largely based on interviews with real Asian Pacific Americans over a period of several years. However, none of the names used in this book is the actual name of any real person interviewed.

2. Richard Herrnstein and Charles Murray authored the recent controversial study, *The Bell Curve: Intelligence and Class Structure in American Life* (New York: Free Press, 1994), a complex book that, in part, relates I.Q. to race. A series of responses to the book can be found in "Race and I.Q.—An Apologia: Murray and Herrnstein," *The New Republic,* 31 October 1994.

3. The statistical tables in *The Bell Curve* were constructed so as to suggest a *disfavorable distribution* for intelligence among persons of African descent and a *favorable correlation* for persons of Chinese and Jewish descent (p. 275). Herrnstein and Murray's assertions resulted in numerous volatile disputes over their flawed statistical data and willful underestimation of research on environmental and intervention factors affecting the reliability of I.Q. tests administered to individuals. Some critics identified *The Bell Curve* with an unqualified and poorly disguised political agenda revisiting Hitler's eugenics. For many,

what makes the book incredible is Herrnstein and Murray's reliance on the work of Canadian psychologist J. Phillipe Rushton. As summarized by Jeffrey Rosen and Charles Lane, writing in *New Republic* (31 October 1994: 14-15), Rushton attributed to Asians not only greater intelligence than Whites, but larger brains, smaller penises, lower sex drives, and a capacity for harder work. "It's a trade-off: more brain or more penis," he states in a *Rolling Stone* interview, "You can't have everything!" For most readers, the only question—a strictly rhetorical one—is whether Asian Pacific Americans (APAs) should feel more honored or more repulsed by the stereotyping.

4. A more detailed treatment of this topic can be found in chapter 11 of *Strangers from a Different Shore* (Boston: Little, Brown, 1989), Ronald Takaki's comparative historical account of Asian Pacific Americans.

5. Carter Goodwin Woodson, born to slave parents, received his Ph.D. from Harvard University, formed the first Association for the Study of Afro-American Life and History, and published sixteen books on black history before his death in 1950.

6. African American Charles Drew, born in 1904 in Washington, D.C., graduated from McGill University Medical School in 1933 and joined the Howard University faculty in 1935. Drew did most of his plasma research at Columbia University from 1938 to 1940. He became medical director of Freedmen's Hospital, which is associated with Howard University, in 1946.

7. Granville T. Woods, born in Columbus, Ohio, was self-taught and also took college engineering courses and worked as a railroad engineer. His inventions include an egg incubator, automatic air brakes, electric battery, telephone transmitter, and various devices for the telegraph.

8. Frederick Jones invented a portable X-ray machine, the auto refrigeration system, and the self-starting gasoline mower. For more information on notes 5-8, read *African American Scientists* by Patricia and Frederick McKissack (Brookfield, CT: Milbrook Press, 1994).

9. The U.S. immigration policy drew many wealthy APA immigrants into America's wealthy neighborhoods because an individual wishing to qualify for investment immigrant status had to possess a minimum of one million dollars in investment assets or to provide jobs to fifteen or more individuals in the U.S.

10. E.Q. is a shortened form of *Emotional Intelligence,* the title of a recent book (New York: Bantam, 1996) by Harvard psychologist Daniel Goleman, who is also a contributing writer to the *New York Times* on scientific matters. Goleman's thesis is, "When it comes to success, I.Q. may actually matter less

than E.Q." Expressed another way, "In the corporate world, I.Q. gets you hired, but E.Q. gets you promoted."

11. In the 1 December 1995 issue of *Asian Week,* Professor Norman Matloff of U.C. Davis raised the question, "When it comes to African Americans, why do so many Asian Americans tolerate intolerance?" Professor Matloff's work depicts only an older, less informed generation of APAs. In another study, Quynh Tran of Stanford University found that students who had grown up in the U.S. were less prejudiced against African Americans than were students who had immigrated at a later age.

12. This is the Cambodian community in Long Beach, California. Residents are predominantly refugees, unemployment is high, and many earn less than the minimum wage. For more information on this group, read S. Gold, *Refugee Communities: A Comparative Field Study* (Newbury Park, CA: Sage, 1992).

13. Congress created the Glass Ceiling Commission as part of the Civil Rights Act of 1991. A twenty-one-member presidential commission investigated the glass ceiling phenomenon and issued a report on 16 March 1994. A copy of the report can be obtained from the U.S. Government Printing Office.

14. Walter R. Nord, ed., *Concepts and Controversy in Organization Behavior* (Santa Monica, CA: Goodyear, 1976).

15. D. Krech, R. S. Crutchfield, and E. L. Ballachey, *Individual and Society* (New York: McGraw-Hill, 1962).

16. This concept is adapted from the work of Larry Hajime Shinagawa, Ph.D., Professor and Chair of the Department of American Multicultural Studies, Sonoma State University.

17. Michael Omi and Howard Winant, *Racial Formation in the United States: From 1960s to the 1990s,* 2d ed. (New York: Routledge, 1994).

18. See Larry Hajime Shinagawa and Gin Yong Pang, "Asian American Pan-Ethnicity and Intermarriage," *Amerasia Journal* 22 (1996): 3, 32. The authors offer a particularly compelling and classic example of perceived race, that of Walter White, executive secretary of the NAACP for twenty years, who had blond hair and blue eyes and came from a light-skinned African American family. Despite his long career as a social activist, White was accused of "selling out" by some African Americans following his marriage to a White American woman. Although in fact his wife's skin was darker than his own, the general public perceived Walter White as an African American and his new wife as White.

19. Normitsu Onishi, "New Sense of Race Arises among Asian Americans," *New York Times* (30 May 1996).

20. After the communist reform took over in China in 1949, about 5,000 college students already studying here received political asylum in the U.S. Between the 1950s and 1962, some 23,000 highly educated Chinese were allowed to enter the U.S. The first 2,000 refugees were admitted under the 1953 Refugee Act; another 1,000 in 1957; then 15,000 entered under a presidential directive of John F. Kennedy in 1962. This group formed the middle class of Chinese Americans today.

21. U.S. Bureau of the Census, "1990 Census of the Population, Asian and Pacific Islanders in the U.S." (Washington, DC: U.S. Government Printing Office, August 1993).

22. Current Population Survey conducted by the U.S. Bureau of the Census, Statistical Branch, 1996 (http://www.census.gov).

23. Larry Hajime Shinagawa, "The Impact of Immigration on the Demography of Asian Pacific Americans," in *Reframing the Immigration Debate,* ed. B. Ong Hing and R. Lee (Los Angeles: LEAP Publications, 1996): 60.

24. American demographics indicated that, since 1980, the White American population has increased by 4.4 percent, the African American population gained by 14 percent, and the U.S. Latino population by 39 percent.

25. According to a government report, "We the Americans: Asians," distributed free upon request by the U.S. Department of Commerce, Economics and Statistics Administration (Washington, DC, September 1993).

26. P. Ong, ed., *The State of Asian Pacific American Economic Diversity, Issues and Policies* (Los Angeles: LEAP Asian Pacific American Public Policy Institute, 1994).

27. In recent years, "NBC Nightly News," CBS's "60 Minutes," *U.S. News & World Report, Newsweek, Fortune,* and *Time* have all devoted special coverage to applauding the success story of Asian Pacific Americans.

28. For those unfamiliar with organization theory, it simply means a set of suppositions or assumptions about the functioning of organizations. It is one of the most interesting and relevant subdisciplines within the behavioral and administrative sciences. For further understanding, the best brief overview, in my opinion, can be found in Diana T. L. Wu, "A Short History and Overview of Organization Theory" (Moraga: Saint Mary's College of California, 1992). A multicultural perspective means that this representation reflects more than the view of a majority group; it encompasses the cultural heterogeneity among all groups in the workplace. The multidisciplinary approach uses principles,

models, theories, and methods from other disciplines—especially psychology, sociology, cultural anthropology, and ethnic studies.

29. See S. Chan, *Asian Americans: An Interpretive History* (Boston: Twayne, 1991); H. Kitano and R. Daniels, *Asian Americans: Emerging Minorities* (Englewood Cliffs, NJ: Prentice Hall, 1988); and R. Takaki, *Strangers from a Different Shore: A History of Asian Americans* (Boston: Little, Brown, 1989).

30. The classic *Grounded Theory: Strategies for Qualitative Research* (Chicago: Aldine, 1973) by B. Glaser and A. Strauss, and the more recent systems approach by V. K. Narayanan and R. Nath, *Organization Theory: A Strategic Approach* (Boston: Irwin, 1994), have been influential in the theoretical approaches of this undertaking.

# Two

# Ethnic Composition
# and Demographics

*"Excuse me. I heard you refer to yourself a few minutes ago as an Asian Pacific American. Could you tell me what that means?"*

*"Well, yes, I can. In my case, I am classified as Chinese American."*

## Asian Pacific American Groups

The classification of human beings is a complex proposition. We have learned that all humans have a common ancestry, that we are all related to each other and belong to the same species, *Homo sapiens*, a name composed of the Latin words for "human" and "wise." Historically, some scholars have divided *Homo sapiens* into three major groupings called the Negroid, Caucasoid, and Mongoloid races, each with its own distinctive appearance and genetic makeup.[1] More recently, scientists[2] have concluded that the number of human groups is far greater than three; anthropologists today generally classify populations into geographical races. There are nine recognized geographical races: African (Negroid), American Indian (American Mongoloid), Asian (Mongoloid), Australian (Australoid), European (Caucasoid), Indian (Asian and European), Melanesian (Asian and African), Micronesian (Small Pacific Islanders), and Polynesian (Tall Pacific Islanders).[3] Each of the nine is associated with different physical characteristics and other genetic traits.

How does all of this fit with the grouping of "Asian Pacific Americans"? According to the above exposition, Asian Pacific Americans are a subgroup composed of multiple groups whose members came to reside in America and whose ancestors came from six of the nine geographical races (the exceptions being African, American Indian, and European). Thus, it is reasonable to say that anyone living in America who can trace his or her family roots to the Asian continent or the Pacific Islands and who is not of American Indian, African, or European descent is an Asian Pacific American. Perhaps to minimize confusion, the U.S. Census Bureau[4] has disaggregated Asian Pacific Americans into nine categories: Chinese, Filipino, Japanese, Asian Indian, Korean, Vietnamese, Hawai'ian, Other Southeast Asian (i.e., Cambodian, Laotian, Thai, and Hmong), and finally, Other Asian and Pacific Islander, which includes Samoans, Guamanians, Tongans, and all other Asian and Pacific Islands ethnicities.

Is it possible to derive commonality for such a diverse human population? This chapter will attempt to provide a frame of reference by first giving a general picture of the whole Asian Pacific American population and the new perception of Asian Pacific Americans since the influx of recent immigrants and the enormous expansion of the Asian Pacific American population following the adoption of the U.S. Immigration Act of 1965. The next section explains where in the U.S. Asian Pacific Americans live and work, followed by a discussion of their educational attainments and economic status. The final section reveals what they do for a living—what kinds of professions they practice and the distribution of professions among different ethnic Asian Pacific American groups. This chapter is arranged to give the reader a clearer answer to the questions of who, what, where, and how.

The facts and figures presented in this chapter are derived as much as possible from official documents such as the U.S. Bureau of the Census reports and Equal Employment files. Much of this official data, however, is less than current due to the fact that an official census is taken only every ten years. The most recent U.S. census was conducted in 1990, and the next one will not be taken until 2000. Consequently, some statistical data are derived from surveys, projections, and estimations. Other sources include books, periodicals, and newspaper accounts that use terms, descriptions, and classifications similar to those used by the census.

## Differentiation: Who Are the Asian Pacific Americans?

In "Racial Classifications of Asian Americans," author Larry Hajime Shinagawa[5] asserts that "Asian Pacific Americans" incorporates thirty Asian American ethnic groups and twenty-one Pacific Islander ethnic groups, all of whom can trace their ancestry to one or more of the nations of eastern Asia and the Pacific Rim. As reported by Cordura and Jensen,[6] the first Asian Pacific Americans were a small number of Filipinos who jumped Spanish merchant ships in Louisiana to make their way to New Orleans in the 1760s, and a few Asian Indians who were brought to the East Coast as indentured servants. The first wave of Asian immigration to the United States occurred more than a century ago and consisted mainly of Chinese and Japanese citizens.[7] Today, the Asian Pacific American population includes descendants of some of these early pioneers as well as more recent immigrants who come not only from China, India, Japan, Korea, and the Philippines but also from places which may be less familiar to many readers, such as the southeast Asian nations of Brunei, Burma, Indonesia, and Malaysia; the south Asian nations of Bangladesh, Pakistan, and Sri Lanka; and from hosts of Pacific Island countries. Many of the newest Asian Pacific Americans are Indochinese refugee immigrants from Cambodia, Laos, Thailand, and Vietnam.[8]

Most Americans, including the Asian Pacific Americans themselves, automatically tend to connect the term "Asian Pacific Americans" with the East Asian populations of China, Japan, and Korea. Although there are many differences in terms of national character, philosophies, and beliefs among these peoples, they share a common East Asian (Mongolian racial) origin and have relatively similar physical appearances. Westerners have long been familiar with these people through Confucian traditions and culture. Other nations, such as India and the Philippines, which have long histories of Western colonization, are also relatively well known to Westerners. In recent years, the general public has become more aware of others as they relate to events such as the accounts of Vietnamese "boat people," refugees of the Indochina War—Khmer, Hmong, Laotian—and other displaced immigrants from Pacific Rim nations.

However, very few Americans, regardless of ancestry, think to include as Asian Pacific Americans the indigenous peoples of the Pacific Islands, namely, the Polynesians (mainly Hawaiians, Samoans, Tahitians, and Tongans), Micronesians (most notably, the Guamanians), and Melanesians (largely consisting of Fijians). Although Pacific Islanders are few in number when compared with Asian Americans who live on the mainland, the majority of them—87 percent according to a 1993 U.S. Census Bureau report—have been U.S. citizens since birth.[9] Guam and American Samoa are even represented in the U.S. Congress, albeit by nonvoting members. According to an article by Nina Chen,[10] Pacific Islanders, in general, have much more pronounced difficulties than the other Asian groups because their cultural traditions do not fit into the perceived "Asian Pacific American" mode. They have a markedly different value system that, for example, emphasizes familial affection and enjoyment of the family more than educational achievements of family members. This contrast is one reason why Pacific Islanders rank at the bottom of the scale scholastically while Asians rank at the top. Being grouped with Asian Americans under affirmative action actually hurts Pacific Islanders' chances for social mobility.

Clearly, then, the makeup of this diverse group called "Asian Pacific Americans" is enormously complex. However, as one would imagine, aside from the differences in language, religious and other beliefs, and cultural values—including some extremely significant differences—between the various population subgroups, there are also differences within each subgroup. Media coverage of current events, for example, has recently brought Korean shopkeepers to public attention or focused on the collective struggles of the Vietnamese, Cambodian, Laotian, and Hmong refugees who are America's newest immigrant group.[11] Among the Japanese American component, there are names for each generation: *Issei*, the pioneers who arrived in the 1880s; *Nisei*, second-generation Japanese Americans—more than 100,000 of whom lived in internment camps during World War II;[12] *Sansei*, third-generation Japanese Americans; and *Yonsei*, fourth-generation Japanese Americans.

However, the largest segment of the Asian Pacific American population remains the Chinese Americans (estimated to be about two million).[13] Yet even within the Chinese American population, there are still a great many significant differences in language, culture, and social class. Because this population is the largest today, it provides an excellent illustration of the complexity of the Asian Pacific American population overall. Subgroups of the Chinese American population include the following.

*American-born members of old, establishment families.* They can date their presence in the U.S. back to the 1800s. Their ancestors were largely brought to the United States as a source of cheap labor for mining and railroad building. Most of these immigrants later settled in the ethnic enclaves known as "Chinatowns" all over the U.S., although some individuals were successful in their struggles to establish themselves as merchants elsewhere. Many of their descendants remain in ethnic enclaves, but far more have left these enclaves and have moved into suburban communities that dot the American landscape.[14] One such descendant, Gary Locke, has even become the first Chinese American governor of a U.S. state and the first Asian American governor of any mainland state (see Box 2.1).

---

Box 2.1
*"One Mile, One Hundred Years"*

[M]y father . . . fought in World War II and participated in the Normandy invasion. . . . My mother . . . raised five children . . . , and . . . returned to school at Seattle Community College when she was nearly 60.

. . . One of my ancestors . . . immigrated to Olympia in 1874. . . . Just a few years after [that] . . . my grandfather [seeking an education] came to America to work as a "house boy" . . . in a house . . . less than a mile from here [the state capital].

. . . [A]lthough I [am] standing less than a mile from where our family started its life in America, we've come a long way. Our journey was possible because . . . of a deep faith in the essential goodness of mainstream American values; the values of hard work, hope, enterprise and opportunity. . . . Our journey was successful because the Locke family embraces three values: Get a good education, work hard, and take care of each other.

*Excerpted from the inaugural address of*
*America's first Chinese American Governor,*
*Gary Locke, State of Washington.*
*January 15, 1997*

---

*The "elite immigrants."* From the late 1940s through the mid-1960s, the majority of immigrants to the U.S. from China were somewhat elite, generally very well-educated refugees who had fled the communist Chinese takeover of mainland China. A few Chinese college students were also stranded here during these years, but the majority of these refugees had their origins in China's upper classes.[15] They did well in America as professionals and entrepreneurs. Many have traveled to China to facilitate technical exchanges and economic development between the two countries.

*"Student immigrants."* In the late 1950s and throughout the 1970s, a large number of students of science and engineering came to prestigious American public universities and to Ivy League institutions from Hong Kong and Taiwan. Many of these individuals settled down in U.S. educational institutions and became professors, researchers, or other professionals. Many of them also stayed to help transform Silicon Valley and the world. A few have become chancellors of colleges and universities. Many others are making substantial contributions in the arts and literature.[16]

*"Investor immigrants" and other recent arrivals.* More recently, many wealthy Chinese investors have emigrated to the U.S. from Hong Kong in anticipation of the communist Chinese takeover there on July 1, 1997. Still other recent Chinese immigrants have included both wealthy venture capitalists from Taiwan, and some 100,000 political refugees from the People's Republic, many of whom have come to the U.S. illegally. As a group, then, the newest Chinese Americans are either very successful or very poor, and there are few in between.[17] According to a July 1995 U.S. Census Bureau report, more than half of the new arrivals are still earning below-average wages.

*The new generation.* The offspring of all of the above groups, this group includes second and higher generation U.S.-born as well as members of the foreign-born "1.5 generation" who immigrated as children. In general, members of this group face no language barrier problem, and more than half attend college. Like other Americans of their generation, they tend toward technological sophistication, and many consider themselves to be "plugged in" to the international circuit. A recent phenomenon is that many in this group who are bilingual and bicultural have found greater opportunities with companies doing business in Asia and are going back to pursue careers in Hong Kong, Taiwan, and China.[18]

Although these five groups can trace their origins to China, each emigrated for different reasons, speaks a different language or dialect, and holds a different view of the world.

"Excuse me. I heard you refer to yourself as Chinese American. Can you tell me, please, what kind of Chinese American you are? PRC? Taiwanese, Toisanese, Cantonese, Shanghainese, or Beijingnese? Perhaps a mainlander via Taiwan? Or Hong Kong Chinese? Vietnamese Chinese, Chinese whose family lives in the Philippines, Malaysia, Indonesia, Singapore, Africa, South America? Are you FOB? ABC?"

The complex makeup of the Chinese American population is only one component of the larger and even more complex population of Asian Pacific Americans. Because of the diversity of their experiences, it would be difficult for Asian Pacific Americans to form an all-encompassing political organization, similar to the NAACP or the Mexican American Legal Defense and Education Fund, which would have a broad, common agenda appealing to every Asian Pacific American, or even to a clear majority of Chinese Americans. Nevertheless, as documented by Espiritu and by Shinagawa and Pang in their recent studies,[19] there is a continuous development of the concept and perception of Asian American pan-ethnicity.

For one thing, there are certain problems which all Asian Pacific Americans have in common. For most, this commonality is particularly evident in the workplace, because most American workers, regardless of their professions, are likely to associate with a more ethnically and culturally diverse group of individuals on the job than they will meet in their neighborhoods or socialize with at home. As a result, the probability of confronting issues involving racial discrimination or stereotyping is greatest while on the job.

According to the common stereotype, Asian Pacific Americans are perceived as a rather peculiar group of overly serious "nerds" that works and studies almost constantly. Ironically, even the most negative stereotype can actually contribute some commonality to its victims, even victims as diverse as the Asian Pacific American population. As one of the individuals interviewed for this book commented, "No matter what differences we [Asian Americans] may have, we all have the same flat facial features that Whites feel compelled to make fun of."

Yet even this statement may no longer hold true. A cultural phenomenon which has been charted over the past two decades is the high rate of intermarriage between Asian Pacific Americans and members of other races. In the fall of 1993, *Time* magazine even reported in a special issue[20] that, since 1981, the number of babies born in the U.S. with one Japanese American parent and one White American parent exceeded the number of babies with two Japanese American parents.[21] This "trend" was in fact an anomaly of brief duration, possibly caused by some phenomenon such as the once-high incidence of war brides. According to "Asian American Pan-Ethnicity and Intermarriage," coauthored by Larry Hajime Shinagawa, a statistician and Chair of American Culture Studies at Sonoma State University, and Gin Yong Pang, even though statistics show that a large number of second- and third-generation Asian Pacific Americans marry ethnic non-Asians, in the past ten years there has been a significant decrease in the proportion of such interracial marriages.

Again, it now appears that there has been a continual development of Asian American pan-ethnicity, reflecting in turn a reaction against pan-ethnic racial discrimination.[22] The fact is that in today's cultural landscape, the question of identity is more complex than ever, in part because the final answer to the question, "Who is an Asian Pacific American?" always depends on the perceptions of others within the society. However, because it facilitates making statistical comparisons, we will use the definition provided by the U.S. Bureau of the Census.


## Distribution: Where Do
## Asian Pacific Americans Choose to Live?

According to the U.S. Census Bureau report of that year, there were 7,273,662 Asian Pacific Americans in 1990, the year of the last official census. In other words, about 2.9 percent of the nation's total population of 248,709,873 citizens were Asian Pacific Americans. By 1 July 1995, the Asian Pacific American population was estimated at 9.8 million and projected to reach 12.1 million, representing about 4.4 percent of the U.S. population, by the year 2000; and 34.4 million, or 8.7 percent, by the year 2050.[23] While this may seem to be a stunning rate of growth, the January 1997 issue of *Asian Week* quotes Shinagawa as predicting that the Asian Pacific American population could in fact reach 12 percent of the national total by 2050. "In the past," Shinagawa explained, "if people were mixed-race they would just identify themselves as White, [but] my guess would be that there will be the possibility of a stronger identification with being Asian in the future."[24]

The Asian Pacific American population is now divided among all fifty states, but 59 percent—or six in ten—live in the western region of the U.S., as shown in Table 2.1. In addition, 87 percent live in one of fifteen metropolitan areas, as detailed in Table 2.2.

As shown in Table 2.1, at the time of the 1990 census, Hawaii, with 685,236 Asian Pacific Americans, was the only state where Asian Pacific Americans made up a majority. Although 1995 statistics indicate a decline in residence, a majority of Hawaii's population remains Asian Pacific American. California, with 2,845,659 Asian Pacific Americans, had the highest concentration in 1990; and this had jumped to nearly four million by 1995. Unofficially, however, it is estimated that the actual number of Asian Pacific Americans in California is now greater than five million.

New York comes in a distant second with an official estimate of nearly 846,000 Asian Pacific Americans and, unofficially, more than one million.

Table 2.1

*U.S. Asian Pacific American (APA) Population by State (Top Fifteen States)*

|  | 1990 Asian or Pacific Islander Population* | 1990 % of State Population | Estimated 1995 APA Population (in thousands) | 1995 % of State Population |
|---|---|---|---|---|
| 1. California | 2,845,659 | 9.6 | 3,908 | 12.6 |
| 2. New York | 695,760 | 3.9 | 846 | 4.7 |
| 3. Hawaii | 685,236 | 61.8 | 679 | 55.6 |
| 4. Texas | 319,459 | 1.9 | 461 | 2.5 |
| 5. Illinois | 285,311 | 2.5 | 383 | 3.2 |
| 6. New Jersey | 272,521 | 3.5 | 356 | 4.5 |
| 7. Washington | 210,958 | 4.3 | 318 | 5.8 |
| 8. Virginia | 159,053 | 2.6 | 220 | 3.3 |
| 9. Florida | 154,302 | 1.2 | 231 | 1.6 |
| 10. Massachusetts | 143,392 | 2.4 | 180 | 3.1 |
| 11. Maryland | 139,719 | 2.9 | 196 | 3.9 |
| 12. Pennsylvania | 137,438 | 1.2 | 185 | 1.5 |
| 13. Michigan | 104,983 | 1.1 | 140 | 1.5 |
| 14. Ohio | 91,179 | 0.8 | 122 | 1.1 |
| 15. Minnesota | 77,886 | 1.8 | 113 | 2.5 |

Source: U.S. Census Bureau.
*The next U.S. census will be taken in the year 2000.

Fourth and fifth both in 1990 and 1995 are Texas and Illinois, both having experienced surging Asian Pacific American populations during the past fifteen years.

Data obtained from the Racial Statistics Branch, Population Division show that Asian Pacific Americans now outnumber African Americans in the states of California, Hawaii, Idaho, Montana, New Hampshire, Oregon, Utah, Vermont, Maine, Alaska, Massachusetts, and Washington. In Wyoming, Minnesota, North Dakota, and South Dakota, the Asian Pacific American and African American populations are approximately equal. Asian Pacific Americans outnumber Latino Americans in Alaska, Hawaii, Minnesota, and Maryland, and the Asian Pacific American and Latino American populations are about equal in Alabama, Maine, Mississippi, New Hampshire, North Dakota, Tennessee, Vermont, Virginia, and Washington.[25]

The fifteen U.S. metropolitan areas most heavily populated by Asian Pacific Americans are shown in Table 2.2. Among these, the area surrounding Los Angeles, California, has the largest Asian Pacific American population.

In the past few years, developers from several Pacific Rim nations have poured capital into southern California, bringing about an unprecedented economic expansion. Monterey Park, a suburb of Los Angeles with about 65,000 people, is now known as Little Taipei, after the capital of Taiwan. However, although the majority of Monterey Park's population is Asian Pacific American, not all are Taiwanese. West of downtown Los Angeles, one sees countless signs and advertisements in Korean. The Vietnamese language can be heard in many parts of California's Orange County; even though the Indochinese refugees were originally placed in 813 separate zip codes in every U.S. state, including Alaska, more than half of them later made their own way to California.[26] In addition, there are now more than 600 Korean eateries, 500 Japanese sushi bars, and 300 Thai restaurants in Los Angeles. There are more ethnic Filipinos in Los Angeles than in any other city except Manila.[27] This highly concentrated population can reasonably be expected to lead to continued future growth of the Asian Pacific American population in the area.

Table 2.2

*Asian Pacific American Population in Fifteen Metropolitan Areas, by Rank*

| | |
|---|---|
| 1.  Los Angeles-Anaheim-Riverside, CA | 1,339,048 |
| 2.  San Francisco-Oakland-San Jose, CA | 926,961 |
| 3.  New York-Northern New Jersey-Long Island, NY-NJ-CT | 873,213 |
| 4.  Honolulu, HI | 526,459 |
| 5.  Chicago-Gary-Lake County, IL-IN-WI | 256,050 |
| 6.  Washington, DC-MD-VA | 202,437 |
| 7.  San Diego, CA | 198,311 |
| 8.  Seattle-Tacoma, WA | 164,286 |
| 9.  Houston-Galveston-Barzoria, TX | 132,131 |
| 10.  Philadelphia-Wilmington-Trenton, PA-NJ-DE-MD | 123,458 |
| 11.  Boston-Lawrence-Salem, MA-NH | 121,405 |
| 12.  Sacramento, CA | 114,520 |
| 13.  Dallas-Fort Worth, TX | 97,578 |
| 14.  Detroit-Ann Arbor, MI | 69,454 |
| 15.  Minneapolis-St. Paul, MN-WI | 65,204 |

Source: "The Asian Pacific American Population in the U.S." U.S. Census Bureau, March 1994.

The five-county San Francisco Bay Area has the second largest concentration of Asian Pacific Americans. The total general population of the region, which includes the cities of San Francisco, Oakland, and San Jose, is approximately five million. Nearly one million—20 percent of the area total—are Asian Pacific Americans. By far the largest component of this population, as well as the Bay Area's most established Asian Pacific American group, is the Bay Area's 350,000 Chinese Americans. The next largest groups, respectively, are comprised of the Bay Area's 230,000 Filipino Americans, 83,000 Vietnamese Americans, 70,000 Japanese Americans, 50,000 Asian Indian Americans, and 40,000 Korean Americans.[28] Because of the presence of several prominent universities and the high-tech community of Silicon Valley, there are a great number of mathematicians, scientists, engineers, and skilled technicians living in the San Francisco area. As we will see later in this chapter, many Asian Pacific Americans are employed in these professions.

Ranking third after Los Angeles and San Francisco is the greater New York metropolitan area. This is the second most popular settlement area, particularly among Chinese, Asian Indian, and Korean immigrants. Although New York's general population has declined in recent years, its Asian Pacific American immigrant population has grown, and the number of Southeast Asian immigrants continues to climb. In comparison with the 1980 Census Bureau report, the Asian Pacific American population in the New York area has more than doubled, growing from 1.8 percent of the state's total to 3.9 percent—an increase of 125 percent.

According to data compiled by the Immigration and Naturalization Service, by 1992, New York City was the most popular city for Asian Pacific American immigrants. Nearly half of the city's Asian Pacific Americans are Chinese Americans. New York City's Chinatown is recognized as the largest overseas Chinatown in the world, even larger than San Francisco's Chinatown! The second largest Asian Pacific American group in the New York area is composed of more than 100,000 Asian Indian Americans, which is the largest Asian Indian American center in the United States.

Although many Asian Pacific immigrants still live in central-city ethnic enclaves, many now also reside in the suburbs. According to 1990 U.S. census data and 1996 estimations, the percentage of Asian Pacific Americans now living in suburban areas is higher than the percentage of the general U.S. population living in suburban areas. In a few suburbs, such as the Bay Area, Milpitas, Monterey Park, Pinole, Arlington, and Silver City, they have created new Pan-Asian-ethnic enclaves.[29] Currently, Asian Pacific Americans comprise only about 4 percent of the total U.S. population overall, but because they are concentrated around major U.S. metropolitan areas, their presence is a highly visible one.

## Profession: What Do Asian Pacific Americans Do for a Living?

The Asian Pacific American job classification distribution data in Table 2.3 reveal that only 8 percent of Asian Pacific Americans were employed in management positions—compared with 12 percent among the general population—even though Asian Pacific Americans were represented among professionals at twice the level of the population as a whole.[30] The data further reveal that Asian Pacific Americans tend to concentrate in professions where quantitative and concrete skills are needed and where competence is affirmed by technical education and ability. Fewer Asian Pacific Americans are in the craft and labor forces, probably due in part to the requirement for union membership.

Table 2.3
*Distribution of Asian Pacific Americans (APAs) According to Job Classification*

|  | All Groups | All APAs | APA Men | APA Women |
|---|---|---|---|---|
| Number of workers | 37,247,280 | 825,812 | 427,537 | 398,275 |
| Officials and managers | 12.2% | 8.2% | 11.1% | 5.1% |
| Professionals | 11.7% | 22.5% | 24.6% | 20.3% |
| Technicians | 5.7% | 8.2% | 9.7% | 6.7% |
| Sales workers | 11.8% | 8.2% | 7.6% | 8.9% |
| Office and clerical workers | 16.7% | 16.9% | 8.0% | 26.4% |
| Craft workers | 9.8% | 5.3% | 8.0% | 2.5% |
| Operatives | 15.7% | 13.6% | 13.5% | 13.7% |
| Laborers | 6.4% | 5.6% | 6.2% | 4.9% |
| Service workers | 10.0% | 11.4% | 11.3% | 11.5% |

Source: U.S. Equal Employment Opportunity Commission, 1994.

The ten industries most popular or prevalent among Asian Pacific Americans are shown in Table 2.4. Here, hospital workers stand out most dramatically. Behind this particular statistic are many Asian Indian American doctors and Filipino American nurses. Ranking below hospitals is the electronics industry. This field is dominated by large numbers of Chinese American, Japanese American, and Korean American workers. Many Asian Indian Americans have also participated in the electronics industry, but greater numbers are concentrated in the hotel and motel industry.

The more recent immigrant Chinese Americans, Vietnamese Americans, and Filipino Americans are employed mainly in the service occupations. A

Table 2.4
*The Ten U.S. Industries with the Most Asian Pacific Americans (In Percentages)*

| Industry | All Workers | Asians Pacific Americans | APA Workers in the industry |
|---|---|---|---|
| Hospitals | 33.9 | 31.8 | 3.3 |
| Electronic components | 7.8 | 13.5 | 7.4 |
| Miscellaneous business services | 15.5 | 12.3 | 3.2 |
| Commercial banking | 14.5 | 12.2 | 3.4 |
| Hotels and motels | 5.7 | 8.7 | 5.8 |
| Office and computing machines | 6.1 | 6.4 | 4.7 |
| Nursing and personal care facilities | 6.0 | 5.8 | 4.2 |
| Communication equipment | 5.9 | 4.2 | 3.1 |
| Measuring and controlling devices | 2.4 | 2.7 | 3.8 |
| Medical instruments and supplies | 2.1 | 2.4 | 4.0 |

Source: U.S. Equal Employment Opportunity Commission, 1994.

study conducted by the East-West Population Institute in Hawaii showed that whereas 71 percent of Filipino Americans work for Whites, 69 percent of Korean Americans work for other Korean Americans.[31] This may be due in part to language barriers; most recent Filipino immigrants learned English in school back in the Philippines, but this was not the case for most Korean Americans. Another factor is the substantial number of Korean American immigrants who own and operate small businesses, such as laundry/dry cleaners or grocery stores.[32] Korean Americans have also demonstrated a high level of entrepreneurial success in ethnic-based businesses. Many other Asian Pacific Americans also find an ethnic-based or other small business to be more satisfying than low-wage employment.[33]

The most popular industries for Asian Pacific American business owners are retail trade, manufacturing, and professional-related services. Approximately 400,000 U.S. firms are owned by Asian Pacific Americans, bringing estimated annual receipts of $33 billion into the U.S. economy.[34]

Yet while the number of affluent Asian Pacific Americans has increased over the past decade, many Asian Pacific Americans remain in low-paying jobs in the service industry and manufacturing. The most significant difference between Asian Pacific American males and White males is in service jobs, where the proportions are 10 percent and 3 percent, respectively. Additional comparisons are shown in Table 2.5.

Table 2.5
*Asian Pacific American Occupational Distribution*
*(Percentage of Workers in Occupation, by Sex)*

|  | Asian Pacific American | | White, not Hispanic | |
|  | Men | Women | Men | Women |
|---|---|---|---|---|
| Total (excluding armed forces) | 100.0 | 100.0 | 100.0 | 100.0 |
| Executive, administrative, and | | | | |
| managerial workers | 16.3 | 17.5 | 18.5 | 18.9 |
| Professional specialty workers | 21.5 | 20.3 | 15.6 | 18.4 |
| Technical and related support | | | | |
| workers | 5.5 | 4.5 | 3.1 | 4.6 |
| Sales workers | 10.9 | 9.6 | 13.0 | 10.8 |
| Administrative support workers, | | | | |
| including clerical | 8.5 | 22.5 | 5.5 | 28.0 |
| Private household workers | | 1.0 | | 0.3 |
| Protective service workers | 1.6 | 0.6 | 3.0 | 0.6 |
| Service workers, except private | | | | |
| household | 10.1 | 11.0 | 3.4 | 8.7 |
| Farming, fishing, and forestry | | | | |
| workers | 2.0 | 0.1 | 3.3 | 0.9 |
| Precision production, craft, and | | | | |
| repair workers | 11.7 | 3.8 | 19.2 | 2.6 |
| Machine operators, assemblers, | | | | |
| and inspectors | 7.0 | 7.8 | 6.1 | 4.7 |
| Transportation and material | | | | |
| moving workers | 3.5 | 0.2 | 6.4 | 0.6 |
| Handlers, equipment cleaners, | | | | |
| helpers, and laborers | 1.4 | 1.1 | 3.1 | 0.9 |

Source: U.S. Department of Commerce, Bureau of the Census, 1994.

Asian Pacific American females consistently lag in high-paying positions in the managerial and professional category. They tend to concentrate in the administrative support, clerical, and service occupations. The proportion of college-educated Asian Pacific American women who worked in this managerial field was twice that for college-educated White females. Cabezas, Shinagawa, and Kawaguchi[35] found that most Asian Pacific American men, and in particular, Filipino American men, were accountants, engineers, and health technologists, whereas the women were overwhelmingly concentrated as registered nurses, elementary school teachers, accounting clerks, and bookkeepers. Nevertheless, few Asian Pacific Americans, male or female, were found among public administrators or managers of large marketing or financial institutions.

Even among Asian Pacific Americans who are employed in the managerial occupations, the tendency has been to manage research and development departments or food services centers.[36] Furthermore, according to the Glass Ceiling Commission report, most of the Asian Pacific American managers who do exist were selected as managers either to oversee a predominantly Asian Pacific American workforce or to accept a foreign job assignment in a Pacific Rim nation. More often than not, Asian Pacific Americans are passed over for promotions. They consequently remain noticeably absent from high-ranking corporate positions, and many depart the corporate world to found their own firms.[37] Currently, there are no Asian Pacific American chief executive officers (CEOs) among the top 1,000 corporations in America, and only 0.4 percent of the Director of Corporate Board seats of Fortune 1000 companies are occupied by Asian Pacific Americans. Only two Asian Pacific Americans currently serve as presidents of major U.S. universities.[38]

## Education: What Do Asian Pacific Americans Study?

Perhaps due to the traditional respect for education and learning in many Asian Pacific cultures, or the belief that a college education opens the doors to opportunity and promotes upward mobility, Asian Pacific Americans tend to attain higher educational goals than the general population. More Asian Pacific Americans have gone to college and to graduate school, and Asian Pacific American students and faculty can be seen on nearly every university campus in the United States.[39]

Although Asian Pacific Americans account for about 3 percent of the U.S. population, they constitute more than 30 percent of the student body at California universities and more than 15 percent at many prestigious Ivy League schools on the East Coast.[40] Moreover, Asian Pacific American enrollments continue to increase and to do so more rapidly than they do for the general population. Naturally, these statistics were influenced in part by the growth of the Asian Pacific American population itself, but Asian Pacific Americans are also considered by many accounts to be superachievers in educational settings. Accordingly, recent controversies have developed as to whether Asian Pacific Americans are overrepresented and should be accepted to colleges at lower rates than other minorities and Whites.[41]

According to a Minorities in Higher Education report of the American Council on Education, Asian Pacific Americans have made significantly larger enrollment gains at four-year colleges and universities in the past ten years than have other ethnic minorities. California, where the largest Asian Pacific American population resides, experienced a 101.3 percent growth in Asian Pacific American enrollments at four-year institutions and a 55.4 percent gain at two-year institutions.[42] Nationwide, as reported by Escueta and O'Brien, the number of Asian Pacific Americans in higher education has nearly doubled, in part due to the increasing immigrant population but also attributable to the increased presence of Asian Pacific American women in higher education. The number of Asian Pacific American female students has doubled at the undergraduate level, increased by 75 percent at the graduate level, and increased by 150 percent at the professional level. Compared with their counterparts in the general population, where half of the women who hold graduate degrees were native U.S. citizens, only one-third of Asian Pacific American women who hold Ph.D.s were born in the U.S.[43]

Table 2.6
*Educational Attainment of Persons 25 Years and Older (Percentage of Population)*

|  | Total Population | Asian Pacific Americans | Whites |
|---|---|---|---|
| Four years of high school or more | 81 | 85 | 85 |
| Four or more years of college | 22 | 41 | 24 |
| Five or more years of college | 9 | 18 | 10 |

Source: U.S. Dept. of Commerce, Bureau of the Census, 1996 (http://www.census.gov).

As shown in Table 2.6, 85 percent of Asian Pacific Americans in 1994 had completed four years of high school, a slightly higher rate than the 81 percent rate for the general population. However, at the collegiate level, the number of Asian Pacific Americans completing four years of college is almost double the rate for the general population. For graduate study, the rate is twice as high.

No doubt this was influenced by the 1965 Immigration Act, which encouraged highly skilled Asian adults to emigrate to the U.S. A closer look at the statistics reveals that almost two-thirds of this latter group of Asian Pacific

Americans were not only foreign-born but also received their postsecondary educations prior to their arrival in the U.S. Thus, the statistics reflect the recruitment of foreign-born, foreign-educated Asians from advantaged backgrounds over the past several decades. They do not, in other words, reflect much upward mobility for U.S.-born descendants of Asian Pacific American immigrants. As further shown in the 1993 summary report on universities by Reis and Thurgood,[44] 75 percent of the Asian doctorate recipients in that year were non-U.S. citizens, compared to a mere 8.5 percent of White doctorate recipients.

Table 2.7
*Fields of Study by Ph.D. Candidates in 1995 (Percentage of Population)*

|                        | All | Asian | Whites |
|------------------------|-----|-------|--------|
| Life sciences          | 18  | 20    | 18     |
| Physical sciences      | 17  | 26    | 15     |
| Social sciences        | 16  | 9     | 18     |
| Education              | 16  | 5     | 20     |
| Engineering            | 14  | 30    | 9      |
| Humanities             | 12  | 4     | 14     |
| Professional and other | 7   | 6     | 6      |

Source: National Center for Educational Statistics (http://www.ed.gov/NCES).

The fields of concentration for Asian Pacific American scholars are frequently engineering and physical and life sciences, as shown in Table 2.7. Almost two-thirds of the Asian doctoral students concentrate in the fields of engineering, life sciences, and physical sciences, in comparison to two-fifths of Whites and less than half for all the other doctoral degrees. Asian Americans appear to shy away from fields in the humanities, education, and social sciences, perhaps due to language usage limitations.

It must be noted that because of the diversity of the Asian Pacific American population, educational attainment varies considerably from group to group. The statistically evident achievements shown in Tables 2.6 and 2.7 can actually mask significant problems relating to educational opportunity facing particular ethnicities or other subgroups within the Asian Pacific American population as a whole. In particular, as shown by Table 2.8, only 11 percent of Pacific Islanders are college graduates, compared with 41 percent for Asian

Table 2.8

*Educational Attainments by Ethnic Group of Persons 25 Years and Older (In Percentages)*

| Group | Bachelor's Degree and Higher | Under Grade 5 | Total Asian Pacific American Population |
|---|---|---|---|
| Asian Indian | 58 | 5 | 12 |
| Chinese | 41 | 9 | 24 |
| Filipino | 39 | 4 | 20 |
| Japanese | 35 | 1 | 12 |
| Korean | 35 | 4 | 11 |
| Thai | 33 | 9 | 1 |
| Vietnamese | 18 | 12 | 9 |
| Pacific Islander | 11 | 3 | 5 |
| Cambodian | 6 | 41 | 2 |
| Laotian | 5 | 24 | 1 |
| Hmong | 5 | 78 | 1 |
| Other Asian[a] | 41 | 4 | 2 |

Source: "We the Americans—Asians," U.S. Dept. of Commerce, Economics & Statistics Administration, Bureau of the Census, September 1993.
a. Includes Pakistani, Indonesian, Malayan, Bangladeshi, Burman, Sri Lankan, etc.

Americans and 22 percent for the general population. Similarly, 82 percent of Vietnamese Americans and 95 percent of other Southeast Asian Americans do not have bachelor's degrees.[45] The illiteracy rate is high among this last group. The Pacific Islanders and Southeast Asian Americans have been hurt in instances where Asians are not eligible for affirmative action.

## Earnings: How Do Asian Pacific Americans Score?

Despite the greater educational attainment of Asian Pacific Americans, their median earnings were less than those of Whites both at the high school and college graduate level. As Table 2.9 shows further, individual earnings for Asian Pacific Americans lag behind earnings for Whites on average. Note also that Asian Pacific American males earn more than women, whether they are of White or Asian Pacific heritage.

A 1995 survey by the U.S. Racial Statistics Branch indicated that the median family income for Asian Pacific Americans was $46,857. In comparison, the median family income was $41,329 for White Americans and $37,159 for the general population. Similarly, census data listed the median household

Table 2.9
*Median Household Income and Individual Earnings*
*by Educational Attainment (In Dollars)*

|  | Asian | White | All |
|---|---|---|---|
| Households: all families | 46,857 | 41,329 | 37,159 |
| Households: homeowners | 49,510 | 45,240 | 38,920 |
| Individuals: high school graduate | 21,868 | 24,336 | 22,917 |
| Individuals: bachelor's degree or higher | 38,167 | 41,278 | 40,414 |

Source: U.S. Census Bureau, Statistical Branch, 1996 (http://www.census.gov).

income for homeowners as $49,240 for Asian Pacific Americans, compared with only $45,510 for Whites and $38,920 for the general population.[46]

However, these averages can be quite misleading; as reported by Shinagawa in a recent article,[47] Asian Pacific Americans tend to have larger, extended family households, with more members of the family working. The average Asian Pacific American household includes 3.8 workers, versus an average of 1.8 workers in the White household. Thus, the higher income figures can represent the combined efforts of several individuals earning wages which are, in fact, lower. We must also consider that Asian Pacific Americans have tended to concentrate in metropolitan areas of New York and California, where wages and salaries, along with the cost of living, are higher than for the rest of the nation.

Furthermore, the socioeconomic conditions of the various Asian Pacific American groups differ greatly. Although 11 percent of Asian Pacific Americans—about one million people—were living in poverty in 1990, compared with 8 percent of White Americans, 17 percent of the impoverished Asian Pacific Americans were Pacific Islanders.[48] Around 50 percent of all Vietnamese, Laotian, and Cambodian refugees lived below the poverty level in 1990. About 90 percent of disadvantaged Asian Pacific Americans are relatively recent immigrants.[49]

The main reason that recent immigrants experience difficulties in finding more preferable employment is centered around their present inability to master the English language. Even "English-speaking" Pacific Islanders experience this language barrier because they come from areas where the only spoken language is Pidgin English, with its limited vocabulary usage and simplified grammatical constructions.[50]

In recent years, there has also been a growing sentiment of intolerance toward immigrants. For example, employers may regard certain foreign accents as

proof of a lack of prerequisite communication skills, and this has dispropor-
tionately affected employment opportunities and the earning capacity of
many Asian Pacific Americans. It is interesting to note that European-born
White Americans typically face no such barriers, even when they do confront
language difficulties. This may either reflect racial discrimination against
Asian Pacific Americans or favorably reflect common American sentiments
regarding European accents.

## Summary

The Asian Pacific American population, which has doubled in the past decade,
incorporates thirty ethnicities, including people from as far west on the Asian
continent as Pakistan, the indigenous peoples of the Pacific Islands, and the
offspring from interracial marriages. There are nearly 8.8 million Asian
Pacific Americans, projected to reach 12.1 million—roughly 4 percent of the
U.S. population—by the year 2000. About six in ten live in the western region
of the U.S., and 87 percent live in one of fifteen metropolitan areas, most
notably the Los Angeles, San Francisco Bay, and greater New York metropolitan areas. The makeup of this group is complex, with differences in
language, religious beliefs, and cultural values existing even among population subgroups.

Compared to Whites, a higher proportion of the Asian Pacific American
population is employed in health care, science, technology, and other technical occupations. Many work in retail trade, manufacturing, and service-
related industries. Some segments of the Asian Pacific American population,
especially recent immigrants, remain in low-paying service and manufacturing jobs. There are many Asian Pacific American entrepreneurs. Some 400,000
Asian Pacific American-owned U.S. firms bring annual receipts of $33 billion
into the U.S. economy.

On average, Asian Pacific Americans are highly educated: 41 percent are
college graduates, compared with 24 percent of Whites. However, Asian
Pacific Americans' median individual earnings average lower. Their median
family household income is higher than that of Whites, but this is often due to
Asian Pacific Americans living in larger, extended family households with
multiple wage earners. Roughly one million Asian Pacific Americans, or 11
percent, live in poverty. About 90 percent of these disadvantaged are recent
immigrants. Half of the Vietnamese, Laotian, and Cambodian refugees live
below the poverty level.

Many Pacific Islanders have experienced more pronounced difficulties than their sister Asian Americans. In some instances, Pacific Islanders have been hurt by being grouped with Asian Americans where Asian Americans were not eligible for affirmative action.

◆  ◆  ◆  ◆  ◆

## CASE FOR CRITICAL THINKING

### Who Am I?

Jose's grandfather was a pure blooded Japanese whose parents had migrated to Peru, in South America, when he was just a small boy. The grandfather later married a Peruvian woman and they had four children—two boys and two girls, in that order. Jose's father was the eldest son. Jose's grandmother died shortly after the birth of her last child, the younger of Jose's two aunts.

During World War II, the American and Peruvian governments worked out an exchange program that entailed sending all of Peru's Japanese immigrants to the United States in exchange for resources needed by the Peruvian government. In a sense, the U.S. government "bought" Peru's ethnic Japanese for use as hostages who could later be traded to the Japanese government in exchange for American prisoners held by Japan. Jose's grandfather and his four children were uprooted overnight and shipped with only a few belongings to an encampment in the United States. They were, of course, shocked by the sudden traumatic experience and bewildered by their new surroundings, but, ironically, their greatest difficulties arose from having to confront a new and completely strange language—Japanese. At home in Peru, they had only learned to speak Spanish.

Despite all these difficulties, the family survived. Years later, Jose's father married an urbanized Native American computer programmer whose ancestors had migrated to America from East Asia hundreds of centuries earlier. Jose is their only child. Jose's uncle married an Australian whose ancestors migrated to Australia from the Caucasus, an area once besieged by the Mongol empire. Jose has two cousins from this marriage.

Jose's younger aunt married a man from France whose adoptive parents are Vietnamese and French. When Jose's uncle was a boy, this couple found him wandering the streets of Saigon and believed him to be the abandoned off-spring of a Vietnamese mother and an African American G.I. father. They brought him up in Europe, then later sent him to college in the United States, where he met Jose's aunt. Jose's uncle is now a widely acclaimed forensic psychologist, and the couple is expecting a child. Jose, meanwhile, is planning to marry a native Hawaiian.

*Questions for Thought and Discussion*

1. Can all of Jose's cousins be classified as Asian Pacific Americans, as defined by the U.S. Census Bureau? As defined by Shinagawa and Pang?
2. What groups or individuals benefit from an inclusive classification system? Who might benefit more from noninclusive classification?
3. What kinds of stereotyping might Jose be likely to encounter in the workplace?
4. Many factors over the centuries have significantly altered human appearances and created new genetic combinations, especially in the United States. Discuss some of the reasons why we continue to group human beings by race.
5. How would ethnic studies and diversity programs benefit individual workers, as well as human resources managers, in American organizations?

◆ ◆ ◆ ◆ ◆

## EXPERIENTIAL EXERCISE

"Asian Pacific Americans in the twenty-first century will have a great impact on the development of our economy. Younger generations of Asian Pacific Americans, if not already there, are on their way to becoming movers and shakers who influence American society."

*Objectives*

To present students with an opportunity to reassess their own assumptions about and understanding of current Asian Pacific American status. Students are to compare their own thoughts with their classmates' understanding and assumptions.

*Before the Class Meeting*

Ask students to choose a topic area such as economics, politics, or social sciences, and ask them to think of as many "Asian Pacific American movers and shakers" in their chosen area as possible.

*Starting the Exercise*

1. Divide the students into groups according to their chosen topic areas, economic, political, social, and so on.
2. Have group members compare their findings and decide whether the opening statement above is true or false.
3. After a specific time period, bring the whole class together for group discussion. Ask each group to reiterate its consensus and to elaborate reasons for the position taken.

## NOTES

1. Additional reasons can be found in Stanley M. Garn, *Human Races,* 3d ed. (Springfield, IL: Charles C Thomas, 1971).

2. Richard A. Goldsby, *Race and Races,* 2d ed. (New York: Macmillan, 1977); Morton Klass and Hal Hellman, *The Kind of Mankind: An Introduction to Race and Racism* (New York: Harper & Row, 1981).

3. The *World Book Encyclopedia* (1991) classified these nine geographical races clearly under the heading "Races, Human." The article indicates that, although no two human beings are exactly alike, members of a single geographical race will tend to resemble one another in various ways. Today, with increasing migration, new genetic combinations have been added to the human population. Roughly half of the people of European descent live outside of Europe. In Hawaii, many people have combined European-Hawaiian-Asian ancestry.

4. Included in the U.S. census data are people who reported themselves as one of the nine categories and other who wrote in another specific Asian Pacific American ethnicity. For further understanding of Asian Pacific American groupings by the U.S. government, refer to "We the Americans: Asians" and "We the Americans: Pacific Islanders in the Unted States." Both reports

were issued in September 1993 by the U.S. Department of Commerce, Economics and Statistics Administration, Bureau of the Census (Washington, DC).

5. Larry Hajime Shinagawa, "Racial Classification of Asian Americans" (Paper presented at the Office of Management and Budget hearing, San Francisco, 15 July 1994).

6. Descriptions of these first Filipino Americans in Louisiana, who established villages outside New Orleans, can be found in *Filipinos: Forgotten Asian Americans* by F. Cordova (Dubuque, IA: Kendall/Hunt, 1983). J. M. Jensen gave an account of how Asian Indians were brought to New England as indentured servants by captains of merchant ships in *Passage from India: Asian Indian Immigrants in North America* (New Haven, CT: Yale University Press, 1988).

7. Records kept by immigration authorities counted about 370,000 Chinese arrivals in Hawaii and California between late 1840 and early 1880. In the subsequent three decades, about 400,000 Japanese landed at Honolulu and part of the U.S. Pacific coast. For more on Chinese emigration, read Sing-Wu Wang, *The Organization of Chinese Emigration, 1848-1888* (San Francisco: Chinese Material Center, 1976) and Robert G. Lee, *The Origins of Chinese Immigration to the United States, 1848-1882* (San Francisco: Chinese Historical Society of America, 1976). For accounts of Japanese emigration, see Hilary E. Conroy, *The Japanese Frontier in Hawaii 1868-1898* (Berkeley: University of California Press, 1953) and Yasui Wakatsuki, "Japanese Emigration to the United States, 1866-1924" in *Perspectives in American History* 12 (1979): 389-516.

8. Works providing understanding of the recent immigration phenomenon include David M. Reimers, *Still the Golden Door: The Third World Comes to America* (New York: Columbia University Press, 1985) and James T. Fawcett and Ben V. Cavino, eds., *Pacific Bridges: The New Immigration from Asia and the Pacific Islands* (New York: Center for Migration Studies, 1987).

9. The 87 percent estimation is derived from the September 1993 report titled "We the Americans: Pacific Islanders in the United States" published by the U.S. Department of Commerce, Bureau of the Census (Washington, DC: U.S. Government Printing Office).

10. Refer to the article by Nina Chen, "Spotlight on Pacific Islanders," *Asian Week,* 7 July 1995.

11. Greater detail can be found in Sung-Nam Cho and Herbert Barringer, *Koreans in the United States* (Honolulu: Center for Korean Studies, 1989); Ivan Light and Edna Bonacich, *Immigrant Entrepreneurs: Koreans in L.A.* (Berkeley: University of California Press, 1988); Barry Wain, *The Refused: The Agony of the Indochina Refugees* (New York: Simon & Schuster, 1981);

Paul J. Strand and Woodrow Jones, Jr., *Indochinese Refugees in America* (Raleigh, NC: Duke University Press, 1985).

12. Roger Daniels, *Concentration Camps USA: Japanese Americans and World War II* (New York: New York University Press, 1971).

13. Claudette E. Bennett, "The Asian and Pacific Islander Population in the United States: March, 1994," Racial Statistics Branch, Population Division, U.S. Bureau of the Census.

14. It is impossible to select only one or two representatives from the many excellent books, both fiction and nonfiction, about this group of immigrants. There are also some fine films on the Asian Pacific American experience; both students and instructors should enjoy viewing "American Chinatown" by Todd Carrel (30 min., color, U.C. Extension Media Center, Berkeley) and "The Gary Locke Story" (CNN, January 1997). In "Chinatown: The Hidden Cities of San Francisco" (Mark Powelson, KQED video, 1996), personal recollections and archival photos chronicle the tumultuous and inspiring history and how the people thrived.

15. See chap. 1, n. 20.

16. *Who's Who among Asian Americans* (Detroit, MI: Gale Research, 1995) lists thousands of high-profile achievers from among this group; space does not permit reproducing them here, and any sampling might accidentally omit someone worthy of inclusion. See also "100 Great Asian American Entrepreneurs," *Transpacific* (December 1994).

17. This information has appeared numerous times in daily newspaper and magazine accounts, including Bruce Nolan's report on illegal immigrants, "Not Quite So Welcome Anymore" (*Time,* Fall 1993) and, more recently, in the San Francisco journal *Asian Week*'s "Asian Pacific American Population Report: January 1996."

18. Althea Yip, "Careers on the Fast Track," *Asian Week,* 7 March 1997.

19. Yen Le Espiritu, *Asian American Panethnicity: Bridging Institutions and Identities* (Philadelphia: Temple University Press, 1992); Larry Hajime Shinagawa and Gin Yong Pang, "Asian American Pan-Ethnicity and Intermarriage," *Amerasia Journal* (1996): 3, 32.

20. Pico Iyer, "The Global Village Finally Arrives," in *Time* special issue, "The New Face of America: How Immigrants Are Shaping the World's First Multinational Society" (Fall 1993).

21. *Time* special issue, "The New Face of America: How Immigrants Are Shaping the World's First Multinational Society" (Fall 1993).

22. Espiritu, *Asian American Panethnicity.*

23. Current Population Survey by U.S. Department of Commerce, Bureau of the Census (Washington, DC, March 1994).

24. Althea Yip, "The Big Picture," *Asian Week,* 3 January 1997.

25. Data obtained from a report titled "The Asian & Pacific Island Population in the United States: March 1994," U.S. Bureau of the Census, Racial Statistics Branch, Population Division (http://www.census.gov).

26. Reported by R. P. Baker and D. S. North in their 1984 study for the New Trans Century Foundation, Washington, DC.

27. Description of Asian Pacific American neighborhoods and restaurant figures from "Capitol of the Rim," *Seattle Times,* 14 August 1985.

28. All statistical tables contained in this section can be retrieved from the U.S. Bureau of the Census, "1990 Census of Population, Asian & Pacific Islanders in the U.S." (Washington, DC: U.S. Government Printing Office, 1993).

29. Larry Hajime Shinagawa, "The Impact of Immigration on Demography of Asian Pacific Americans," in Bill Ong Hing and Ronald Lee, eds., *Reframing the Immigration Debate* (Los Angeles: LEAP Asian Pacific American Public Policy Institute and UCLA Asian American Studies Center, 1996).

30. Job Classification Guide, to be used with Employer Information Report EEO-1 (Washington, DC: Office of Program Operations, ORPP-Program Research and Surveys Division, U.S. Equal Employment Opportunity Commission, 1994).

31. The 1991 study conducted by the East-West Publications Institute further details the large percentage of Korean-owned ethnic businesses.

32. Pyong Gap Min, "Korean Americans," in *Asian Americans: Contemporary Trends and Issues* (Thousand Oaks, CA: Sage, 1995).

33. In addition, Peterson stated that the influx of Asian immigrants, many educated in the U.S., are bringing jobs and innovation to the U.S. market. See J. Peterson, "Asian Entrepreneurs," *Los Angeles Times,* 6 August 1989.

34. "1990 Census of the Population, General Social and Economic Characteristics in the United States," U.S. Bureau of the Census (Washington, DC: U.S. Government Printing Office, 1994).

35. A. Cabezas, L. Shinagawa, and G. Kawaguchi, "New Inquiries into the Socioeconomic Status of Pilipino Americans in California," *Amerasia Journal* 13 (1986-1987): 1-12.

36. This is derived from the U.S. census report, September 1993, as well as from personal observations. Furthermore, Pauline Fong and Amado Cabezas noted this phenomenon as early as 1980 and reported their findings in "Economic and Employment Status of Asian Pacific Women" (U.S. Department of

Education Conference on the Educational and Occupational Needs of Asian Pacific American Women, October 1980).

37. This is also documented in the fact-finding March 1995 report of the federal Glass Ceiling Commission in the focus groups with Asian, African American, and Latino executives.

38. Deborah Woo, "The Glass Ceiling and Asian Americans" (Research report funded for the U.S. Department of Labor, Glass Ceiling Commission, July 1994).

39. In comparison, examine the statistical data provided by the U.S. Department of Education. To gain further knowledge about the aspirations and perceptions of Asian Pacific Americans in higher education, read Jayzia Hsia, *Asian Americans in Higher Education and at Work* (Hillsdale, NJ: Lawrence Erlbaum, 1988).

40. Further discussion and statistical data can be found in chap. 3 of Paul Ong, ed., *The State of Asian Pacific American Economic Diversity, Issues and Policies* (Los Angeles: LEAP Asian Pacific American Public Policy Institute, 1994).

41. Dana Takagi debated the admissions controversy surrounding Asian Pacific Americans at Berkeley, UCLA, Stanford, Harvard, Brown, and Princeton in *The Retreat from Race: Asian American Admissions and Racial Politics* (New Brunswick, NJ: Rutgers University Press, 1992).

42. This 1992 report is titled *Minorities in Higher Education* and was prepared by Deborah Carter and Reginald Wilson and funded by the American Council on Education.

43. Eugenia Escueta and Eileen O'Brien, "Asian Americans in Higher Education: Trends and Issues" (Research report for the American Council on Education, 1991).

44. Paula Reiss and Delores Thurgood, *Summary Report of Doctorate Recipients from United States Universities* (Washington, DC: National Academy Press, 1993).

45. "We the Americans: Asians" (Washington, DC: U.S. Department of Commerce, Economic and Statistics Administration, Bureau of the Census, 1993).

46. "The Asian Pacific American Population in the U.S.," 1-32. (Washington, DC: U.S. Bureau of the Census, Racial Statistics Branch, Population Division, March 1994).

47. Shinagawa, in Hing and Lee, *Reframing the Immigration Debate.*

48. "1990 Census of the Population, Asian and Pacific Islanders in the U.S.," U.S. Bureau of the Census (Washington, DC: U.S. Government Printing Office, 1993).

49. Shinagawa, in Hing and Lee, *Reframing the Immigration Debate.*

50. Chen, "Spotlight on Pacific Islanders."

# Individual Attributes, Group Interactions, and Organization Issues

# Three

# Personal Development
# of Asian Pacific Americans
## *Motivation, Perception, and Role Theories*

"I always heard my parents talking about college. Never bringing shame upon the family played an important role," said Dr. Yue, a fourth-generation Chinese American who can trace her roots to the California railroad-building days.

"I would have liked very much to get a college degree . . . but since my brother is more the intellectual type and one of us had to work . . . we thought it's best to cultivate him, the smart one in the family," said Mr. Phan, a refugee from Vietnam who now owns a chain of grocery stores.

"We were obscenely rich . . . a maid would help us dress for school. . . . Until I left home, I had never put on my own socks. Then overnight, all our property was confiscated by the government," said Ivy, a successful securities broker who came as an immigrant from Indonesia via Guam in the early 1970s.

"My father's untimely death enabled me to gain insight into human nature. . . . Asian cultures emphasize learning and achievement, . . . but most were brought up with the 'Fear of Power' syndrome," said Dr. N., a world-renowned scholar who occupies a top administrative position in higher education.

In the following pages, you will find the stories of the individuals introduced above and learn more about the forces that motivate highly accomplished Asian Pacific Americans. As we have seen from the statistical data, many Asian Pacific Americans have established careers both in higher education and in various other, mostly technical professions. Behind such statistics, there are individuals working extremely hard to achieve specific predetermined goals and doing so despite a number of formidable obstacles. Knowing what made these individuals willing to work so hard to achieve their goals is, of course, of great interest to organizational managers and others interested in human behavior.

In this chapter, we will provide insight into factors that motivate a number of Asian Pacific Americans. To what do achievement-oriented Asian Pacific Americans owe their accomplishments? How do these people perceive themselves and the roles[1] they play in society in general, and within an organization or workplace in particular?

To begin with, we must ask what motivates anyone to undertake challenging and difficult tasks. Do people go to work only because they need the money? Or do some also work hard for security, status, a sense of belonging, or even an opportunity to learn and grow?

Many theorists, including Campbell, Dunnette, Lawler, and Weick,[2] and more recently Robbins,[3] have tried to explain the motivation to work and have tried to identify factors within individuals or personality types that energize and direct human behaviors. One of the most widely discussed motivation theories is the *need hierarchy model* of Abraham Maslow.[4] Clayton Alderfer[5] later modified Maslow's model and proposed the *ERG theory*. Both theories (see Box 3.1) are derived from similar general assumptions about human needs. Organizational managers can use these models as guides for understanding human motivations so that they will be able to establish systems which promote employee satisfaction by responding to varying levels of employee needs.[6]

Another researcher, Frederick Herzberg, derived the *two-factor theory*.[7] Herzberg and his associates concluded that two different sets of factors affect one's experiences at work, namely, hygiene factors and satisfiers. Hygiene factors, also called extrinsic conditions, are those which encourage workers to

---

Box 3.1
*Needs Theories*

The most widely cited and discussed motivation theory is Abraham Maslow's five-level hierarchy of needs, consisting of (1) physiological needs, (2) the need for safety, (3) a sense of belonging, (4) esteem needs, and (5) self-actualization needs. According to Maslow, a person attempts to satisfy the more basic, physiological needs for food and shelter before directing behavior upward toward the next level of needs and ultimately satisfying higher level needs for self-actualization and the fulfillment of one's abilities and potentials.

Alderfer's ERG theory similarly categorizes needs using the simpler hierarchy: (1) Existence, (2) Relating to others, and (3) Growth. This accords with Maslow's hierarchy generally but differs in that if higher needs are being blocked it is possible for managers to redirect subordinates' efforts toward lower level needs.

---

keep (or quit) their jobs. These are pay or wages, job security, working conditions, company policies, and interpersonal relations. The satisfiers, or intrinsic conditions, include achievement, recognition, responsibility, advancement, and the nature of the work itself. The satisfiers are the factors which actually motivate workers. Herzberg's theory seems to have universal appeal with managers in the international arena.[8]

Skinner and Locke are among the most notable process theorists.[9] Process theorists believe that willingness to work is essentially an instinctive or primarily unconscious reaction. For example, in response to a physical stimulus such as hunger, people go in search of food, whereas in response to a psychological stimulus such as feeling threatened, people will seek security. There is not a great deal of free will involved in this approach, although different personality types may be motivated by dissimilar stimuli. For example, some individuals may be dominated by their more aggressive and sexual impulses, whereas others will tend to follow the endless pursuit of higher wisdom or a utopian dream.

The theories cited above suggest that motivation is primarily a matter of a response to a stimulus. However, it may be the case that willingness to work hard is, conversely, primarily the result of a conscious, deliberate decision to do so.

According to Charles B. Handy's motivational calculus theory[10] (see Box 3.2), which deals with the way an individual decides either to do something or not do it, motivation may result from a mixture of all of the various elements and forces which constitute any individual's internal decision-making process. For example, differences in upbringing, childhood experiences and environment, and predominant cultural values would obviously result in individuals with different aspirations and potentially dissimilar responses to similar opportunities and challenges.

---

Box 3.2

Charles B. Handy, Professor at the London Graduate School of Business Studies, widened the application of motivation theory by asserting that motivation calculus is the mechanism by which one decides how much of "E" one will expend on any particular activity or set of activities. The "E" stands in part for "Energy," but it also includes Expenditures of time and money as well as the Enthusiasm and Excitement one brings to the task at hand and one's Emotional reactions. This approach is based on the idea that a person is a self-actualizing organism who can, to some degree, control his or her own destiny and select the response to a set of needs that is most likely to achieve the desired results.

---

One theory that has practical, functional applications for managers is D. C. McClelland's learned needs theory[11] (see Box 3.3). McClelland's work suggests that people work in order to compensate for something specific that is lacking in their lives, either something tangible—whether it be food or a new sports car—or something intangible such as a need for affiliation, achievement, or power. He further maintains that motivation is clearly associated with learning concepts; that many needs are learned during childhood and acquired from the culture of the surrounding society.[12] He also contends that motivation can be taught in organizations.[13] The most interesting research study directed by McClelland and his associates led to the "fear of success" hypothesis.[14] According to the conclusion of that study, most women express conflict over success because of reaction to fears of social rejection or a negative self-image.

The "fear of success" for many women and minority members in this society is not a personality trait but rather a learned supposition triggered by certain socioeconomic historical conditions.

An exploratory study based on McClelland's theory and conducted by Professor Wu and her students during the spring of 1997 found that Asian Pacific Americans[15] raised with traditional Asian cultural values tend to score

---

Box 3.3

D. C. McClelland's learned needs theory assumes that many needs are acquired from one's social culture. Three of these learned needs are the need for affiliation (nAff); the need for power (nPow), and the need for achievement (nAch).

When a particular need is strong in a person, it will direct that person's behavior so as to achieve satisfaction of that particular need. Most people have all of the above needs, but seldom do they have equal strength.

*The need for power (nPow).* As a result of his TAT tests, a projective technique that encourages respondents to reveal their needs, McClelland concluded that most managers have a high need for power. In general, individuals high in nPow are competitive, aggressive, and interested in prestige possessions. They are also action-oriented and, although they join many groups, are unconcerned with developing close relations with others.

*The need for affiliation (nAff).* Individuals high in nAff tend to be more concerned with developing and maintaining good relationships than with utilizing their power. They are not task-oriented. Although some need for affiliation is present in most managers, it is seldom dominant in successful managers.

*The need for achievement (nAch).* Individuals with high nAch will set challenging goals and then use their skills and abilities, along with hard work, to attain them. The nAch motive is necessary for a person to achieve success, but it does not equate with being a good manager because the satisfaction of nAch often means a focus on personal improvement and a tendency to do things themselves rather than delegate them.

McClelland seems to believe that a society's economic growth is based on the level of nAch inherent in its people, and, further, that the need to achieve can be taught within organizations.

---

high on the need for achievement, with great concentration on the goals they think they can achieve, and low on the need for power, perhaps due to negative traditional cultural assessment of the individual power seeker.

As you read the following case histories of Asian Pacific Americans and some of the difficulties they have faced in the American workplace, remember to think about the factors that motivated each of these individuals as well as their self-perceptions (self-image) and the role concepts each holds. Considering the experiences and values of these Asian Pacific Americans will also enable you to think about your own personal experiences and motivational calculus: the rules by which you live your life, how your personality responds to challenge and rewards and the changing external environment, and whether its positive or negative force affects your perceptions and behavior in the workplace.


## Case #1: The Dutiful Daughter

"I always heard my parents talking about college," said Dr. Yue, "and how children who went to college made a worthwhile contribution to society and made their families proud. There was no question in my mind, as I was growing up, that I would become a college graduate so that I, too, could make my parents proud of me."

Dr. Yue is a 34-year-old dentist. She was born to a third-generation Chinese American family and can trace her roots to the California railroad-building days. Her parents own a highly successful small business.

"By the time I was in high school, we didn't question whether we would go to college or join the workforce instead. The conversations we had with relatives and friends of the family were always the same—never, 'Are you going to college?' but always 'Which colleges are you applying to?'

"However," sighed Yue, "I was not a particularly bright student—not like my cousins who have SAT scores of 1500. I always felt intimidated by my relatives' scholastic achievements. The thought of causing my parents shame was so dreadful that I even used to dream of running away to the country. I imagined that there was some rural and backwards place where I could hide and not be exposed as a 'low achiever.'

"Of course, really running away was an impossibility. I had no alternative but to try as hard as I could, so I gave up all the things that a normal American teenager enjoys. I don't mean only that I just gave up going to parties and dating; I gave up having friends. I gave up all the activities that develop social skills and devoted my time exclusively to studying. I had to attend an SAT workshop to improve my SAT scores, go to math workshops so that I could get good grades and live up to the image of me I wanted other people to have. More than anything else, I was afraid of disappointing my parents.

"I graduated with honors from high school, but my SAT score was still only 1150. I remember my parents praising me lavishly for being awarded honors, but also reminding me that my cousin William's SAT score was 1510."

Dr. Yue studied teacher's education and taught junior high for several years. "Being a teacher was the most respected profession in the traditions of old China. I expected my career choice to please my parents, but I discovered that all I was really doing was displeasing the parents of my students. In retrospect, what I failed to do was to develop the social and human relations skills needed to communicate most effectively with other people. I was too direct in my approach to my students and to others and so was perceived as blunt and insensitive. In my evaluations, I was told that I do not have a caring personality. No one could see me for the sensitive, caring person I really am. The entire experience became very painful to me, and I knew that I had to choose a different path. It took a lot of soul searching, but in the end I made up my mind to go to dental school.

"One summer some years earlier, I had helped out in a dental office and had liked it. Once I made up my mind, both of my parents supported me one hundred percent, financially and emotionally. It took a lot of hard work and determination to change careers in my thirties, but it was worth it. Now," grinned Dr. Yue, "my parents are very proud of me.

"So, in answer to the question of who or what motivated me to work harder, I guess the answer has always definitely been my parents, and the kind of environment in which they raised me. I suppose the traditional stress on never bringing shame upon the family also played a much more important role than I once realized. I feel happy to have fulfilled my parents' expectations of me. I think I feel happy, too, because my self-image is closer to other people's expectations now. My own expectations are better reconciled with the role I play in society."

## Case #2: The Pious Son

"What motivates me to work harder?" asked Mr. Phan. "I think it is definitely something I learned in early childhood, part of my upbringing as well as my subsequent experience." Mr. Phan is an ethnic Chinese who came to the U.S. as a refugee from Vietnam in 1979, about four years after the Vietnam War ended. Today, Phan owns a chain of grocery stores in southern California.

"My father was always a small business man in Vietnam. Ever since I can remember, I followed him around in his store. I watched how hard he worked during the war, amidst the devastating economic conditions brought by conflict. When we left Vietnam, we had nothing of our own. We lost everything except each other, the family. Even then, my mother died on the refugee boat in the Gulf of Thailand.

"Eventually, the three of us—my younger brother, my father, and I—arrived in Arkansas. We immediately went to work for a manufacturing company. The work was very difficult and we only earned minimum wage, yet it was like heaven compared to what we had gone through in the four previous years. Even on minimum wages, we saved enough to move to California, where one of my father's former business associates, a businessman originally from Taiwan, had already established himself. He operated a produce market in San Jose."

Phan and his father both went to work in the produce market as soon as they made their way to San Jose. The family decided, however, that Phan's younger brother should continue his schooling.

"I would have liked very much to get a college degree," said Phan, "but I knew that, between my brother and myself, one of us had to work. All three of us couldn't live solely on my father's wages, and since my brother is more the intellectual type than I am, we thought it would be best to cultivate the smart one in the family." Mr. Phan speaks five languages fluently—Vietnamese, Cantonese, Mandarin, English, and French—yet presents himself as a man of modest intelligence. In his own perceptions, he is a practical-minded "doer" and not the best candidate for a life of scholarly pursuits.

"Two years after we arrived in San Jose, my father was found to have cancer. He died only three months later. There was a rumor that many Vietnamese from my father's village died from cancer, because millions of gallons of the defoliant Agent Orange had been dumped nearby. The long-term effects of such dumping are still unknown.[16]

"Before my father died, I was never truly afraid. We came close to death many times, but I always felt that I had someone I could count on. No matter how painful things were or how much devastation we endured, it seemed my father could make everything come out all right."

Although it had been twelve years since his father's death, Mr. Phan's eyes filled with tears as he spoke. "I would have done anything for him, and he could motivate me to do the impossible. All that kept me going after I lost him was the sense of responsibility he had instilled in us. That is what motivated me to get up in the morning and go to work. I had promised him that I would take care of my younger brother and support him while he got a good education."

Mr. Phan kept his promise to his father; indeed, he did not even date for as long as his brother remained in school. It was not until six years ago, when his brother had graduated from college with a degree in computer technology, that Mr. Phan finally married.

Today, Phan's brother lives in Texas and works for an international corporation. "My father would have been proud of him," said Mr. Phan. He paused a moment and seemed to be fighting more tears. "My father would have been proud of me, too," he said. "How I wish he could see my wonderful wife and our two beautiful sons."

Mr. Phan works today at his chain of retail stores. His wife has also left her position as an office manager for a financial institution and helps him manage his business. Her mother provides child care for the Phans' two sons, ages four and five. Mr. Phan's mother-in-law teaches the two children her native languages, reads to them every morning, and teaches them to tend a small patch of vegetables in the garden. Every afternoon, the boys go with her to visit the park or library or go shopping. Soon they will begin taking music lessons.

"We believe in forming good habits while they are still young. Even though my wife and I are extremely busy with a twelve-hour working day, we still make sure that we both spend enough time with them. I want them to love me just as I loved my father. No matter what else changes, this tradition has to continue.

"Both of my sons love to sit on my lap at night on the porch, just gazing at the stars in the big, dark sky. I think one of them will be an astronomer, and the other a mathematician because he is constantly counting things and trying to figure out sizes, shapes, and patterns of everything." Mr. Phan gave a laugh of pleasure, then suddenly became very quiet.

"Do you believe in ghosts or spirits?" he asked. "When we sit in the dark, I can always feel my father's presence, as if he were right here with us, still guiding us all through life, helping us stay on the correct path."

## Case #3: The Poor Rich Maiden

Ivy came to the U.S. from Guam in the early 1970s. She was born into a very wealthy family living in Indonesia. Her ancestors were originally from China.

"We were obscenely rich," Ivy explained. "There were five servants assigned just to the family's three children. We rode in chauffeur-driven cars and were spoon-fed by maids even when we were old enough to start kindergarten. A maid would help us get dressed for school in the morning. Until I left home, I had never put on my own socks. Can you believe it? The servants did everything for us.

"Then, overnight, the Indonesian government confiscated all we owned and expelled us from the country. Within three more years, my parents were divorced. My father took my brother to live in Japan and married a Japanese national. She is a successful entrepreneur. My mother married an Australian and took my sister to live with them. They now live in Papua New Guinea. I was the one whom no one wanted. I ended up living in Guam with my aunt.

"My aunt's husband was a White American G.I. The couple had no children of their own, so they adopted me. It was a tremendously difficult and traumatic time in my life, both physically and emotionally. I cried myself to sleep each night; I lost my sense of belonging, and my sense of self-esteem had been turned into feelings of inferiority. Without the help of servants, I did not yet know how to perform even the most everyday tasks.

"My aunt and her husband were amazed at my incompetence. They forced me to learn things in a hurry, and, in a way, they forced me to regain my sense of self-worth pretty quickly. But a feeling of insecurity has followed me throughout my life, even to this day."

Ivy gave a nervous laugh and lit a cigarette. A securities broker with a major stock brokerage firm, Ivy is highly successful by conventional accounts. She has an annual income of more than six figures and lives in a million-dollar home overlooking a lake and a golf course.

"The strange thing is that, somehow, the fact that my parents caused my devastating childhood provided my motivation. As soon as I recovered from the initial shock of the abandonment, I vowed that some day I would be rich again and that my parents would see they had made a mistake when they gave me away. My dream was that somehow, some day, I would amass a fortune of fifty million dollars. This was literally my only goal.

"My aunt and her husband were not the easiest people to live with. They were very set in their ways. They made high demands on me as far as schoolwork was concerned. But they never really wanted me to be wealthy or a career woman. I figured out all on my own to major in finance at college and to get a securities trading license. Step by step, I saved all my paychecks while continuing to live with my aunt. My aunt had a terrible temper. It took a lot of patience to live with her, but I endured everything for the sake of my dream and kept saving every penny I could.

"The first fifty thousand dollars were the hardest to save. It took four years, but once I had that kind of capital, it took only two more years to save the second fifty thousand. From then on, it all fell into place. I had a carefully devised master financial investment plan. I was also blessed with very good luck.''

Ivy's aunt and uncle died within a year of one another, seven years ago. They left her their house and an apartment building as well.

"One day five years ago, I had just posted an equity of five million dollars in my account—only ten percent of what I had originally planned—when I received the news from Japan of my father's death. At that very same moment, I completely lost the drive to fulfill my ambition.

"Since then, I have reconciled with my mother, and she has come to visit me once. She was profoundly apologetic, trying hard to explain to me why she and my father had acted as they had. I told my mother to let bygones be bygones. I said, 'Let's not relive all the agony; let's live for the future.' But the perplexing thing is, I don't know anymore what kind of future awaits me. Over the years, all I have wanted and all I have learned how to do is to make money!''

Ivy is now in her mid-forties. She was frank enough to admit that she has had several love affairs and almost got married ten years ago to an investor from Hong Kong, but he had wanted her to move to his home. Ivy had been unwilling to change her job or give up her fifty-million-dollar dream. She didn't think her potential husband would be able to make her dream come true alone, so she let him go.

"Thinking back, it seems so odd to have given up what was probably my best chance for real happiness in exchange for such an incredible dream. At that time, my whole conscious being was driven and motivated exclusively by just that one single, narrow vision. That fifty million dollars was a curse upon me. Then, suddenly, without any struggle, it was lifted by my father's death. With no one left to whom I could prove myself, my motivation simply evaporated.''

Ivy's present lover is a married Roman Catholic. He will never divorce his wife to marry Ivy, and, since she is past child-bearing age, Ivy will never have children of her own.

"Well, maybe I should cut down on the hours I work and volunteer some time to a charity or social welfare group. When everything has been said and done, there is no question that this country has been good to me. Perhaps it is time for me to pay something back.''


## Case #4: The Power Behind the Power Broker

Dr. N came to the U.S. to study for a graduate degree and received his Ph.D. in science from an Ivy League college on the East Coast. Today, he is a world-renowned scholar who occupies a top position in educational administration. Such accomplishments did not come to him easily; on the contrary, Dr. N has worked extremely hard. He is an exceptionally intelligent, diligent, and organized person who has trained himself to remember facts, not only the most minute details and statistical data pertinent to his work but also, for example, the characteristics, faces, and names of everyone he has met throughout his career.

Dr. N pursues perfection relentlessly. He learned to speak with barely a trace of an Asian accent by going to a speech therapist and faithfully practicing his English with a tape recorder every day. He also learned how to cultivate effective relationships with the people in his organization who held key business positions or political power. He carefully advanced his position in the organization by learning office etiquette and socializing within a network of important and influential contacts. He worked an average of sixteen to eighteen hours each day.

Asked to discuss the source of the motivation behind such a powerful drive for achievement, Dr. N explained, "First of all, I am a very healthy person. I only need four hours of sleep per night, and I have the mental and emotional intelligence for quick and sound judgment. But above all else, I enjoy being in a powerful position.

"My family was in high society, back in the old country. My father held a cabinet position in the government. We had banquet dinners regularly, with key political figures as our honored guests. My father helped countless other people, both politically and financially. Yet all the while he was in power, he steadfastly refused to accept either gifts or favors. He was a man of honesty, with genuine integrity. He and my mother had four children. I am the second youngest son."

Dr. N has been unable to maintain the close relations with his three siblings that he would have liked. He has an older brother living in the U.S. who is an engineer and married to a Eurasian, but this couple does not have close relations with either of their extended families because the sister-in-law places a rather low value on kinship bonds. Dr. N also has an older sister who remained behind in their native country. She married into a well-to-do family and works at home; she also supports her husband's career by serving as hostess to his influential clients. The youngest brother, who also lives in the U.S., was the family "black sheep" and seemed disinterested in studying or bettering himself. However, after a brief membership in a gang, and with Dr. N's help both financially and emotionally, this young man turned himself around and now operates a fast food restaurant.

"When my father suddenly died of a heart attack," Dr. N explained, "he left us penniless. I was a junior in college and my brother was still in high school. Do you think a single one of my father's business friends and associates would lend us a hand? No one even bothered to show up at our home again. Overnight we had become paupers, unable even to pay our daily living expenses. It was a great blow to my mother, but an important lesson to me. I learned that power is one of the most essential ingredients in a successful career. Unless you are in a position of power, you are nobody.

"I also think that my father's untimely death contributed to my younger brother's later troubles. My brother couldn't adjust to being reduced to nothingness. At least, in a gang, he could feel 'different,' and the gang situation offered him a sense of brotherhood, even though it was a false brotherhood."

To continue his college education, Dr. N became a tutor. He found a position as a mathematics tutor to the children of a rich family. Over time, he and one of his pupils fell in love. After they were married, her parents agreed to help Dr. N finance his continued studies.

Despite his scientific background, Dr. N claims a strong belief in fate. "I believe in destiny, karma, fate, God's blessing—whatever you wish to call it. My father's early death made me a stronger person, which also indirectly led me to marry my wife. More importantly, the tragedy of losing my father enabled me to gain insights into human nature. It gave me a more realistic view of what human relationships are all about and motivated me to seek out a position of leadership.

"I think one of the reasons that fewer Asian Pacific Americans are in leadership positions is the negative image in Asian cultures of power-seeking individuals. Most Asian Pacific Americans also have the 'fear of power' syndrome, a strong avoidance reaction resulting from fear of the negative consequences they associate with any deviation, under normal circumstances, from the traditional culture in which they were brought up.

"In my view—and I have been a living example of this—Asian Pacific Americans may be excellent candidates for management positions because they were brought up to esteem good relationships with others. Our value systems typically emphasize learning and achievement, and consequently, Asian Pacific Americans might be better suited to motivate other employees than are some of the autocratic, traditional White managers."

## Discussion and Analysis

The first two cases presented above, "The Dutiful Daughter" and "The Pious Son," describe individuals who were influenced by the traditional Asian cultural values of filial piety, perseverance, hard work, and avoiding feelings of shame. Although Dr. Yue was born in the United States and Mr. Phan was an immigrant from Vietnam, both viewed their elders—Dr. Yue's parents and Mr. Phan's father—as the most important factor in motivating them to work harder.

This sentiment coincides with the feelings expressed by the other individuals interviewed for this study, more than two-thirds of whom expressed strong feelings with regard to meeting parental expectations and other family obligations. In Dr. Yue's case, short-term pleasures and immediate gratification were sacrificed in favor of long-term gain and development. As found in the study by De Vos,[17] this kind of future orientation, including a willingness to postpone immediate gratification and to endure adversity, is one of the characteristics of Asian culture. One may also argue that future orientation is a coping mechanism to achieve upward mobility in a society which generally discriminates against Asians. Moynihan and Glazer[18] state that many European immigrant groups, including Italians, Irish, Poles, and Jews, also used occupation as a means of overcoming unfavorable caste classification.

As for Mr. Phan, he was willing to sacrifice his own potential intellectual development and channel the self-actualization to his brother's advantage and the well-being of his family as a whole. The different life experiences encountered by Yue and Phan appear less influential than the commonalities they shared, such as childhood upbringings within the tenets of Confucianism, which translates in his case as a shared belief that hard work and persistence will result in successful accomplishment of whatever task is at hand.[19] This important principle, which guided the development of Yue and Phan and motivated their attitudes and behavior toward work, could also be the major influence guiding many other Asian Pacific American workers today. It is no exaggeration to say that the motivating principles expressed in the stories of Dr. Yue and Mr. Phan can be found at work in the stories of many thousands of Asian Pacific Americans.[20]

In recent years, influenced by globalization of business and aided by the advancement of technology—including easy access to transportation and communication—researchers have become increasingly interested in understanding the cultural dimension of motivation and the possible impact of the cultural environment on organizational behavior and managerial style.[21]

In their cross-cultural study of workers in twenty-two countries,[22] researchers Geert Hofstede and Michael Bond "discovered" one particular cultural dimension, which they labeled "Confucian Dynamism." Confucian Dynamism is essentially a measure of the importance ascribed within a given cultural setting to the values espoused in Confucian thought—persistence, status, and thrift; avoidance of shame and face-saving behavior; respect for tradition and reciprocity of favors and gifts; and subordination of one's personal or private concerns. Thus, Confucian Dynamism measures the importance a person might ascribe to ethical principles in a social setting as well as the manner in which he or she will act upon his or her principles when engaged in role behavior.[23]

The traditional role of organizational managers in the United States may have to be broadened and made more sensitive to greater diversity in the American workforce and the consequent changing of organizational culture and global perspectives. Asian Pacific Americans could very well serve as an important link in the period of change and transition.

To contrast the stories of Dr. Yue and Mr. Phan, the cases of Ivy and Dr. N also have been presented. Ivy and Dr. N are also of Asian ancestry and origin, but because of their strong personalities, both turned away from the "typical Asian" role and image and asserted themselves in an effort to be transformed and to reach a "higher level" of accomplishment. Although both Ivy and Dr. N worked to create better lives for themselves through education and by acquiring new skills, as well as through persistent hard work and devotion to goals, neither of these individuals' experiences can be called uniquely Asian. On the contrary, both Ivy and Dr. N endeavored to break away from a traditional path and out of the stereotypical Asian mode. The fact that both were Asian Pacific Americans seems coincidental to their stories. They seem to share personality traits and other qualities that are almost universally associated with highly accomplished, self-determining individuals.

It is predictable that, as the culture of the American workplace continues to change and, at the same time, Asian Pacific Americans in the workforce become more culturally savvy and sophisticated—for example, taking greater advantage of techniques such as networking to gain entry into the "inner circle"— there will be a more substantial number of Asian Pacific Americans moving up the corporate ladder. Nevertheless, for the foreseeable future, the majority of Asian Pacific Americans will probably continue to find themselves employed in nonmanagerial positions. More than half of the people interviewed for this study, whether Southeast Asian Americans or East Asian Americans—that is, Chinese Americans, Japanese Americans, and Korean Americans—confessed that they could not see themselves becoming upper-level managers of large corporations. It may be true that times have changed and organizations have become much more diverse, but some of the more traditional perceptions remain, as does racism, both indisputable and discerned.

The majority of American workers, by and large, are likely to live, marry, raise their children, and work within the same community in which they were born. Such communities tend to be relatively homogeneous in terms of social class, lifestyle, and race. The majority of Americans, in this respect, have led simple, secure lives up to now; they are consequently self-assured and tend to have a consistent self-image.[24] In contrast, the many Asian Pacific Americans who are either immigrants or the children of immigrants have experienced more complex and far more turbulent lives. Not knowing what behavior is socially acceptable or expected of one in the larger setting outside of one's own family can be extremely stressful and lead to a confused self-image and low self-esteem.

By living through the experience of learning to cope with an entirely new environment and a different culture, as well as working to overcome language and other social barriers, Asian Pacific Americans have also broadened their perceptions and increased the complexity of their perceived roles.[25] The difficulties of coping with the work role, family role, career role, and social role expressed by many of the Asian Pacific Americans are understandable. Furthermore, the image of Asian Pacific Americans as members of a "model minority" has caused definite, additional role stress due to the expectation that society in general will make heightened demands upon Asian Pacific Americans relative to members of other groups.

One of the ways of coping with the complexity of life as an Asian Pacific American is to choose a professional career. Because the roles played by doctors, accountants, engineers, and other professionals are clearly defined in cultural terms, the U.S. population in general shares standardized, favorable perceptions about the professions. Becoming a professional can thus lessen role conflict and act to stabilize the ambiguity and uncertainty of being in a foreign culture. Stabilizing the role one plays at work can help individuals lessen the ambiguity and distress caused by feelings of insecurity and lack of self-confidence. By following the clearly prescribed role behavior associated with a given profession, one can fit in comfortably with society's expectations. This may very well be the same phenomenon experienced earlier by some Jewish Americans and certain other European ethnic immigrant groups.[26]

However, not all individuals have the same perception of the behavior associated with a given role. Thus, accuracy in role perception has a definite impact on performance. For example, consider Dr. Yue's first job as a junior high school teacher. Her perception of that role was very different from her parents' perception, and the discrepancies resulted in role conflict.[27] To alleviate the conflict, Yue changed to an occupation with a more clearly defined role that was more suited to her personality and expectations. Fortunately, this sort of reconciliation can still be made fairly easily in our American society.

Let's examine two more cases involving members of a younger generation. Linda and Nathan are both in their mid-thirties. Linda, upon graduating from college, went into the management training program offered by her employer, a large, high-tech organization. Linda had a clear image of herself and was able to match her personal goal with an organizational goal. Nathan, on the other hand, never clearly understood the demands of his organization.

"Yeah, sure, my parents have influenced me somewhat," said Linda, "but I don't think they were the sole motivators." Today, Linda is a section manager who supervises ten highly skilled, technical employees. She is one of the relatively few Asian Pacific Americans who have attained a managerial position. "I love my job," she said. "Being able to do what I wanted was motivation enough. My parents never told me what to study or what to major in. I won an award in my high school science fair, and that prompted me to major in computer science." Linda is married to a White American who also works for a high-tech industry.[28] They have two young sons.

"I have never, ever felt that I was being discriminated against. If anything, the personnel department said they love the fact that I'm a woman and also a minority; it's an added bonus. But I know I am the best when it comes to my skills, both technical skills and in terms of human relations and communications. I am surrounded by men, but I have never had any problems managing them."[29]

Linda was three years old when her parents decided to immigrate to the United States from Singapore. "My mother told me that one of the main reasons for moving was seeing how all the Asian husbands entertain their business associates in places frequented by 'loose women.' Although my father never did anything disloyal to my mother, she still worried that some day he might be tempted."

The saying "Men are like cats; when they smell fish, it's awfully hard for them not to eat it" seems to summarize a worrisome problem for many Asian wives.[30] In a way, Linda's family, and in particular her mother's decision to move to the United States seeking relatively better living conditions for women, inadvertently provided Linda with the environment where she could establish a career in a field that she enjoys. Linda considers herself successful and attributes her success to her inborn abilities, her abundant energy, and her intelligence, as well as to the environment that enabled her to fulfill her potential.

On the opposite side of the spectrum is Nathan. His family came to the United States from Taiwan, and both of his parents are highly educated professionals. Nathan is a supervisor in a bank.

"The anti-Asian sentiment is really strong in this country right now," Nathan said. "I have been passed over many times for promotions, just because I have an Asian heritage. I was born in this country and educated here." Nathan received his bachelor's degree from a school in the same community where he has spent his entire life.

"You don't have to be a genius to figure it out. Even though the Census Bureau says Asian Americans make the highest achievements in education— almost double the figure for White Americans—Asian men still make only eighty-seven cents for every dollar that a White male makes.[31] If that's not discrimination, I'd like to know what it is!"

Nathan strongly perceives that significant factors for achieving his goals are determined by external or environmental factors. Yet we have also seen individuals such as Dr. N, who believed that, if he worked conscientiously and methodically and devoted his time and energy to constructive ends, he could control his environment. He studied his situation, assessed his strengths and weaknesses and his opportunities, and mapped out strategies to accomplish his goals. When the right moment appeared, he was ready.

Further light may be shed on the behavior of individuals such as Nathan and Dr. N by the work of behavioral scientists, most notably Rotter's *locus of control theory*[32] and Bandura's *self-efficacy theory*[33] (see Box 3.4). According to the behaviorists, individuals such as Nathan are "externals"; they view themselves as helpless against certain powerful forces outside of themselves and beyond their personal control. On the other hand, individuals more like Dr. N. are "internals" who believe themselves to be responsible for their own fates. They believe that they are controlled primarily by internal forces such as the will and intellect. Individuals who are "internals" and who accomplish the goals they set for themselves develop a strong sense of self-efficacy. The behaviors displayed by someone with high self-efficacy and an internal locus of control tend to be positivistic and goal-oriented.[34]

Studies have shown that cultural values can have a significant impact on locus of control and sense of self-efficacy.[35] As an increasingly diverse workforce enters the workplace, perhaps, as suggested by Gist,[36] companies should sponsor efficacy training programs to help minority group members better understand company expectations. Any individual whose worldview resembles Nathan's would likely benefit from studying a less passive model of behavior.

---

Box 3.4

*Locus of Control:* People who believe that they have control over their own lives, which comes from within the self, are internalizers. People who believe that their lives are controlled by outside factors are externalizers. A study by Mitchell, Smyser, and Weed[37] of 900 employees in a public utility found that internally controlled employees were more content with their jobs and more likely to be in managerial positions than were those who perceived themselves to be externally controlled.

*Self-Efficacy:* The belief that one can perform adequately in a situation. The behaviors of individuals with high self-efficacy tend to be associated with strong motivation and high levels of attainment. Sam Walton, founder of Wal-Mart, exemplifies a person with high self-efficacy.

*Adapted from J. Gibson, J. Ivancevich,*
*and J. Donnelly,* Organizations *(1997).*

---

## Summary

This chapter has introduced the motivation theories of Maslow, Alderfer, Herzberg, and McClelland; the motivational calculus theory as viewed by Charles Handy; and the concepts of perception and role theories as tools for understanding how individuals function in organizations. The idea of a *self-concept* is emphasized, since how the *self* is determined underlies all the scholarly work on motivation. How one envisions the self and what that perceived self is capable of doing determine one's basic motivational drive.

The formation of *self-concept* is further influenced by one's selection of role models and peer groups, as well as societal norms, values, and culture. Thus, even though societal discrimination may cast unfavorable perceptions on Asian Pacific Americans and even inflict unwarranted feelings of inferiority on some individuals, not all individuals will be so affected. Many have risen above difficult external impediments by virtue of a strong self-concept, the setting of specific goals, and the indomitable support of their families. This was shown in the presentation of the cases of four Asian Pacific American individuals whose experiences are generally consistent with this model.

The first two cases, "The Dutiful Daughter" and "The Pious Son," are manifestations of a Confucian upbringing which cultivates the desire to meet parental expectations and family obligations, stresses the value of persistent hard work, and a sacrifice of short-term gratification in favor of long-term gain. The concept of Confucian Dynamism was introduced. The third and fourth cases show that, with a strong personality and some good luck, it is possible to achieve one's goals and break out of the stereotypical roles often assigned to Asian Pacific Americans by mainstream America.

Finally, Asian Pacific Americans may be greatly motivated by the traditional cultures in which their parents raised them, but no individual's basic personality and self-concept can be ignored in the motivational calculus process. External factors such as an organizational culture, the socialization process, and assigned role expectations in the workforce are also important elements. Organizations intending to support and develop an effective Asian Pacific American workforce and encourage Asian Pacific Americans to aim for management are advised to include motivational factors in their training programs. More discussion and suggestions regarding the various diversity training programs will be brought up in later chapters.

## CASE FOR CRITICAL THINKING

### *To Be or Not to Be*

Peter Jung is a 1.5-generation Korean American. His family immigrated to the U.S. in 1970, when Peter was twelve years old. He is now in his mid-thirties and has worked for six years for a national corporation in the high-tech industry. Everyone who knows Peter thinks highly of him; he is diligent, well-organized, punctual, conscientious, and personable. As a supervisor, he is well-liked by his subordinates.

Peter supervises ten people in the parts manufacturing department. Peter and his group work closely with the engineering department, and his group members often come up with creative ideas to improve the production line as a whole. Peter's group has also developed many new projects. The group members freely credit their successes to Peter's ability to transform their old ways of thinking and bring out the innovative spirit in everyone. Because of the group's innovations and creative approach to problem solving, the company has enjoyed some substantial cost savings over the years.

Peter's boss is Audrey Chapman, the production manager. Audrey has a degree in engineering as well as an MBA from one of the country's top business schools. She is well-respected in the company and often works late into the night and all weekend long. She and Peter have always had a good working relationship and, over time, have also become friends. Recently, Audrey was selected to receive a promotion to one of the three top executive vice president positions at company headquarters. Audrey has met with all of the company's other key executives, and they have accepted her recommendation that Peter be named to replace her as production manager. This promotion will give Peter more authority, more intrapreneurial opportunities, and, of course, more money and prestige within the company.

After careful consideration, Audrey called Peter into her office and prepared to give him the good news.

**Audrey:** How is your group doing with the new order?

**Peter:** Very well, thank you. I am fortunate to have a good group of people working for me. Every one of them is cooperative and hard working.

**Audrey:** I'm glad to hear it. It's important to have good working relationships with your team members. I've always been impressed by your leadership abilities in that regard.

**Peter:** I'm just lucky to have a good group, a real first-class team.

**Audrey:** I have some good news for you, Peter. As you've probably already heard through the grapevine, I am about to become one of the top vice presidents at headquarters. I'll be leaving in about two weeks.

**Peter:** Congratulations! That is indeed very good news. I am delighted to hear of your promotion, although of course, I am also sad that you will be leaving us.

**Audrey:** But that isn't the good news I meant! The good news is that the executive selection committee has unanimously chosen you to replace me as the new production manager. And I couldn't be more delighted!

**Peter:** They have? This is very unexpected; I'm really too surprised to say anything, just now.

**Audrey:** No need to say anything right now, Peter. Just prepare yourself to make an acceptance speech in two weeks, when the official announcement is made.

**Peter:** But what I mean to say is, I don't think I can accept such an honor. I am very flattered by your offer. I believe I have the ability, the knowledge, and the skills to undertake such a challenge.

**Audrey:** Then why the hesitation? Of course you understand there will be sizable increases in salary and benefits.

**Peter:**    Yes, I imagine so. My hesitation is due to a different cause. There is a problem of a personal nature involved.

**Audrey:**    I see. Please feel free to speak freely, Peter. You know I feel that you and I are friends, not just co-workers. If there's anything either I or the company can do to help you . . .

**Peter:**    I don't think so. You see, I am the oldest son in my family. This is a great responsibility. We recently learned that my father is gravely ill. My mother's health is also not good. She has a weak heart and also arthritis, so she cannot handle my father by herself. My own wife is so busy with our two boys that she already thinks I spend too much time with my folks and not enough with her and our kids.

**Audrey:**    But I know you have sisters and brothers. Don't they help out?

**Peter:**    My younger brother is studying at the University of Texas. He must spend most of his time studying. My younger sister has her own problems, and she also expects me to help her solve them. I have no choice but to help my sister, no matter how many mistakes she makes.

**Audrey:**    Peter, I'm very sorry to hear about all this. But I am sure you'll be able to separate your personal problems from the work situation. . . .

**Peter:**    No. I am sorry. My wife is so mad at me right now for meddling in my sister's affairs, she has threatened to take our children and go back to her family if I don't start spending more time at home. I just can't afford to take on additional responsibilities just now.

**Audrey:**    But Peter, with the extra money, you'll be able to afford outside help for your family. For one thing, you can hire someone to stay with your parents. You have to think of your future with the company. This kind of opportunity may not come again. Can't you at least talk it over with your wife and family? I understand that some of your traditions may be unfamiliar to me, but I can't believe your family wouldn't all agree on what's best for you.

*Remarks:* Individuals who were brought up within the traditional Confucian culture are greatly influenced by a strong sense of responsibility and family obligations. Self-sacrifice for one's family is considered normal, and therefore, behavior such as Peter's is expected.

## Questions for Thought and Discussion

1. What would you do in Peter's position? Can a decision not to accept a promotion be considered honorable in today's workplace? Can Peter simply take the new job—and the additional money, status, and authority—but

devote no extra time to the new job? What might happen if he put his family relationships on hold and started working late nights and weekends? Is he wise to jeopardize his career for the sake of family?

2. If Peter turns down the new job, has he, from Audrey's perspective, failed to achieve an organizational goal?
3. Do you consider organizational needs more important than personal needs? Should the company force Peter to fit their plan?
4. Might Peter's behavior be different if he were not an Asian Pacific American? How important are cultural influences in this case?
5. What aspects of traditional culture affected Peter's decision-making and motivational processes?

◆ ◆ ◆ ◆ ◆

## EXPERIENTIAL EXERCISE

*What Does Commitment Do to One's Self-Concept?*

Commitment in any situation forces us to behave in a consistent manner, just as a lack of commitment suggests inconsistent or even unreliable behavior. Over time, a commitment we have made becomes part of our self-concept, as do the behaviors which are part of that commitment.

Individuals who grow up under the influence of a traditional Asian culture tend to make commitments early in life—to a career, a profession, a family, a prescribed social role. Such commitments constrain these individuals' behavior and enable them to define themselves rather narrowly by many Western standards but within clear boundaries that are understood and accepted by the society in which they live. A society which expects high levels of personal commitment from its members will generally include a stable family life with correspondingly high feelings of responsibility to family members, including distant relatives.

Individuals who grow up in a society such as the contemporary United States, where they are expected to make fewer commitments and to make them later in life, probably develop a less stable self-concept. A society which encourages lower commitments may therefore experience a higher divorce rate, lowered feelings of personal responsibility toward dependents, increasing joblessness—and an ever-increasing number of people who have unstable self-concepts.

*Starting the Exercise*

1. Ask each student to make up a list of ten things that he or she remembers from childhood and that his or her parents expected to see performed on a regular basis.
2. Divide the students into two separate groups, "Pros" and "Cons."
3. Now ask the students to make a second list. "Pros" should identify ways in which the ten items listed in step 1 have contributed to their success as students. "Cons" should instead identify ways in which the ten things restricted their activities, their thinking, or their later development.
4. When each student has completed his or her list, divide the class into four-person groups of two "Pros" and two "Cons" each. Ask each group to compare and contrast its lists.
5. Allow twenty minutes for small group discussion. Each group should try to reach a consensus regarding commitment, based on the statement which begins this exercise.
6. Ask each small group to present its findings to the class, including the most important factors that led to the group's conclusion and any new discoveries it may have made regarding the statement.

## NOTES

1. The term "role" as used here refers to the expected behavioral patterns attributable to the particular position one occupies in an organization or other social structure. Nearly all of us perform multiple roles in our lives. For example, one may simultaneously be a parent, a child, a friend, a supervisor, and a subordinate. For good sources for the basic studies, read Charles B. Handy, *On Roles and Interactions* (London: Hazall Watson & Viney Ltd., 1976) and J. H. Greenhaus and N. J. Beutell, "Sources of Conflict between Work and Family Roles," *Academy of Management Review* 10 (January 1985): 76-88.

2.  John P. Campbell, Marvin D. Dunnette, Edward E. Lawler III, and Karl E. Weick, *Managerial Behavior Performance and Effectiveness* (New York: McGraw-Hill, 1970).

3.  Stephen P. Robbins's basic concept of motivation in *Essentials of Organization Behavior* (Englewood Cliffs, NJ: Prentice Hall, 1997).

4.  Further understanding can be found in A. Maslow, *Motivation and Personality* (New York: Harper & Row, 1954).

5.  Clayton P. Alderfer, *Existence, Relatedness, and Growth: Human Needs in Organizational Settings* (New York: Free Press, 1972).

6.  A number of research studies have tested the needs hierarchy theory. The first, conducted by Lyman Porter, resulted in the articles "A Study of Perceived Need Satisfaction in Bottom and Middle Management Jobs," *Journal of Applied Psychology* (February 1961): 1-10; and "Job Attitudes in Management: Perceived Deficiencies in Need Fulfillment as a Function of Size of the Company," *Journal of Applied Psychology* (December 1963): 386-97. Other noteworthy articles include John Ivancevich, "Perceived Need Satisfaction of Domestic Versus Overseas Managers," *Journal of Applied Psychology* (August 1969): 274-8; and Edward Lawler and J. L. Suttle, "A Casual Correction Test of the Need Hierarchy Concept," *Organization Behavior and Human Performance* (April 1972): 265-87. The hierarchy model does explain aspects of human behavior but is not accurate for all individuals.

7.  For a more detailed reading and understanding of Herzberg's two-factor theory, please see F. Herzberg, B. Mausner, and B. Syndman, *The Motivation to Work* (New York: John Wiley, 1959).

8.  According to J. L. Gibson, J. H. Ivancevich, and J. H. Donnelly in *Organizations* (Homewood, IL: Irwin, 1997), more frequent reference is made to Herzberg's theory in Europe, the Pacific Rim, and Latin America.

9.  Among the author's many notable works, a classic example is B. F. Skinner, *Beyond Freedom and Dignity* (New York: Knopf, 1971).

10.  Charles B. Handy, Professor of Organization Behavior at the London Graduate School of Business Studies, has written numerous works. *On the Motivation to Work* was written for the Penguin Modern Management Text series in 1986 and spells out the proposition of motivational calculus.

11.  David McClelland has been one of the most influential thinkers in the field. He has written many articles to promote the understanding of motivation theories. For basic reading, see *Human Motivation* (Cambridge, UK: Cambridge University Press, 1988).

12.  David C. McClelland, "Business Drive and National Achievement," *Harvard Business Review* (July/August 1962): 99-112.

13. David C. McClelland, "Toward a Theory of Motive Acquisition," *American Psychologist* (May 1965): 321-33.

14. The "fear of success hypothesis" was sensationalized by the press in the 1970s as an example of a personality type created by sexist ideology. Since then, more than 200 studies have followed up on various aspects of women's fear of success. For further detail, read David Tresemer, ed., "Current Trends in Research on Fear of Success," *Sex Roles* (Spring 1976).

15. The study was based on survey and interview methods involving 160 Asian Pacific Americans of various groups. Two-thirds of the subjects were born in Asian countries.

16. This subject has garnered public attention in recent years. For more information on this form of chemical warfare, read "Agent Orange in Vietnam: The Persisting Poison," by P. Korn, *The Nation,* 8 April 1991.

17. George A. De Vos contributed a recognition of this characteristic as developed by the apprenticeship system. For more detail, read his work, *Socialization for Achievement: The Cultural Psychology of the Japanese* (Berkeley: University of California Press, 1973).

18. Nathan Glazer and Daniel Moynihan, *Beyond the Melting Pot* (Cambridge: MIT Press, 1963).

19. Confucianism is a vast subject with multiple cultural and ethnic manifestations. But in many quarters, part of the "Golden Rules" equate well with the Christian work ethic. For further reading, see Francis Sue, *Confucians* (Newbury Park, CA: Sage, 1991); Chu Chai and Winberg Chai, *Confucianism* (Hauppauge, NY: *Barons* educational series, 1973).

20. As stated in chap. 1, many "success stories" such as these have been reported by the news media in recent years.

21. This concept has flourished in the past decade. Countless news accounts and articles and books have been written relating to this issue. It has even been included in several of President Clinton's public speeches.

22. Geert Hofstede and Michael H. Bond have examined cultural attitude and values in twenty-two countries. Their findings appear in "The Confucius Connection: From Cultural Roots to Economic Growth," *Organizational Dynamics* (Spring 1988): 4-21.

23. The term "Confucian Asian" is a relatively new one which refers collectively to peoples of Chinese, Korean, and Japanese origin who have been influenced by Confucianist thought and practice for nearly 2,000 years. Most notably in Hofstede's studies, the author claims that cultural characteristics explain why managers behave as they do in terms of managerial practices. Suggested readings are Geert Hofstede, *Cultures and Organizations: Software*

*of the Mind* (London: McGraw-Hill, 1991) and "Cultural Constraints in Management Theories" (Presentation at the National Academy of Management, 11 August 1992).

24. Taylor H. Cox, Jr., *Cultural Diversity in Organizations: Theory, Research & Practice* (San Francisco: Berrett-Koehler, 1994).

25. Diana Ting Liu Wu, "Immigrant Women in Professional Occupations: Inherent Abilities or Focused Energy?" (Working paper, Saint Mary's College of California, 1981).

26. More knowledge can be gained by reading George A. De Vos, "Ethnic Pluralism: Conflict and Accommodations" in *Ethnic Identity,* ed. Lola Romanucci-Ross and George A. De Vos (Walnut Creek, CA: AltaMira, 1995).

27. "Role conflict" is a term used to describe the experience of trying to play conflicting or overlapping roles in an organizational setting. Here, the term is used in the same sense as by Nevitt Sanford in chap. 9 of his work, *Family Impact on Personality* (Champaign: University of Illinois Press, 1964).

28. According to the 1990 research findings of Shinagawa and Pang in "Asian American Pan-Ethnicity and Intermarriage," 9.9 percent of Asian Pacific American husbands and 20.8 percent of Asian Pacific American wives are married to Whites. However, the interview samples compiled for this book indicate that, in business circles and in high-tech industry, the percentage of Asian Pacific Americans married to Whites is much higher.

29. With the many female Asian Pacific American presenters seen on TV in recent years, some individuals may feel that mainstream society is more accepting of Asian women than of Asian men, resulting in faster upward mobility for Asian Pacific American females in many cases. This will be considered further in chap. 5.

30. In many traditional Asian cultures, men are treated as superior to women, and polygamy is still practiced in today's society in some Asian countries. The societal system sets up many temptations, especially for the businessman, Business meetings often take place in bars and nightclubs, where opportunities to engage in extramarital liaisons are plentiful. It is still fashionable to keep mistresses in many parts of Asia, where the masculine self-concept and the male ego construct are equated with the number of women one can conquer, and wealth can be flaunted through the number of women one can afford to keep.

31. Claudette E. Bennett, "The Asian and Pacific Islander Population in the United States: March 1994," Racial Statistics Branch, Population Division, U.S. Bureau of the Census.

32. For more information, see Julian B. Rotter, "Generalized Expectancies for Internal vs. External Control of Reinforcement," *Psychological Monographs* 1:609 (1966): 80.

33. A. Bandura, "Self-Efficacy Mechanism in Human Behavior," *American Psychologist* (February 1982): 122-47.

34. Kathy G. Shaver, "The Entrepreneurial Personality Myth," *Business and Economic Review* (June 1995): 20-3.

35. See details in Christopher Earley, "Self or Group? Cultural Effects on Training on Self-Efficacy and Performance," *Administrative Science Quarterly* (March 1994): 89-117; Michael Frese, Wolfgang Kring, Andrea Soose, and Jeannette Zempel, "Personal Initiative at Work: Differences between East and West Germany," *Academy of Management Journal* 9 (February 1966): 37-63.

36. Marilyn E. Gist, "Self-Efficacy: Implications for Organization Behavior and Human Resources Management," *Academy of Management Review* 12 (July 1987): 472-85.

37. T. T. Mitchell, C. M. Smyser, and S. E. Weed, "Locus of Control: Supervision and Work Satisfaction," *Academy of Management Journal* 18 (September 1975): 623-31.

# Four

# Challenges Experienced
# in the American Workplace

Managing the enterprise of one's working life is a major endeavor for any individual. Cognitive maps must be constantly revised and strategies for goal accomplishment continually altered to accommodate challenges experienced. Research on work generally leads to very diverse fields of knowledge because an individual's ability to manage work is determined by an extremely complex network of factors. Some of these factors relate to events and circumstances within the life history of the individual, whereas others appear to reflect the history of the entire human society. Likewise, some of the factors affecting work management are internal, such as perceptions, motivation, self-efficacy, cognition, and so on. Others are external, such as cultural, social, and physical environment.

In this chapter, we will examine the life histories and work experiences of five Asian Pacific Americans. By considering their perceptions of the American workplace and exploring the challenges they encountered, we hope to gain greater understanding of Asian Pacific Americans in the workplace. Another important feature of this chapter is that it begins to suggest the complexity of comparing individuals who have differing Asian ethnic backgrounds.

To protect confidentiality and the anonymity of our five subjects, specific information about their work situations (such as company names, locations, and names of co-workers) have been omitted. Wherever possible, comments supporting the historical accuracy of subjects' stories have been presented in the notes section at the end of the chapter. The notes also incorporate selected references to key scholarly research works and relevant theoretical writings which can significantly enhance the reader's knowledge and understanding. Many of the inner workings of organization processes and structures are incorporated throughout these case studies. Whenever a technical term or special jargon is presented, an explanatory note is used to provide a definition or information for further understanding.

The five cases are presented in the following order: "Seeking Distributive Justice" the story of a fourth-generation Filipino American; "A Speck in the White Laboratory" the story of a Hmong woman, one of the newest Americans; "Making It in a Hairy Business" the story of a 1.5-generation Korean American woman; "Wealthy by Comparison" the good fortune of an Asian Indian American entrepreneur; and "All Vultures Must Be the Same Color" the misfortunes of a Chinese American would-be scholar.

As you read these cases, keep in mind the factors that appear to influence these Asian Pacific American mainstream workers. How were their work experiences affected by *external forces* such as the American economic system, the actions of employers and managers, or the overall social and political environment surrounding them? In some cases, the profound effects of public policy and even major historical events will be obvious. Think as well about the unique traditions and history that underlie each of the different Asian Pacific backgrounds illustrated by these examples. To what extent did family and culture determine the roles these five individuals played in the American workforce?

Finally, how important are personality and individual character in each of the five stories? How important are societal constraints in the making of individual career decisions? Do these cases seem to typify the experiences of many Americans, or does each of these five individuals somehow stand out from the crowd?

A series of more specific discussion questions follows at the end of the chapter. By thinking about and trying to answer these, it is hoped that the reader will gain additional insights into these five Asian Pacific Americans and the organizations in which they worked. At the same time, students may wish to reflect upon their own aspirations and the organizations that lie ahead on their own future career paths.

To capture the flow and narrative intensity of these five subjects' life histories and work experiences, the stories are presented primarily as first-person narratives. We will begin with the story of Carlos.

## Seeking Distributive Justice (Carlos's Story)

"The Philippines is an archipelago of several thousand islands named after King Philip of Spain. The name reflects Spanish colonialism. People who leave the Philippines to come to America tend to prefer calling themselves Filipino Americans.[1] Currently, there are about two million of us in the United States,"[2] said Carlos, a fourth-generation Filipino American.

Carlos is an accountant for a nonprofit corporation. His ethnicity can be traced back to ancestors of Chinese, Spanish, and American Indian origin, but his surname is Hispanic and Carlos is often mistaken for a Latino American. "In fact," he added, "many Filipino Americans intermarry with Latinos. We have the same Catholic beliefs and many similarities in our food, music, and dances because of Spanish colonial rule. Even more importantly, both cultures emphasize strong family ties and loyalty to kinship."[3]

Carlos's grandfather was of mixed American Indian and Chinese ancestry. He came to the United States in the 1920s for an education, and while here he met and married Carlos's grandmother. Carlos's grandmother was descended from the earliest Filipino settlers in the United States, men who had been forced to work as sailors on Spanish ships during the late eighteenth century. Some of them had jumped ship in Louisiana and settled permanently in New Orleans.[4] In time, some of their descendants drifted toward the East or West Coasts. Many became farm laborers in California, lured by the state's warm climate, rich soil, and low cost of living, especially in rural Kern County, where the population is now 20 percent Filipino American.[5]

"My mother was a mail-order bride," Carlos said, "although not the current sort who advertise themselves in the American newspapers and magazines or through some catalog agency.[6] My two sets of grandparents were good friends back in Manila, and they encouraged their son and daughter to correspond while they were still in high school. When the Philippines became independent in 1946, my father went back and married my mother and brought her back to the United States. Subsequently, she brought her parents and brothers and sisters here. We have a large extended family.[7] We've always gathered frequently for festivities, with a hundred dishes of food piled high on buffet tables. My wife, Glenna, is White. We've been married for ten years and have two children; she is still amazed by the extravagance of our family gatherings."

Carlos attended a parochial high school, where his wife was also a student. They have known each other since junior high but didn't date until he was a senior in college. Carlos admits that he has experienced racial prejudice and has been called a few names, even though, he says, he is "totally American-ized: look, walk, talk, act like any other American. Of course," he adds, "there are still always a few who have to say something like, 'How come your eyes are slanted like a Japanese, but you have an olive complexion and a broad nose like a Mexican? Where are you from, anyway?'

"Our household was bilingual; we were raised speaking both English and Tagalog at home, and it never occurred to me that this might be at all unusual. It wasn't until one day when I was called names in school that I became aware of my different ethnicity. It hurt a little, but it passed soon.

"The real pain came when my wife Glenna and I first started dating. Her Anglo-Saxon, European relatives said much worse things, like 'Why a Fili-pino? Even a Japanese or Chinese would have been better!'

"Glenna was furious. I told her that next time anyone said anything like that she should just tell them we *are* Americans and, 'Carlos is so American-ized, he can actually sh-- apple pie!'

"My jokes made her laugh, but on the inside, behind the laughter, I was hurting a lot."

After ten years of marriage and two healthy children, Glenna's relatives did come to take a more accommodating view. Without exception, they all recognize Carlos's intelligence, generosity, empathy, and gentleness. "But what impressed them, finally, was my college degree, my ability to make a good living and provide Glenna and our children with a comfortable home."

Aside from personal relationships, Carlos also spoke about prejudice and stereotyping that exist in the workplace. "I have experienced quite a few faulty perceptions on employment interviews. People believe the erroneous stereotype that Asians are good with numbers but, being a Filipino, I didn't seem to count as that kind of Asian. 'Why didn't you major in art or music?' or 'Are you sure you're not Chinese?' After many rejections, I finally caught on. The next time I had to fill out the 'Race' portion of an employment application, I checked the 'Other' box, then told them I was part Chinese, part White, and part Spanish. I don't know whether it was a coincidence, but I did get hired the very next day."

Carlos's first position was as an assistant to the chief accounting manager for a manufacturing company. In today's increasingly complex business environment, and with the rapid growth of computer technology, the importance of the accounting function is rarely underestimated. Yet until very recently, and with the exception of public accounting firms, most organizations traditionally have regarded their accounting departments as "staff" working in a supportive function. Accounting managers thus have been treated as support staff rather than members of the team of essential management personnel. Accounting managers were further regarded essentially as messengers who brought financial data to the decision makers and whose other achievements went largely ignored or unrecognized.

Like other manufacturing firms, the company where Carlos worked was organized around its production department. The production line is the traditional core of this kind of enterprise, and line managers, who contribute directly to the basic work of manufacturing a product, tend to rise to the most significant positions in the company. Other departments, such as research and development, marketing and sales, legal counsel, human resources, public relations, or the cafeteria and mail room, were seen as supporting the production line, and their roles were seen as secondary and advisory only. In other words, line managers had the authority and power.[8] Specialists employed on the staff, even when more highly trained or better educated, had little or no authority within the company's hierarchical structure. As an inexperienced employee learning organizational politics on the job, Carlos found this phenomenon amazing.

"I was also very surprised by the kinds of stereotyping that existed within the company. There were no women or minorities employed as line managers. Nearly all of the minority employees worked on the production line as simple operatives. There were a few Asian Americans who were specialists in the research and accounting departments.

"I soon found out that the Asian Pacific Americans were all, without exception, earning 20 to 30 percent less than their White American counterparts in similar positions and at comparable educational levels. What seemed even stranger was that, among Asian Pacific Americans who were employed to work identical jobs, Filipino Americans earned less than all the other Asian Americans, except for the Cambodians and Vietnamese.[9]

"Feeling frustrated, I gathered all the relevant information, organized it into a very clear chart, and presented it to my manager, along with a request for salary adjustments. The manager pretended that he'd had no idea of what was going on and promised to talk to the vice president of finance and operations. I was young and naive; the possibility of retaliation or retribution by the higher-ups never crossed my mind. But the following week, I was transferred to the warehouse to do inventory control. In those days, there wasn't any federal law to protect whistle-blowers.[10] I actually had no intention of taking company information to outside sources, and I hadn't bypassed the organization's hierarchical structure or tried to go over my manager's head. I had simply thought of bringing an injustice to management attention and expected the company to be receptive to the idea of treating employees fairly and equitably rather than on the basis of questionable, arbitrary, or outright discriminatory practices. My inexperience at handling that kind of situation resulted in my demotion."

Carlos felt humiliated and, soon afterwards, changed to a job in a service industry. He was hired as a general ledger accountant for a department store.

"The department store even had an international division, but I found the same unfair labor practices. Few non-Whites were in managerial positions, and, although there were more women in supervisory positions, nearly all of them were White Americans. Asians mostly held technical support and sales positions. I often heard comments such as 'Asians [workers] are satisfied and happy where they are. Why bother to arouse their ambitions?'

"Whenever the opportunity arose to promote an employee, a White American male was first choice, followed by a White American female. As for Asian Pacific Americans, again, the order was Japanese and Chinese Americans first, then Filipinos. This overt prejudice really puzzled me, since most Filipino Americans are well-assimilated and largely Westernized. Nearly all Filipino Americans speak English perfectly, have no problems socializing with Whites, and yet, as a group, they are viewed as the least preferred.[11] I've even read articles that claim Filipino Americans are partially responsible for their own condition because, having 'inherited' a colonial mentality from their parents, they are content with being exploited within a White power structure and with being members of an oppressed minority.[12] Personally, I find this sort of explanation unacceptable."

After being passed over twice for promotions, Carlos decided to change jobs once again, this time to a nonprofit agency where more than half of the workers were members of minority groups.

"I am very happy with my present situation now. The competition is less, and the office atmosphere is much more relaxed. Since more than half of the workers are minorities, the pay is based on seniority and there is no inequity in the pay scales. Although there are many rules and regulations, I don't feel discrimination here. After so many years of facing reality in the working world, I am fully aware that discriminatory practices exist elsewhere, in the society in general.

"Recently, I've been thinking that the most effective way to fight discrimination and make a change in people's negative perceptions is to gain a larger power base. Knowledge-based power is the most pleasant one to obtain. I need to prepare my children for college." Carlos paused for a moment and smiled mischievously. "Since Filipino Americans, like Chinese Americans, are no longer considered eligible for affirmative action in college admissions, I think that when my children are ready for college, I may have to change their ethnicity on application forms to 'Hispanic—White.'"

*Comment*

The implications of Carlos's story are complex indeed. He began by perceiving himself as no different from other American children. Through his experiences, he gradually developed a self-concept of himself as a minority and was forced to confront a predominantly White society in a variety of ways. Although he did not always intend to do so, Carlos often learned that other people perceived him as challenging the status quo and "making trouble." Not surprisingly, Carlos is uncertain what ethnic identity his own children will develop and how society will perceive them.

Although many Asian Pacific Americans feel that affirmative action programs should continue to be used to help minority groups in our society, others believe such programs may actually hamper their advancement in areas such as college admissions and in job placement in certain fields and organizations. The seeming abundance of Asian Pacific Americans in our universities, especially Chinese Americans, can mean tougher admissions standards for other qualified Asian Pacific Americans.[13] If the American social fabric remains unchanged and affirmative action policies continue to use racial quotas to correct racial imbalance, Asian Pacific Americans, like Carlos, may be tempted for pragmatic reasons to metamorphose into Latino Americans if they can.

A more creative solution might well be one which could consider the socioeconomic backgrounds of applicants. As inferred above and discussed in previous chapters, Asian Pacific Americans are a highly diverse group and differ from one another in many fundamental ways. When policymakers use only statistical information and categorize Asian Pacific Americans as a unified whole, problems arise for subgroups which can be easily overlooked or erroneously interpreted. As early as 1973, Sue and Kitano[14] reported overly positive interpretations of Asian Pacific American social progress. Today's managers, however, cannot afford to rely on oversimplified stereotypes[15] about their workers. Stereotyping, as demonstrated by many of the managers in Carlos's story, results in unsuitable motivational programs and inadequate methods for performance evaluation and promotion. Effective contemporary managers remain cognizant of a worker's cultural background and value individual differences in their workers during performance evaluations.

## A Speck in the White Laboratory (Mila's Story)

"I was eight years old when my mother, older sister, and older brother came to America," said Mila. "My parents were farmers in the highlands of Laos. We were the Hmong people, a very simple agrarian family. The war forced us to flee our home on foot, living an upside-down life for years before we finally received permission, in 1979, to come to America.[16] Because my father had died, we did not have kinship ties in the United States. Along with other refugees in similar situations, we were randomly relocated by the Immigration Service using a zip code dispersal program.[17] We ended up in the state of Louisiana.

"Later, we learned that most of the Hmong immigrants had somehow found their way to California. The largest Hmong American community is around Fresno, California, which makes sense because of the agreeable weather and the agriculture-based lifestyle of the San Joaquin Valley. In Louisiana, there were very few Asian Americans at the time, although we did feel lucky that we didn't get relocated to the East Coast. Some of my parents' friends were placed in Wisconsin and Minnesota.[18] They all had frostbite and almost froze to death during the first winter season—not surprising, since none of our people had ever before seen snow in their entire lives.

"At the time, my sister was fourteen, my brother was sixteen years old, and I was eight years younger than him. My parents had other children between my sister and myself, but all of them died in infancy. My mother always called me the quiet, strong one, the one who could endure any hardship without being affected by it. How could I let her know what was inside of me, when she, who has suffered so much grief and torment, keeps her composure and hides her sorrow? My tears for my father were flowing only on the inside.

"When we arrived in Louisiana, we learned that many other East Asian refugees were working in the local manufacturing plants. My mother, however, received sponsorship to do domestic work for a Vietnamese American restaurant owner. Part of the deal was that my sister and brother helped out at the restaurant after school. I remember that all of us were miserable at school. Because there were so few Asian Americans, we were treated as if we came from outer space, and the situation was compounded by the fact that we couldn't speak English fluently or dress fashionably.

"The Vietnamese restaurant owner was not much help. He kept telling us not to make friends with anyone. He said such stupid things, like 'African Americans are bad, White people are even worse.' He had experienced horrors during the Vietnam War and had been poisoned with hatefulness—but the main reason I think he said these things was to keep us isolated, so that we had to depend on his mercy for our survival in this new country.

"Everyone in our family was working extremely hard, especially my mother, who worked fourteen to sixteen hours every day. Under those circumstances, I thought the only thing I could do was to study hard and give my mother some pride in my good grades. I was very lonely; my only friends were the characters from books I borrowed from the library. I studied and studied, because I didn't know what else I could do to please my family and put a smile on my mother's disheartened face. My father was never mentioned after his death. I was too young to remember if he was involved in the Cambodian 'killing field' or during the Pol Pot period.[19]

"My sister and brother never did well in school. They were kept back, attributing their failure to the language problem. In retrospect, they might have suffered many psychological problems. Not knowing how to deal with the extreme form of culture shock prevented them from learning and excelling in school. I remember mastering the English language within one year and helping my sister and brother with their homework, even though they were two and three grades ahead of me.

"I skipped one grade and graduated from high school with honors. My interests had turned to science, and I had excellent science teachers who kept me fascinated. My school counselor, a truly kind and patient African American, gave very generously of his time and experience to all of us. He further helped me to apply for a four-year scholarship to study chemistry at the University of Texas. It was at college that I came to realize that, although I have an obligation towards my family, I also have a responsibility to myself. I met many new friends on campus, particularly new Asian American friends, and I discovered that my family was not the only one which had endured tormenting experiences and tremendous hardships throughout life. I began to turn what seemed like a pathetic situation into a more hopeful and positive one. Although I continued to seek solace in my studies, I also looked outward and sought reconciliation with my environment. I am not a void, not a nerd either. I can be an Asian, or an American, or both, and I can find meaning in both.

"Because I had 22 units of Advanced Placement credits going into the university, it took me only three years to graduate. During that time, I met many great teachers and made great friends. After college, I was accepted into graduate school and worked part-time as a research assistant in the university laboratory. I think this is the story you wish me to tell, but please keep all the names anonymous.

"I was assigned to one of the best laboratories in the United States. I was elated to find out that a nationally known professor would want to put me in the laboratory, working with a group on a special project, devising specific procedures in testing unusual chemical properties. Unfortunately, when I told my advisor about this exceptional opportunity, he did not show any signs of enthusiasm. As I recall, after I broke the news to him, he thought for a second and then said reluctantly, 'Well, try your best. Who knows, you may learn something.'

"Little did I suspect what was in store for me. I soon found out that my laboratory supervisor, Dr. Oy, was a Chinese American who had come to America in the late 1950s as a foreign student and then changed to permanent residency. Years of residing in the States still couldn't alter her native Chinese accent when she spoke English.

"Dr. Oy was a perfectionist; she was also very strict and would not hesitate to reprimand a person in front of others if she thought the person had made a mistake. She did not allow any food or drink in the laboratory, not even chewing gum. She seldom smiled, always looked stern and serious in her demeanor. Once, I was told, she caught a student taking something out of the laboratory and she fired him, right then and there. She was also very arrogant toward the professors, even Professor Frank, who was the principal investigator in our laboratory. But Dr. Oy was very professional, intelligent, and absolutely brilliant. Her mind was like an encyclopedia; in all the time I worked there, I never ceased to wonder how it was possible for so much knowledge to be stored in her brain! And she worked hard. She was always the first one to arrive, even though the previous night she might have stayed until midnight.

"There were seven research assistants in our group. Two White American male Ph.D. students, Dale and Mark, were both under Professor Frank and worked separately; our group of five consisted of two White American female staff members, one East Indian male research assistant, one part-time master's student from Taiwan, and myself. The group was very task oriented, but no one particularly liked Dr. Oy, not even the Taiwanese student. When he tried to speak to her in Chinese, she always looked annoyed and would answer in English. Aside from her seriousness and inflexibility, she was demanding and difficult to follow because her mind was always ten paces ahead of everyone else's. When Professor Frank came into the laboratory, he always humored her and tried to please her, and he must have instructed his two Ph.D. students to do the same because it was obvious that they had no idea what was going on.

"I soon developed a strong admiration for Dr. Oy. I had never met any Asian, let alone an Asian woman, with such authority and self-assurance in front of White people. I even called my sister and told her what an extraordinary lady Dr. Oy was. By then, my sister was working as a hostess in a restaurant and living with my mother, who, by then, was only working six hours a day, cooking and cleaning for a newly established nursery school in town. My brother had left Louisiana for California with an Amerasian bride whose mother was Vietnamese and whose father served in Vietnam during the Vietnam War. Back home, these children were called 'bui doi,' which literally translates to 'dust of life.' They were greatly discriminated against and looked down upon.[20]

"Several weeks after I began working in the laboratory, I found the real Dr. Oy under her stern exterior. She was really a very caring person. One day, I accidentally knocked over a bottle of solution which ruined my laboratory coat, my sweater, and slacks. Just as I was thinking, 'Great, here goes a week's pay to replace this,' Dr. Oy came over, assessed the damage, and said, 'Good, you are not hurt. I'll bring a new coat for you tomorrow. Be more careful from now on.' Next day, she not only brought a new lab coat, but a sweater and a pair of slacks as well, all as presents for me! I was speechless. She knew that I was living on limited means and had recognized that I was a conscientious worker. From that day on, I felt I had developed a special bond with her. Although others criticized her behind her back, I always thought otherwise.

"Several months into our project, we were still not able to define the proper procedures. One day, Dr. Oy came to my work station and said, 'I suspect there is a flaw in Professor Frank's assumption. Would you check all of these pages? I asked Dale and Mark to double-check, but it has been two weeks and they still can't give me an answer. See what you can do.'

For the next 48 hours, I stopped everything and worked only on the project, thinking what an honor it was that Dr. Oy would trust me to redefine such an important concept. It was tedious, difficult work requiring lots of persistence and concentration, but I did finally pinpoint a possible problem area and reported my findings to Dr. Oy. She immediately started to construct a new experiment. Everyone in the lab worked with renewed excitement. By the end of the week, Dr. Oy said to us with resolution, 'I think we've got it!' She wrote the new procedure and the resulting report, including her acknowledgments of my participation and that of the others, and she gave the report to Professor Frank.

"A month later, Dr. Oy's report was published in the most prestigious scientific journal—except that her name was not on it. None of our group members' names were even mentioned; Professor Frank was named as chief investigator, assisted by Mark and Dale, neither of whom had any knowledge or understanding of the work. Our group couldn't comprehend what had taken place. Of course it was a theft of intellectual property, but at the time this whole concept was unfamiliar.

"Dr. Oy went to the university's ethics committee but was told that Professor Frank could never have done such a thing. Mark and Dale vouched for him, and besides, he was the grant recipient. Dr. Oy and her staff had gotten paid, hadn't they? No one would trust an Asian woman to receive a grant. She should be grateful; why make trouble for everyone?

"I kept thinking about the verdict, asking myself, What's wrong here? Was it because of Dr. Oy's attitude and demeanor? Did people wish to dump her because they did not perceive her as being a 'team player'? Or was it because she is an Asian woman? When it comes down to it, is it really money and power that matter in the American system? Whatever happened to the moral principles, honesty and trust, that are supposed to go hand in hand with the freedom and other privileges here in this land of opportunity?

"I told myself that, for every rotten apple, there are ten good ones. I shouldn't be so disillusioned; I am young and have time and the ability to change things.

"Dr. Oy ultimately resigned from her post because of the university's unconscionable treatment of her. I transferred to another school to continue my graduate work, and Dr. Oy was kind enough to send me a note, which I still have. She wrote, 'It is the University's loss; they have lost two brilliant researchers. They have neither the intellect nor the foresight to see that what they think is only a speck can become spectacular. You are the future of the world.' "

*Comment*

Although many accounts of individual struggles are quite touching, Mila's story of inner resolve versus dispassionate external forces is particularly so.

Mila's homeland was destroyed by warfare and other acts promulgated by inept and shortsighted leaders, many of them White Americans, whose decisions had also cost 60,000 young American lives. Mila's scientific career was sabotaged by supervisors who also happened to be White. Would it not have been understandable for Mila to blame at least some of her many misfortunes on White Americans as a whole? And yet she does not view her past as a racial tragedy; she harbors no bitterness, outward anger, or despair but instead is confident and upbeat. She maintains her *locus of control* and *high self-efficacy.*[21] She recognizes that knowledge is power, and that as long as she equips herself with knowledge, the future will be there for her.

Note that although Mila's methods are nonconfrontational and she chose not to vent her anger publicly, her attitude is not one of apathy or passive resignation. Perhaps a childhood ravaged by war taught her to maintain serenity amid adversity and, if things do not work out, to move on to the next opportunity. Referring to the APA typology model (see chap. 1), we may define Mila as an Autonomist: self-contained and self-governing. She chose to devote her time to a pursuit of knowledge and focused her efforts to improve society by selecting professions in which she could use her expertise and make a contribution to her field.

## Making It in a Hairy Business (Kim's Story)

*"Your hair looks gorgeous! Is it yours?"*

*"Of course it is. I already made the full payment!"*

Conversations such as this one might have been overheard at many different social gatherings in the United States during the 1960s and 1970s. At that time, fashion wigs were considered chic and were very popular. Because of the fine workmanship and quality, Korean wig manufacturers were among the best in the world.

Kim's uncle was the chief operating manager of a wig factory in Korea exporting primarily to the United States. He concentrated his export accounts in the southern part of this country.[22] When one of the company's biggest buyers, a Louisiana firm, experienced financial trouble, Kim's uncle came to the U.S. Soon after, the uncle took over the troubled company's entire retail wig business.

"My uncle was considered to be one of the pioneer business immigrants in the United States. It was not until the late 60s and early 70s that there was a significant increase in Korean exports to the United States and the massive influx of Korean immigrants began. Almost all of the Korean immigrants came here to establish businesses dealing with imported Korean merchandise. Very few people realize that 90 percent of the Koreans living in this country came here after 1970."[23]

Kim graduated from high school at about that same time, and her uncle brought her to the U.S. He enrolled her at the University of Louisiana at Baton Rouge. "I also had a relative by marriage on my mother's side of the family—the younger sister of my aunt's husband—who was living in Louisiana at that time. She came to the U.S. in the late 1950s. Actually, she was a war bride. Her husband was an African American U.S. serviceman stationed in Seoul during the Korean War. They did not have any children of their own at first, but they no sooner adopted two war orphans[24] than they had a son of their own. They are devoted Christians and the nicest family I have ever encountered. I adore their children, especially the little son who has such beautiful olive skin and lovely manners. I enjoyed baby-sitting with them."

Before coming to Louisiana, Kim had considered attending the University of Hawaii. "I heard that the Korean community in Hawaii was very well-established. There are many more Korean Christian churches in Hawaii than Louisiana,[25] but in Louisiana I would be with my own family, which was very important, so I thought I should accept my uncle's very generous offer." Kim's uncle had offered to train her to work in the various wig shops around town in exchange for her tuition, plus room and board at his house.

"I had studied English in high school but had difficulties speaking the language fluently and, if I had to try to find a job on my own, I would probably have been forced to accept menial labor and be a cleaning woman or restaurant worker, something like that. I know that many people who were white-collar professionals back in Korea were unable to find work in their professions in this country. That's why so many turn to running their own small business, to avoid taking blue-collar work."[26]

Kim's decision to help her uncle and to learn the wig business turned out to be not only profitable but very interesting to Kim. "I learned the technical, business end of things as well as developing skills for dealing with customers. Back in Korea, there was no such thing as being assertive and polite at the same time. I was taught to believe that a lady waited quietly until someone wanted something and then attended to their needs. This does not work in the United States; you must show that you have self-confidence.

If you do not show enthusiasm and belief in your product, no one else will believe in it."

Soon after she began working in the wig stores, Kim also began learning about American culture and intergroup relations. Among all of her uncle's stores, the most lucrative ones—and the ones Kim found most comfortable—were the ones located in predominantly African American neighborhoods.

"The African Americans didn't look down at us because of our accents and imperfect English," Kim paused in reflection, "and they were the best customers; they were not as choosy, they were more generous in their spending, and they tended to buy more because of the nature of their hair. We had many repeat customers in those stores. We [Koreans] all agreed it was much more profitable to open stores in the African American neighborhoods."

When the fashion wig trade began to show signs of decline, Kim's uncle closed down many stores in other areas, but kept the stores in the African American community. Another relative, one who had left the wig business because of "downsizing," was approached by a financial institution with the prospect of opening grocery stores in the African American community with 90 percent financing. The financial institution was backed by the U.S. Small Business Administration, which encouraged loans enabling minority and women business owners to establish businesses in "deprived" areas.[27]

"During the early days, the Korean American community and church groups served as a very important source of financing for small business owners. They used a system that had been practiced in the old country for centuries and had been carried to this country by the immigrants. It works like a Christmas club, with a rotating Christmas. For instance, if someone needed to borrow ten thousand dollars for seed money, he or she would organize a ten-member club. Each of the ten members would chip in one thousand dollars a month. Then, for each of the succeeding ten months, each member would have a chance to bid for the use of the money by offering an unspecified interest rate, depending upon how badly the person needed financing. The greater the need, the higher the interest payment offered. In the subsequent months, the borrower would pay the agreed-upon rate of interest to the other club members. Usually, the club member who had the least need to borrow the club's funds would make the largest profit by collecting bonus interest in the final months."

The offer from the U.S. Small Business Administration was quite different in that it put the immigrants directly into the mainstream of American business finance. Kim's relative jumped at the opportunity to get established in business and was closely followed by several other cousins.

"We all thought it was a great chance." The idea that the clientele of a specialty store might be significantly different from that of a convenience store never entered their thoughts until much later. "In the wig business, you get chosen customers who care about their appearance, who are aware of the importance of their self-image, who want their behavior to fit in with mainstream America. But anybody and just about everybody goes into a grocery store. I guess we just didn't expect that. As a result, we mishandled the situation and compounded many errors," sighed Kim.

"What happened in recent years—the friction between some members of the African American community and the Korean American grocers—is really unfortunate. I am not condescending in saying that some of my best friends are African Americans—I even have African American relatives! My early experiences taught me to understand that every person is an individual. I made many good friends through the wig stores. We later socialized and kept in touch and got to know each other very well. Some of these friends taught me how to handle difficult situations that arise from living in America."

Kim also thought that Korean American entrepreneurs such as her relatives play a very important economic role, that of a "minority middleman"[28] serving the needs of lower-income minority customers.

"The Korean American entrepreneurs are actually distributing products marketed initially by large U.S. corporations. We began by providing needed services that no one else was willing to provide or even become involved with, and ended as scapegoats in what is actually a Black-White racial conflict. The ironic thing is that, with so much hostility and conflict surrounding us, solidarity among Korean American entrepreneurs as a group has actually been enhanced."

After Kim received a bachelor's degree in sociology from the University of Louisiana, she wanted to leave her uncle's business, but for fear of offending him, she remained. It was only with her friends' encouragement that she finally found a job and left her uncle's household, her stronghold for so many years.

Unfortunately, her first encounter with the "White" working environment and organizational culture was not very positive. "There were a lot of nice co-workers, but many treated me as an imbecile because of my accent." Without any signs of bitterness, she continued, "The funniest part was that the people who said I didn't speak English properly were the ones who constantly used improper and grammatically incorrect English. Many of my college-graduate co-workers couldn't even write a simple report!

"But what upset me the most at the time was the behavior of my male co-workers. Most have an erroneous concept of Asian Pacific American females. I was physically touched. My male supervisor grabbed me and pinched me whenever he had a chance.''

When asked if the thought of sexual harassment charges had ever occurred to her, Kim replied, ''I did not dare to tell anyone. In those days, I had never heard of sexual harassment. I was miserable. I even thought about swallowing my pride and going back to work for my uncle again.''

Finally, one day, she confided in an African American friend about the harassment. The friend not only encouraged Kim to confront her supervisor, but to do so in a daring and dramatic way. Seeing Kim's hesitation, the friend agreed to coach Kim, helping her choose the words she would say and rehearsing the confrontation with her, step by step.

''I was very scared at first, but I finally walked into my supervisor's office one morning, shut the door, and pulled out a pocket knife.'' She laughed. ''My supervisor was so stunned.''

Bolstered by her friend's support, Kim told her supervisor that she didn't like the way she was being treated on the job. ''I cut my finger with the pocket knife, squeezed out a drop of blood in front of him, and said, 'Look! Our outward appearances might be different, yet we have the same insides—the same color of blood and the same feelings.'

''He never touched me again!''

Kim is now married with two college-age daughters. Her husband, who is also Korean American, has an optometry practice, and Kim manages the office for him as a part-time job. She devotes a great deal of her time to performing social work with minority groups and remains very active in community affairs, even serving one community action group as a volunteer ombudsperson.

### Comment

Korean immigrants are unique in the sense that most of them are Christians who were influenced by American missionaries to Korea.[29] Many Korean immigrants were orphans or ''war brides'' of U.S. servicemen. Today, a large number of them, perhaps as many as 75 percent, are either self-employed or work for Korean-owned firms due to limited English language proficiency.[30] Kim's description of her early experiences in the U.S. coincide with case studies done by Choy, Patterson, Kim and Hurh, Min, and others.[31]

One fact which makes Kim's story striking is that her encounter was not only with racism, but with sexism as well. This exemplifies the belief of many that racism is gendered and gender is racialized (i.e., a stereotype is specific to its victim's race and sex). Bigotry, then, is essentially a complex intersection of both.

In our typology model, Kim is a fascinating example of one who was an Abnegator when she first arrived, became an Assimilator, and ended as a Pragmatist whose approach to social change is helping others through activities such as coaching and mentoring.

## Wealthy by Comparison (Mr. Patel's Story)

"Most of the recent Asian Indian immigrants are not as fortunate as I have been," says Mr. Patel, the owner of several motels on the East Coast. In recent years, he has also purchased properties on the West Coast.[32] "Now that I have two children in the University of California system, I may choose to retire some day in California.

"My father came to study engineering in the early 1940s and went back after Indian independence in 1947 to marry my mother. My mother used to tell us the story of how my father, having been educated in the West, refused to accept a dowry from my mother's family, which absolutely infuriated my more traditional grandmother. In those days in India, no one would marry a woman without a dowry. My grandmother somehow considered the unfamiliar situation to be my mother's fault. This conflict between my father's family and my mother's family somehow escalated into an intolerable situation. My father decided to leave India once again and return to the U.S. to get a Ph.D. Here, he also encouraged my mother to continue a college education.

"Over the years, my father became a college professor, and my mother bore three sons and earned a Ph.D. in clinical psychology as well. I am the youngest son.

"When I was eleven years old, my father died of cancer. His physician and best friend—they had been best friends since high school back in India—later married my mother. My stepfather had two children, a son and a daughter, from a previous marriage to an Englishwoman. This Englishwoman had divorced my stepfather to become a nun, leaving the children in his care. Later, he and my mother had a daughter together."

Mr. Patel's two older brothers and his stepbrother are all physicians.[33] The stepsister is a professor of health administration, and the youngest sister is interning to become an ophthalmologist.

"I am the black sheep in the family. It was very difficult for me to grow up in a family full of high achievers. They all have a doctoral degree except me. I got sick a lot when I was young, and I hate the smell of medicine and hospitals, sometimes even the smell of my stepfather when he comes home from hospital. I tried to avoid him as much as possible. My mother shed many tears on account of me. My self-esteem was low. At school, teachers were always comparing me with my brothers and saying, 'How come you are not like them?' I was always made to feel ashamed, although I have never done anything shameful.

"The first break came with the arrival of my cousins. My mother's brother and his family immigrated to the U.S. in 1972. My grandparents had passed away in 1964, and my mother had wanted the rest of her family to come to this country, but it was not until the 1965 Immigration Act that Asians were allowed to come and my mother could apply for them. It took almost seven years.

"My uncle has two sons and a daughter, and they are all average people like me! I was so relieved to be in their company. Although my uncle has a bachelor's degree from India, he couldn't find any job at first. He spoke fluent English.[34] One of his friends, a man he knew from college in India, was driving a taxi in New York City and wanted my uncle to join him. My mother and stepfather were violently opposed to the idea.

"Finally, my stepfather found my uncle a job in a gas station. The owner of the gas station, another Asian Indian, was one of my stepfather's patients. He was also an engineer. For fifteen years, he had worked for a large American engineering firm and had watched as his White American subordinates, one by one, received promotions. Several of them, in turn, even became his supervisor. Finally, the poor man couldn't take the humiliation any longer and decided to try to escape discrimination by working independently. He took my uncle into business with him, but it didn't last long. As I understand it, they belonged to two different subcultural groups and simply could not get along.[35]

"My mother eventually found her brother a job in a major hotel in the city where she knew one of the owners. I used to visit him sometimes at the hotel, and eventually I decided that I wanted to major in hotel management in college.

"My second lucky break came from one of my business professors in college. She was an Asian American woman who understood what it is like to grow up in a high-achieving family, how the high pressure and expectations caused unconscious anxiety for me. I was always extremely quiet and followed the rule that if one had nothing good to say, one shouldn't say anything, but my stepfather carried this rule to an extreme. I felt that every single word I spoke was being judged, as if to see whether anything I had to say was worthy of expressing. We never gave expression to our personal feelings.

"One day after school, someone I barely knew called to me, out of the blue, 'Hey there! How many ragheads do you have at home?' I had never heard the word 'raghead' and didn't know what it meant, so that night at the dinner table, I asked my family.

"My stepsister was kind to me and said just to ignore such unpleasantness. She had been called worse names before and had been fortunate enough to avoid firsthand experience of the 'Dot Buster' incidents that were common in New Jersey and other states.[36] But my brother said only, 'What did you do to deserve such an insult?'

"Whenever someone mistreated me, my family seemed to blame me automatically for the misfortune and accuse me of not handling things correctly. I was frustrated to the point that I actually thought of ending my own life. But my religion[37] teaches that if I did such a thing, I would suffer far greater misfortune in my next life, and this preserved me.

"My new professor had keen insights into my traditional Asian upbringing and understood my feelings. She encouraged me to speak up and ask questions, helped me develop my communication skills, and restored my self-confidence. After some twenty years, she and I are still good friends.

"A third lucky break came when I met my wife, Nina, and her family. They were Italian American; Nina's father had been a chef in a small town. No member of Nina's family had ever gone to college, and they treated me like I was the smartest person they had ever met! I was honored, respected, and admired. My future father-in-law even pointed me out to his son and said, 'You will make us so happy and proud if you go to college like he did!' Their warmth and respect were things I had never dreamed of having because I hadn't even known such things existed. I was practically a celebrity in their part of the world, and Nina adored me! My self-esteem improved almost to the point of arrogance, but I liked this change a good deal.

"After I proposed to Nina, I had a hard time telling my mother. Intermarriage was still frowned upon in our culture, but to marry into a working-class family was unthinkable, a much bigger offense.[38] But to my surprise, my family accepted Nina wholeheartedly for her warm and loving personality and because she had made such a change in me, had opened me up to life and helped me to become a productive member of society. We were married upon my graduation.

"My family immediately wanted me to start my own business, but I felt I first needed to gain some working experience. I applied for work in a large hotel, part of a major international chain, and for the next six years I traveled all over. I was assigned to work with the organization's Job Enrichment team, which was implementing a management-by-objective program.

"My supervisors managed their workforce using what is called the path-goal method.[39] I saw that this method really enabled me to combine my personal needs with organizational goals in such a way that both could be attained equally successfully.

"While I worked in this position, I was never made aware of any outward discrimination. The only incident in recent years happened when I was on assignment in Hong Kong and was mistaken for a doorman. There were a great many Pakistanis and Bangladeshis and refugees from Sri Lanka who worked in Hong Kong as laborers and security guards, so people there were used to seeing people from that part of Asia in menial positions.

"In 1985, my uncle and I bought our first motel. He had always wanted to be his own boss and invited me to be his partner. I found it difficult to work for my own relations, however, and the second year I sold my share to him and started my own chain of businesses. I was able to utilize everything I learned from college as well as the six years' experience working in the hospitality industry. I use a customer-based structure for my business, and business is good. I am grateful that I have the opportunity to be a free entrepreneur in this great country.

"Our culture encouraged us to work hard at school and take on higher education. Our parents believed that the only way to secure a place in this world is through a career and professional accomplishments. Furthermore, they set good examples for us to emulate, which many of the young people in our society today are lacking. For this, I am grateful to my parents' generation.

"However, I think that in the twentieth century, we need to redefine 'our place.' What we have not been taught at home is the understanding of the changing political environment. Perhaps they don't quite know themselves how to teach this.

"In my capacities as a businessman, an entrepreneur, I do not do as I am told like a 'good' Asian American worker. I must work beyond the expectations of everyone around me to build an impression of competence and to shape the environment around me. For example, if I need to stay in business in a community, I must establish good relations with all the constituencies. I join the community groups, contribute to the community welfare, enlist the support of allies within the business community. In short, I do networking, build up a reputation for integrity, sensitivity, a caring attitude—all the good qualities that people value.

"There is no question in my mind that the United States has improved opportunities for minorities, especially those who have the initiative and innovative spirit to contribute to their community's economic growth and to the welfare of the community at large. In time, minorities will also receive equal rewards. Any person who proves able to improve the quality of life and bring about mutually beneficial changes will inevitably win the respect and admiration of the rest."

*Comment*

As a minority entrepreneur in American society, Mr. Patel has developed the appropriate business concepts of effectiveness and sound management. He understands that the managerial process is inherently a human process, and he recognizes the importance of relating well to others. Businesses exist to satisfy the demands of many constituencies, be they individual customers, institutions, or the community. Each constituency has its expectations, and the key to a successful business venture is the kind of performance that satisfies all of them. Whereas the older generation relies on technical skills and competence to achieve its goals, more and more Asian Pacific Americans like Mr. Patel have found that the key criteria for effectively reaching their goals are human relations skills and effective management practices.

An interesting note is that, among Asian Pacific Americans, East Indians have the highest average educational attainments. India's traditional caste culture places a high value on doctors, scientists, and other professionals. According to the values of Mr. Patel's own family, he was "less competent and least successful." Yet when he began to socialize with working-class White Americans, he suddenly discovered his dual ethnic-social class identity[40] to be enhancing. His wife's White, working-class gestalt actually accorded to him considerable respect, not surprisingly elevating his self-esteem as well.

In his early development, Mr. Patel was forced to accept a caste-ethnic identity, which may have contributed to low self-efficacy. Later, an improved self-identity altered his perceptions and increased his self-efficacy. It also empowered him to foster change in the traditional operations of an organization. Mr. Patel could be identified as a Progressivist in our typology, one who tries to bring improvements and general betterment to the lives of others. His

efforts to further people's understanding of business and organizations constitute an invaluable contribution to society.


## All Vultures Must Be the Same Color (Andre's Story)

The story of Andre took a different turn. Andre was one of seven children born
to a Chinese family. His father was in the Chinese military in 1948, when
Chiang's regime fled to Taiwan before the advancing force of Mao's communist revolution. The family left mainland China in the nick of time and arrived
in Taiwan in a state of complete destitution. Yet the Chinese tradition of
respect for learning continued to dominate the children's lives. Even if the
family was short of food, the children were expected to study and memorize
their lessons. Each morning, they had to recite poetry. Andre remembers being
so poor in those days that he and his brother had to share a single pair of pants
presentable enough to wear in public. This meant that, if one went out, the
other had to stay at home and wait.

Despite the economic hardships, the family survived and the children
continued to study. Andre was a good student, although his oldest sister was
the most intelligent and the most competent scholar. In the early 1960s, she
received a Catholic nursing scholarship to study in Spain. A year later, she
transferred to a U.S. university. Following her marriage, she encouraged
Andre to join her in the U.S. to undertake his graduate study. Andre waited
until he had earned a bachelor's degree from a Taiwanese university, then
began applying to U.S. graduate schools. Andre planned to study mechanical
engineering.

In those days in Taiwan, male college graduates were required to devote a
year to military training before they were allowed either to enter graduate
school or to join the workforce. Just as Andre was completing his military
obligation, he met Professor Chang.

Professor Chang was a teacher at a major U.S. university who had originally gone to the U.S. as a Taiwanese exchange student.[41] After receiving a
Ph.D. in one of the scientific fields, Chang had stayed to teach and became a
permanent U.S. resident. While on sabbatical, he had returned to Taiwan on a
visit, and there he met Andre. He offered to assist Andre in applying to his
home university.

Needless to say, Andre was delighted and grateful for his good fortune.
Andre's parents, who by then had greatly improved their financial condition,
were able to wine and dine Professor Chang at his favorite restaurants during

his visit to Taiwan. The parents were led to believe that their son's future had been secured.

Three months later, Andre arrived in the U.S., and Professor Chang immediately enrolled Andre in the Ph.D. program, took him under his wing, and assigned him to a research project. He promised that, if Andre could complete all of his courses and the research work on time, he could graduate and receive his Ph.D. in only three years' time. The single condition was that Andre's research project had to deliver results and that these would be published under Dr. Chang's name. The arrangement seemed unusual, but Andre was well aware that he had a lot to learn about the inner workings of academic institutions and so agreed.

Then, year after year, on a research assistant's $12,000 annual salary— well below the poverty level—Andre sweated out one research project after another for Professor Chang. In all but one case, the resulting research papers were published under Chang's name. Finally, after the seventh year, Andre went to Chang and begged for a chance to graduate. He had reached the point where his life felt meaningless, and his entire existence seemed to consist of burying himself under steadily mounting piles of paper. He had allowed himself to remain isolated in America and had learned nothing outside of his research work.[42]

At last, Andre knew he had begun to lose his concentration. After the extreme poverty of his childhood, Andre found it increasingly difficult to endure living below the poverty level with no foreseeable change in sight. For seven years, he had been unable to buy any new clothing, go to a movie, or enjoy even the most simple of pleasures, such as going out with a friend for a cup of coffee or tea. And meanwhile, Andre watched Professor Chang receive promotions and research grants because of the work that he, Andre, had accomplished. Andre's papers had brought honors and rewards to Chang— but where were Andre's rewards?

Andre spent a lot of time thinking. He felt exploited and victimized. Andre's father had telephoned Chang several times on Andre's behalf, but each time Chang would answer, "The time is coming soon, but not yet," or "The committee for Ph.D. oral exams this year is really tough. Better to wait until next year. Your time will come; just be patient." Andre and his father felt they had no choice but to be obedient and continue to wait. Professor Chang was almost certainly aware that he was exploiting the Chinese traditional respect for teachers to gain what he wanted in a new world.

Gradually, Andre sunk into profound depression. He forgot to eat and neglected to get out of bed or to keep his appointments. He lost track of time completely and showed signs of mental breakdown. Finally, Professor Chang told Andre, "Come to my home tomorrow and we will discuss your future."

At the appointed hour, Andre went to meet his professor. Chang said, "I hear that your sister and her husband are doing very well investing in the stock market. Can you ask them for a gift of $40,000?"

Andre was stunned. His mind was hopelessly confused as he left Chang's home. How could Dr. Chang have asked for such a thing? How could this be happening?

Reluctantly, Andre called his sister. Both she and her husband found Chang's request outrageous—and now Andre was even more confused. Shouldn't his sister and brother-in-law be trying to save him? Who would help him now? Andre went back to Chang empty-handed and confessed his failure. "My sister says she does not have $40,000 to give you. Please have pity on me. I have slaved for you for seven years. Consider the contributions I have already made to your career! Please let me graduate. I can't function like this any longer. I am no use to you in any way."

Professor Chang's reply echoed with ironic truth: "You are a fool. In the American system, only the strongest survive. Weak people like you don't deserve a Ph.D."

Andre flunked out of his program and spent many months in a sanitarium. He could not go back home to Taiwan and his family because, according to Chinese tradition, he, not Dr. Chang, was the one who had lost face. At the time he was interviewed for this study, his sister had found him a job working as a translator for a major international corporation.

Contacted by telephone, Professor Chang was willing to discuss Andre's case, although he had his own perspective on events. "It is unfortunate that Andy would speak such ills. He is mentally unbalanced. I thought he had great potential when I first met him, but his work was terribly disappointing and he has such a strange personality. He lacked self-confidence, buried his head in the sand, oblivious to what's going on in the world, the changes taking place in his field. Even when there were people in the same room with him, no one would notice him.

"When I brought him along to research conferences, he rarely spoke to anyone and always kept to himself. He could never bring himself to answer even the simplest questions. What was I supposed to do?"

Asked why he waited so long before dismissing Andre and why he didn't try to advise Andre regarding his shortcomings, Chang replied, "At first, I did not see his shortcomings. I thought he needed an adjustment period for culture shock. He had good quantitative skills, but that is not enough in the academic world or the work situation. His research work in general was of poor quality. We couldn't use his reports since he also lacked proficiency in both oral and written communications.

"When we finally gave up on him and told him so, he was devastated and threatened to kill himself. So, out of compassion for a fellow countryman, we carried him on the payroll for as long as we could. What would you do if you had to deal with such a serious case of passivity, lack of initiative, and lack of competence?

"This is a highly competitive country, a dog-eat-dog society. You don't belong if you can't handle the playing field. You've got to have the brains to figure out a successful strategy. This is America!"

### Comment

That exploitation can occur at the hands of a member of one's own racial or ethnic group is truly unfortunate. Should the victim also take some of the responsibility? Should some of the blame also be on parents who failed to teach adequate real-world survival skills? In Andre's case, it is clear that he had never learned how to cope with negative circumstances or how to negotiate with others, especially those who do not behave ethically. Perhaps his family and cultural traditions overemphasized scholarly achievement and neglected development in other areas.

Aside from Chang's unethical willingness to take full advantage of Andre's situation, we might also conclude that the institution's organizational systems, particularly its evaluation program, and perhaps even the capitalist system in general, also contributed to the outcome of this story. In our typology model, Andre is an Abnegator. Although equipped with a college degree, he lacked development of the skills which would have allowed him to socialize outside of his intellectualized ethnic enclave. Chang, on the other hand, is a Pragmatist—indeed, an almost Machiavellian manipulator who both understands the system and has learned to take full advantage of human nature.

## Summary

Challenges experienced in the work place by five Asian Pacific Americans were presented in this chapter. These cases represent individuals with different ethnic backgrounds, unique origins and beginnings, all of whom entered different fields and professions. However, a common thread between all five is that each experienced discrimination and other forms of adversity in his or her life and, in particular, in the work setting. What distinguishes these five individuals is neither ethnicity nor education but how they handled adversity and crises in their lives.

Carlos, a fourth-generation Filipino American who can trace his mixed ethnicity to ancestors of Chinese, Spanish, and American Indian origin, showed us the complexity of ethnic identity and the oversimplified, overgeneralized method of using statistical information or stereotypes to group the diversity of Asian Pacific Americans by a single term. Carlos had always considered himself simply an "American" until subjected to discrimination at school and later in the workplace. His coping mechanism at first was to confront the offending institution; later, he sought ways to avoid a negative external environment, at the same time improving his portable job skills. Finally, he fantasized for pragmatic reasons about metamorphosing into a Latino American.

Mila, a Hmong woman—one of the newest group of immigrants—came from a very simple agrarian culture. When war upturned her family's life together, they became refugees until placed in Louisiana by the U.S. Immigration Service's zip code dispersal system. As a child, Mila learned survival skills subconsciously and sharpened her sensitivity toward the environment, developing in turn an inner strength.

Kim, a 1.5-generation Korean immigrant woman, recalled how her culture's family and kinship values have shepherded her life. She also gave some understanding of how the influence of American missionaries resulted in a higher number of Christians among Korean Americans than among other Asian American groups, as well as how language barriers have caused almost 75 percent of Korean Americans to be involved in small businesses. It is interesting that Kim's courageous, head-on confrontation of sexism and racism was supported by her trusted African American friend. Kim's progression from a dependent child with an abnegator nature to a progressivist working to help others better their lives is encouraging.

Mr. Patel, an Asian Indian American entrepreneur, relates how the caste system not only governs social relationships in India but also influences emigration to the United States. Having grown up in the household of a physician—a profession to which high status is accorded in the U.S.—Mr. Patel felt unable to meet the expectations of his family members and others in their social circle. Marriage to a woman from a working-class European background enhanced his self-identity and increased his self-efficacy. Mr. Patel understands that the managerial process is inherently a human one: the key criteria for organizational effectiveness are the development of human relations skills and the recognition of individual uniqueness among the organization's constituencies.

Andre, a Chinese American from Taiwan, was dominated by his aspiration to become an accomplished scholar in accord with family expectations. His technical skills and formal education were excellent but insufficient to enable him to cope with the complications of American society and institutions. Because his interpersonal skills and judgment were poorly developed, his technical expertise actually imprisoned him within an elite ethnic enclave, virtually enslaving him to another member of his own race whose perception of America was as a highly competitive, dog-eat-dog society in which those who fail to figure out a winning strategy are fair game for those who do.

On the following pages is a set of discussion questions designed to enable readers to think further about several things, among them the implications of being identified as a member of an ethnic minority in the American workplace; ways that individuals can cope with organizational life; and ways that employees and organizations can cooperate and interact in the workplace to improve the quality of life for the organization's entire membership.

◆ ◆ ◆ ◆ ◆

## DISCUSSION QUESTIONS

*Carlos's Story*

1. Why are Filipino Americans among the most Westernized of all Asian Pacific American immigrant groups? When and where were the first Filipino American settlements in the United States?
2. Most Filipino Americans have no difficulties expressing themselves in English and are culturally "pre-Americanized." Why do they still sometimes face discrimination in the workplace and elsewhere?
3. Identify some internal factors and external forces that influenced Carlos. Do you think his intermarriage has any bearing on his work experiences?
4. In what ways is Carlos's story unique? In what ways can we see him as representative of a larger social trend or pattern?

## Mila's Story

1. Why does the U.S. government feel obligated to allow the Hmong refugees to settle in the United States?
2. As a group, more than one-third of the Hmong population is American born. How do they fare in terms of education and professional attainments, compared to other Asian Pacific Americans?
3. Mila excelled in her academic work. What gave her the incentive she needed to succeed academically? Why did her older sister and brother do less well?
4. Expand on Mila's statement, "I can be an Asian, or an American, or both, and I can find meaning in both."
5. Mila and Dr. Oy both decided to leave the laboratory and try their prospects elsewhere. Did they have any other options?

## Kim's Story

1. Discuss the relationship between American Christian missionaries and Korean immigration to the U.S. What forces caused such a large number of Koreans to emigrate? How might the practice of the Christian religion make them unique among most Asian Pacific American groups?
2. What sorts of social and economic networks are used in Korean American communities? What kind of credit system do Korean immigrants use to help out one another?
3. In Kim's story, how accurate was Kim's assessment of relations between Korean Americans and African Americans? Can you suggest ways of improving relations between Korean Americans and other minority groups?
4. In Kim's confrontation with her supervisor, was she too forceful? Was she not forceful enough?
5. What would you do if forced to confront racism and sexism as overt as what Kim experienced? How can the level of consciousness to these issues be raised within corporate cultures—particularly considering that the ranks of managers these days are less diverse than those of workers?

## Mr. Patel's Story

1. Based on the 1990 census, all subgroups of Asian Indians are more highly educated than the U.S. population as a whole. They are also more highly

represented in professional occupations than other groups. What factors do you think contributed to this form of success?

2. Despite their attainments in terms of education and professional advancement, Asian Indian immigrants continue to suffer prejudice and discrimination in the workplace. Asian Indian-owned businesses are concentrated in the service and retail areas, especially in the hotel/motel business. What observations can you make concerning these facts?

3. Mr. Patel married outside his ethnicity. Is it unusual for Asian Indians to intermarry, even in today's cultural landscape? (Hint: see note 38.) What sort of ethnic identity might he be likely to develop in time?

4. According to Mr. Patel's point of view, which criteria contribute to success in most American organizations? What are the key criteria for achieving one's goals in a small business?

### Andre's Story

1. In your experience, how are Chinese Americans different from other Asian Pacific American groups? Is "losing face" common to all Asians, or particular to Chinese culture?

2. Who and what might have caused Andre to fail in his aspiration to be a scholar? Was he ultimately responsible for his own failure? If so, in what ways?

3. Are you aware of many cases of new immigrants being exploited or taken advantage of by opportunistic members of their own racial and ethnic groups?

4. Do you agree with Professor Chang that, in America, only the strongest survive? How important are communication skills and human relations skills in the workplace?

◆ ◆ ◆ ◆ ◆

### EXPERIENTIAL EXERCISE

### Objectives

1. To explore the common beliefs and expectations held in the workplace toward Asian Pacific Americans of different ethnic backgrounds

2. To compare and contrast the major myths and actual sociocultural differences confronting Asian Pacific American workers in today's environment
3. To consider whether individual personality differences rather than ethnic backgrounds affect behavior and work outcome in organizations

*Procedures*

Before class meeting
   1. Organize students into groups of three or four.
   2. Ask each group to interview three or four Asian Pacific American workers with different ethnic backgrounds.
   3. Ask students to make a list of common beliefs and expectations from the interviews.

On the day of the class
   1. Have the groups bring the interview results to class.
   2. Have each group compare the questions on its list with the actual answers from Asian Pacific American workers interviewed.
   3. In class discussion, compile a list of individual differences found.
   4. How would the class account for these differences?
   5. How would the class account for the commonalities?

## NOTES

1. Filipino Americans have a unique historical background among Asian Pacific Americans. Because the Philippines was ruled by the U.S. for forty-five years (after 400 years of Spanish colonial rule), Filipinos were legally considered Americans until Philippine independence in 1946. English remains the common language in schools. Interesting accounts can be found in Ester G. and Joel M. Maring, *Historical and Cultural Dictionary of the Philippines* (New York: Harper & Row, 1977).

2. Filipino Americans are currently the second largest Asian Pacific American group. A more detailed description of this population (derived from U.S. census data) is presented in chap. 2.

3. In *Cultural Awareness in the Human Services* (Englewood Cliffs, NJ: Prentice Hall, 1982), authors C. Tagaki and T. Ishisaka indicate that, among the Filipino American cultural values, family solidarity and cooperation among family members are stressed over individualism, even to the present day.

4. A fascinating and detailed account of the Louisiana settlers can be found in F. Cordova, *Filipinos: Forgotten Asian Americans* (Dubuque, IA: Kendall/Hunt, 1983).

5. U.S. Census Bureau, 1995. For an account of early settlers on the East and West Coasts and also more recent information, read L. L. Pido, *The Pilipinos in America: Macro/Micro Dimensions of Immigration and Integration* (New York: Center for Migration Studies, 1986); J. Liu, P. Ong, and C. Rosenstein, "Filipino Immigration to the United States," *International Migration Review* 25 (1991): 487-517.

6. According to a *Wall Street Journal* article by R. Joseph dated 24 January 1994 (as well as recent coverage by local newspapers and other media), almost 90 percent of Asian mail-order brides in the U.S. were Filipinas. Depressed by the lack of economic opportunity in the Philippines, many of these women turned to mail-order marriage as a way of escaping the poverty at home.

7. To understand more about the traditional culture and family values, read E. Yu and W. T. Liu, *Fertility and Kinship in the Philippines* (Notre Dame, IN: University of Notre Dame Press, 1980); P. Agbayani-Siewert, "Filipino American Families" (Paper presented at the Thirty-Sixth Annual Meeting of the Council of Social Work Education, New Orleans, 1990).

8. The roles of line and staff in organizations are an important concept in the study of organizations. Students who are interested in learning more about the structure of organizations should see Henry Mintzberg, "The Five Basic Parts of the Organization, in *Classics of Organization Theory,* ed. J. M. Shafritz and T. S. Ott (Belmont, CA: Wadsworth, 1995).

9. According to the 1994 census report, "Household Income by Ethnicity," the median family income for Filipino Americans in 1994 was $43,780, the second highest among all Asian Pacific American groups, surpassed only by the $44,696 median family income of Asian Indians, and followed by that of Japanese Americans at $41,626. However, the seeming affluence of Filipino American households correlates not with high wages, but with the fact that, on average, they have the largest number of household members. In terms of per capita income, Japanese Americans ranked highest among the Asian ethnic groups, with average individual earnings of $19,373 (corresponding to 46.5 percent of the median family income figure), whereas Filipino Americans

ranked only ninth, with average individual incomes of only $13,616, or about 31 percent of the median family income figure.

10. Although current federal law protects whistle-blowers' rights, many organizations continue to practice retaliation against informants. More information can be obtained from the article by Marcia P. Miceli and Janet P. Near, "The Incidence of Wrongdoing, Whistle-Blowing, and Retaliation," *Employee Responsibilities and Rights Journal* (June 1989): 91-108.

11. This may be due to educational achievement rates, which are much lower on average for Filipino Americans than for other Asian groups. The 1990 census report indicates that only 22.3 percent of U.S.-born Filipinos have college degrees, as compared to 51 percent of U.S.-born Chinese Americans and 35 percent of U.S.-born Japanese and Korean Americans. A 1988 study, *Reflections on Shattered Windows: Promises and Prospects for Asian American Studies* by E. B. Almirol (Seattle: Washington State University Press, 1988), found that only 0.6 percent of the master's degree students in the University of California system were Filipino Americans.

12. A. Cabezas, L. Shinagawa, and G. Kawaguchi, "New Inquiries into the Socioeconomic Status of Pilipino Americans in California," *Amerasia Journal* 13 (1987): 1-22.

13. On 1 July 1996, the Supreme Court refused to review a Fifth Circuit Court ruling invalidating a racial preferences program to increase African and Latino American enrollments at the University of Texas Law School, generating a good deal of publicity and renewed controversy. California voters passed Proposition 209 in November 1996, a bill abolishing all affirmative action.

14. S. Sue and H. Kitano, "Stereotypes as a Measure of Success," *Journal of Social Issues* 29:2 (1973): 83-98.

15. Stereotyping simplifies the comparative process in group identity categorization by ascribing group traits to individuals. Research on stereotyping to racioethnicity and nationality has been extensive; one of the classic works is G. W. Allport, *The Nature of Prejudice* (Reading, MA: Addison-Wesley, 1954).

16. The first Hmong arrived in 1975; most of them came as refugees rather than immigrants. Out of the 100,000 Hmong currently living in this country, about one-third are American-born. Their median age is thirteen, compared to thirty-three years for the general American population, according to the Racial Statistics Branch, Population Division, U.S. Bureau of the Census (Washington, DC, March 1994).

17. Studies by R. Baker and D. North, *The 1975 Refugees* (Washington, DC: New Trans Century Foundation, 1984), and by C. R. Finnan and R. A.

Cooperstein, *Southeast Asian Refugee Resettlement at the Local Level* (Menlo Park, CA: SRI International, 1983) both confirm a governmental policy of dispersing refugees without family ties away from high-impact areas by placing them in 813 separate zip code areas in every state, including Alaska. Coauthor Ruben G. Rumbaut further indicates, in P. G. Min's book, *Asian Americans: Contemporary Trends and Issues* (Thousand Oaks, CA: Sage, 1995), that, despite the government policy of settling two-thirds of the refugees in zip codes where fewer than 500 refugees lived already, most of the resettled population later found their own way to states that had more highly concentrated Asian Pacific American populations.

18. According to the U.S. Bureau of the Census survey report (1993), about 94,000 Hmong reside in the U.S. half of this population lives in California; about 20,000 each live in the states of Wisconsin and Minnesota.

19. The Khmer Rouge communists, led by Pol Pot, killed vast numbers of the Cambodian people. In R. G. Rumbaut's 1989 study, "Portraits, Patterns and Predictors of the Refugee Adaptation Process" (in *Refugees as Immigrants,* ed. D. W. Haines. Totowa, NJ: Rowman & Littlefield, 1989), the author found that 20 percent of Cambodian women were widows whose husbands had been killed during the Pol Pot period in the late 1970s.

20. During her interview, Mila took pains to explain that, although the interracial "bui doi" orphans were generally looked down upon by society, this had not been the case in her own family. Mila also confirmed that the Hmong marriage tradition of kidnapping one's bride and paying off her family (recently featured in the television show "Picket Fences") still occurs but is not acceptable among Hmong Americans. Her brother and his bride had fallen in love, and their move to California had involved neither kidnapping nor flight.

21. To refresh the memory on the terms "locus of control" and "self-efficacy," see chap. 3, Box 3.4.

22. Various studies, notably "Korean Immigrant Entrepreneurship: A Multivariate Analysis" by P. G. Min, *Journal of Urban Affairs* 10 (1989): 197-212, and *Immigration and Entrepreneurship* by I. Light and P. Bhachu (New York: Transaction Books, 1993) indicate that most Korean American businesses are in southern California. There are also numerous Korean American entrepreneurs in the New York metropolitan area, Atlanta, Philadelphia, and Seattle. Most of the merchandise is imported from South Korea, which enjoys active trade relationships with major U.S. corporations all over the United States.

23. According to the 1970 census, the Korean population in the United States was 69,130. the official count of Korean Americans in the 1990 census was close to 800,000. Unofficially, the actual number of Koreans in the United

States has been estimated as closer to one million by D. J. Fein in "Racial and Ethnic Differences in U.S. Census Omission Rates," *Demography* (March 1990): 285-301.

24. The Immigration and Naturalization Service reported in 1971 that Korean War orphans made up for about 60 percent of all foreign children adopted by U.S. citizens. Between 1950 and 1964, most Koreans admitted to the United States as legal immigrants were either wives of U.S. citizens (generally in interracial marriages) or adopted Korean orphans.

25. Most of the early Korean immigrants who came to Hawaii as contract labor in the 1900s were Christians before they left Korea. Exposure to American missionaries in Korean cities was a major factor influencing Korean immigration to the U.S. at the turn of the century. Further interesting accounts of Christian influences can be found in B. Y. Choy, *Koreans in America* (Chicago: Nelson-Hall, 1979) and W. Patterson, *The Korean Frontier in America: Immigration to Hawaii, 1896-1910* (Honolulu: University of Hawaii Press, 1988).

26. Based on the 1990 census report, among Asian Pacific Americans, the Korean communities have the highest levels of self-employment. It has been estimated that only one out of four Korean workers works for a non-Korean firm. For further studies, see K. C. Kim and W. M. Hurh, "Ethnic Resources Utilization of Korean Immigrant Entrepreneurs in the Chicago Minority Area," *International Migration Review* 19 (1985): 82-111; I. S. Kim, *New Urban Immigrants: The Korean Community* (Princeton, NJ: Princeton University Press, 1981); P. G. Min, "Cultural and Economic Boundaries of Korean Ethnicity," *Ethnic and Racial Studies* 14 (1991): 225-41.

27. According to a 1994 survey by P. G. Min, the most common Korean American-owned business is a grocery-liquor retail store serving non-Korean and, in particular, low-income African American customers.

28. The middle minorities theory postulates that the ruling group encourages alien groups to play an intermediate role between the ruling class and the masses by distributing products to bridge the status gap. For further understanding, see E. Bonacich, *A Theory of Middleman Minority* (New York: John Wiley, 1973); W. Zenner, *Minorities in the Middle: A Cross-Cultural Analysis* (Albany: State University of New York Press, 1991).

29. See W. M. Hurh and K. C. Kim, "Religious Participation of Korean Immigrants in the U.S.," *Journal of the Scientific Study of Religion* 19 (1990): 19-34.

30. See Min, "Korean Immigrant Entrepreneurship."

31. See authors and works cited in notes 25-30.

32. According to the U.S. Bureau of the Census report, in 1990 there were about 800,000 Asian Indian Americans, 35 percent of whom lived on the East Coast in states such as New York, New Jersey, and Pennsylvania; 23 percent lived on the West Coast, most notably in California; another 24 percent lived in the states of Texas, Florida, Virginia, and Maryland; and 18 percent lived in the Midwest.

33. As a group, based on the 1990 U.S. census, Asian Indians have the highest educational level among all Asians. in 1990, 45 percent of Asian Indian Americans held a bachelor's degree, compared to 39 percent of all Asian Americans and 22 percent of all Americans. In addition, 21 percent of Indian Americans hold master's or professional degrees, compared to 19 percent of all Asian groups and only 8 percent of the total U.S. population; 30 percent of Asian Indians have professional occupations, compared to 14 percent of White American workers; and 17 percent of Asian Indian Americans are in the health professions and constitute the largest component of U.S. health workers. A large number of Asian Indian engineers and scientists hold key academic posts on college campuses across the U.S.

34. Generally, people from India have no language problem in the U.S. because, although some may speak with an accent, almost all Asian Indians learn English as children, either at home or in school.

35. Although the majority of Indian Americans are Hindus, many are from Gujarat, Punjab, or Kerala. For detailed information about their religious practices and linguistic groups, see A. Helweg and U. Helweg, *The Immigrant Success Story: East Indians* (Pittsburgh: University of Pennsylvania Press, 1990).

36. The "dot" refers to the mark worn on a Hindu woman's forehead, a protecting third eye from Lord Shiva. Asian Indian American women were harassed in New Jersey and other states. Ron Takaki, in his book *From Different Shores: Perspectives on Race and Ethnicity in America* (New York: Oxford University Press, 1987), has portrayed this as a sad example of the deep mindset of White Americans against Asian Indians.

37. Partially for the sake of maintaining their ethnic group identity in the U.S., many Asian Indian immigrants are more openly devout than they had been in India. In India, Hindus comprise 83 percent of the population; Muslims, 11 percent; Christians, 3 percent; and Sikhs, 2 percent. Hinduism, first introduced to the U.S. in 1893, remains the most prevalent religion among Asian Indian Americans. For more information, see R. B. Williams, *Religions of Immigrants from India and Pakistan: New Threads in the American Tapestry* (Cambridge, UK: Cambridge University Press, 1988).

38. For more details regarding intermarriage patterns of Asian Indian Americans, see the article "Patterns of Asian American Intermarriage and Marital Assimilation" by S. M. Lee and K. Yamanaka, *Journal of Comparative Family Studies* 21 (December 1990): 287-305.

39. The path-goal model attempts to influence employees' perceptions of work goals, self-development goals, and paths to goal attainment. The model was developed by Robert House; see his article "The Path-Goal Theory of Leadership Effectiveness," *Administrative Science Quarterly* (September 1977): 321-39.

40. The idea of dual ethnic-social class identity among minority professionals was offered by Nathan Glazer and Daniel Moynihan in *Beyond the Melting Pot* (Cambridge: MIT Press, 1963).

41. Although the McCarran-Walter Act, passed in 1952, barred race as a criterion for immigration, it still restricted Chinese immigrants to a quota of 105 people per year. Most Chinese immigrants gained entrance to the U.S. via exchange student programs. For further study of Chinese immigrants during that period, read J. Chen, *The Chinese of America* (New York: Harper & Row, 1980); M. G. Wong, "Post-1965 Immigrants: Where Do They Come from, Where Are They Now, and Where Are They Going?" *The Annals of the American Academy of Political and Social Science* 487 (1986): 150-68.

42. Perhaps due to parental pressure and childhood upbringing, many Chinese American students, especially those born overseas, learned to devote themselves to academic studies to the exclusion of virtually all other concerns. Many gained entrance to prestigious universities and graduate schools, where they excelled in advanced courses in science and mathematics, only to face severe problems later in their careers and lives because of the lack of attention paid to the interpersonal dimension. More light is shed on this phenomenon in B. Fischer, "Whiz Kid Image Masks Problems of Asian Americans," *NEA Today* (June 1988): 14-5; and J. Hsia, *Asian Americans in Higher Education and at Work* (Hillsdale, NJ: Lawrence Erlbaum, 1988).

# Five

# Generation, Gender, Identity, and the Perception of the Work Environment

## Prelude

An elderly Filipino American man sits on a bench in Portsmouth Square, near San Francisco's famous Chinatown, watching the people bustling by. The sun is bright but the air is still cold, early on a Monday afternoon in January. By and by, an elderly Chinese American woman approaches the bench. She is all bundled up in layers and layers of clothing and carries a shopping bag with the Chinese characters for "Tien Sun Market" printed upon it. She takes a seat on the other end of the bench and, in a short while, she produces a piece of dried bread from her bag and holds it in her hand.

"Better not," says the man sitting beside her. "No pigeons here. Better go down to Market Street."

The woman at first looks startled, then smiles. "Not for pigeon. I eat. Lunch," she says.

A halting conversation begins in pidgin English.

"See that long hair young man just passing by? I thought he was a girl until he turned around and I saw his mustache. Asian men shouldn't do that," says the old man, shaking his head and muttering about the 1960s.

"Ahh! You been in America long?"

"Since 1928. Came up from Stockton fifteen years ago. Wife died, son here. Now son moved East. Too cold back East. I stay here."

"I, thirty years. Husband, daughter died, cancer. Grandchildren all gone." She held up three of her fingers, made a long and serious face, and shook her head. "Thirty years, my daughter want me come from Macau. Take care her baby. She was smart in college, work big job. Her *Fan Gui* [foreign ghost] husband left."

An Asian American girl passes by dressed in short shorts and a T-shirt; she carries a portable radio and is playing loud music. The old man again shakes his head. "She will catch her death of cold, headache. The music . . . "

"Ahh! Hip-hops,[1] the music, my granddaughter listen. Very good, she is in number one college. We family very educated," she says with obvious pride.

"Back in 1930," the man replies, "my half-Chinese cousin from my mother's side studied engineering, graduated from Stanford. So proud, but he could not find any professional work, so my parents kept me working down on the farm. Why bother to get an education?" he says aloud, remembering, no doubt talking partly to himself.

"Yeah? Me, no education, no English, after daughter died, no money. Work in sewing factory. Very hard, fifteen dollars, twelve hours a day. Some days fourteen hours. No sick leave, no vacation.[2] Only eat bread and drink water; no time to cook rice. I save money for granddaughter get education."

A group of teenaged Asian Americans passes by, laughing and chasing each other down the street in a playful manner. "They no good. School time, should study hard in school, not fool around in street." Both nod their heads and gradually fade into silence.

*     *     *     *     *

Conversations such as this one, carried out by Asian Pacific Americans who are 65 years or more in age—the "Depression generation"—are common-place. Perhaps they are also not too different from the conversations of non-Asian immigrants of their generation. The "silent generation" of Asian Pacific Americans—those between 50 and 64 years of age—are sometimes called the generation of technicians, regardless of whether they are first-, second-, or third-generation Americans, because so many found positions in engineering, science, education, or business. The baby boomers, born after World War II and today in their mid-thirties to early fifties, have the honor of being the basis of the "model minority myth." The generation of Asian Pacific Americans ranging in age from eighteen to their early thirties, sometimes called "Generation X," have also coined the term "GenerAsian" to define themselves as a distinct pan-ethnic social force.

Many young Asian Pacific Americans today clearly expect a massive transformation of the American cultural landscape, and they enjoy both watching for signs of this process and participating in it. Yet another term, "yappies"—for young Asian professionals—has been applied mainly to the offspring of Asian Pacific American professionals and technicians and depicts the young as a generation that drives foreign sports cars, wears designer clothes, frequents fashionable coffee bars and continental restaurants, navigates the "information superhighway" and surfs the World Wide Web with the latest equipment, and even responds enthusiastically to surveys about its sexual practices.[3] But as we have already seen, not all young Asian Pacific Americans enjoy such an affluent lifestyle. How reliable are generalizations about the generations?

What follows are five interviews providing glimpses of how some Asian Pacific Americans view their own generations,[4] with particular emphasis on their views of the American workplace.


## Sitting in Two Chairs at Once: The Second Generation

"I think Asian Pacific American women, in general, have a relatively easier time getting along in the American workplace. They count double under affirmative action as both women and minorities, and other people are much more receptive to Asian American women [than men] due to their greater media exposure as television news anchors and reporters.[5] The majority of Americans are used to seeing female Asian faces, so they're also more comfortable working with them as colleagues.

"I also think that the older generation of Asian Americans, the ones who got to enjoy the robust economy of the boom years, are much better off than our generation."

The speaker is Nevin, a 22-year-old, second-generation college graduate whose parents immigrated to the United States from Thailand during the 1960s. Nevin is, by any standard, an extremely sensitive and intelligent young man. At the time he was interviewed for this study, he had been searching for a job in advertising for several months. Although he had just been hired as a graphic designer, many of the comments he made reflected his recent job searching difficulties. Nevertheless, they are fairly typical of the sentiments of many Asian Pacific Americans of his generation. As a group, the younger generation of Asian Pacific Americans tend to feel that, despite their American educations and thorough familiarity with American institutions and values, they still face extremely difficult or unfair competition.

For one thing, it is a matter of historical record that every time the American economy takes a downward turn, part of the blame has always been placed on the most recent populations of immigrants.[6] Therefore, in a poor economy, anyone who "looks different" is likely to suffer.

"My parents were first-generation immigrants," continued Nevin. "Although they had to overcome a language barrier and make other adjustments to living in a new country, they made it in the workforce because it happened to be a Golden Age for the United States. The skills that American industries needed were exactly the skills my parents brought with them."[7]

Until his recent retirement, Nevin's father had worked as an engineer with a major oil company. His mother continues to work as a laboratory technician. They own a comfortable home in an upscale suburban neighborhood.

"My father worked for the same company for thirty-two years; my mother has been in the same lab for nineteen years, the first ten working part-time. During all that time, the whole environment was relatively stable. Life was simpler; you learned a technical skill, got hired by a reputable firm, and as long as you were conscientious in your work, showed some loyalty to the company, and obeyed the company rules and policies, you were set for life. Sure, there was plenty of bureaucracy and also racism to contend with in the big companies, but most employers actually based everything on the seniority system. The longer you stayed with your job, the more security you got. Today, times have changed."

When reminded that times had changed for all younger Americans, not only for second-generation Asian Pacific Americans, Nevin responded, "True, but being Asian American entails extra burdens. My parents, like most immigrants, had lower expectations for themselves than they have for me today. Their psyches were geared simply for survival, so they were very content with a small-scale version of the American Dream: a stable job, a nice home, a normal family. I believe they also both got a lot of satisfaction from knowing that people valued their skills and they were contributing something to the community and the American economy.

"Just because we were U.S.-born and didn't have the language difficulties to contend with, our parents expected us automatically to do better than they did. It's a very high-pressure situation. It may be invisible to most people most of the time, but the pressure is always there and never lets up.

"One time, I actually mentioned this to my parents, and they acted completely surprised. 'When did we ever pressure you to do anything? We only wanted to give you and your brothers a better life, a better education than we had, a better life than ours.' I told them, 'That's the pressure I'm talking about, right there! I have to out-do my parents or be considered a failure, not living up to their expectations.' Don't get me wrong—my parents are great. I can't tell you how much I appreciate the values they taught me, the work ethic, the capacity for self-discipline, and especially even this drive to do something meaningful with my life. But the world we live in today is different, much more complicated than anything my parents ever experienced."

This same pressure to excel was cited by many members of Nevin's generation. It is implicit in their daily behavior, both as adults and throughout their childhoods.[8] For the most part, it remained unspoken; Asian Pacific Americans learn to sense and feel the pressure to succeed through nonverbal messages.

"Asian Pacific Americans of my parents' generation were allowed to hide behind their professionalism. They got away with not having to come to terms with the stereotyping we face today, such as all Asians are meek, weak, computer nerds, and so on.[9] My parents didn't have to make the same kind of inner adjustments; their cultural values, like discipline and hard work, along with their technical expertise were enough that no one questioned their identities, who they really were on the inside. They were able to keep their old role models from their traditional culture, and, at the same time, as they learned to socialize in the American workplace, they have become pretty well versed in both cultures. They learned to fit into their working roles, to fulfill their bosses' and co-workers' expectations, but still they maintained their old identities on the inside. They managed to sit in two chairs at the same time, and comfortably.[10]

"Young people today don't have such luxuries. There aren't really any U.S.-born Asian or Pacific Islander role models for us to emulate. All of my friends talk about this same thing—anyone whose background is about the same as mine, we all agree on one thing: that none of us can fit into either one of our parents' two chairs comfortably. We are neither Americans nor Asians; we don't get along with the 'FOB'[11] Asians, but we also don't feel accepted by White Americans, not 100 percent accepted. We are not Whites, after all—not just in appearance, but also on the inside. My 'traditional family values' reflect another tradition.

"My mother always reminded me that I was different, so my connection to a traditional culture sets me apart from most Americans, yet I don't really know enough about the older culture to feel a sense of belonging to it. I do not have a deeper connection to my own heritage, only a superficial one.

"I have witnessed how my parents and their friends have had the inner strength to manage to sit in both chairs successfully, in spite of discrimination and sometimes even blatantly unfair treatment they received from this society. But I don't have that kind of confidence. Right now, I feel like I'm actually sitting in between the two chairs, in a gray zone, and not quite accepted by either world. The ironic thing is that people have the perception that we are an 'antigeneration,' always going around speaking against everything and everybody. The media calls my generation 'Generation X' and says we are party-goers and pleasure seekers. How much more wrong could they be?"

Nevin's perspective is no doubt directly related to his social class and other aspects of his background. His parents are highly educated and financially successful. They came to the U.S. as "urgently needed professionals"[12] during a time when this nation was experiencing unprecedented economic growth and unparalleled prosperity on a global scale. For the child, however, it can be difficult to have high-achieving parents, regardless of ethnic background and social status. It is possible that Nevin and his peers are simply still too young to have completed the process of "finding themselves"—that is, of self-exploration leading to a clear self-identity.

Professor Sucheng Chan, in her scholarly research and the resulting book *Asian Americans,*[13] suggests that younger Asian Pacific Americans do not have to choose between either an "Asian" or an "American" culture, but can forge a new culture of their own, one arising out of their own American experiences and blending not only traditional elements of East and West but also incorporating elements from White American, African American, and Latino traditions. She further states that, through Asian American studies programs and other courses at academic institutions as well as corporate training programs, second-generation Asian Pacific Americans can help to create a new, unique pan-ethnic identity.

This view is shared by many other scholars and people currently involved in ethnic studies and other social sciences.[14] A majority of the subjects interviewed for this book agreed that younger Asian Pacific Americans have greater freedom to choose and to form their own beliefs and lifestyle. But many also feel that freedom without direction can lead to social decay or collapse and, therefore, that much stronger forms of responsible guidance and leadership are needed, not just for Asian Pacific American youth but for all younger Americans.

An interesting counterpoint to this "new freedom" perspective, however, is that many members of the second generation claim to have almost no freedom at all. As shown by the following tongue-in-cheek sampling from the Internet, many second-generation Asian Pacific Americans still feel a great deal of pressure to satisfy the extraordinary demands for near-perfection made by their parents and other relatives (see Box 5.1).

---

Box 5.1

*How to Be a Perfect Chinese Parent (from the second-generation perspective)*

1. Be a little more lenient on the 7:00 P.M. curfew.
2. Don't ask "Where's the other point?" when your child comes home with a 99 on a test.
3. Don't "ai-yoh" loudly at your kid's dress habits.
4. Don't blatantly hint about the merits of Hah-phoo (Harvard), Yale-uh (Yale), Stan-phoo (Stanford), and Emeh-I-Tee (MIT).
5. Don't reveal all the intimate details of your kid's life to the entire Chinese community.
6. Don't ask your child, "What are you going to do with your life" if he or she majors in a non-science field.
7. Don't give your son a bowl haircut or your daughter two acres of bangs.
8. Don't try to set your child up on a date in anticipation of his or her poor taste or inept social skills.
9. Incorporate phrases other than "Did you study yet?" into your daily conversations with your children.
10. Don't ask all your kid's friends over the age of 21 if they have a boyfriend or girlfriend yet.

*How to Be a Perfect Chinese Kid (from the first-generation perspective)*

1. Score 1600 on the SAT.
2. Play the violin or piano on the level of a concert performer.
3. Apply to and be accepted by 27 colleges.
4. Have three hobbies: studying, studying, and studying.
5. Go to a prestigious Ivy League university and win enough scholarships to pay for it.
6. Love classical music and detest talking on the telephone.
7. Become a Westinghouse, Presidential, and eventually a Rhodes Scholar.
8. Aspire to be a brain surgeon.
9. Marry a Chinese American doctor and have perfect, successful children (grandkids for ahma and ah-gongh!)
10. Love to hear stories about your parents' childhood—especially the one about walking 7 miles to school without shoes.

*Received via the Internet; author unknown*

## The Nouveau: The One-and-a-Half Generation

Is there a "new Asian Pacific American" of the sort envisioned by some futurists? There does at least seem to be a definite movement in that direction—fueled in large part by the coming together of the newest wave of Asian immigration and the 1.5 generation of Asian Pacific Americans. Technically, "one-and-a-half-generation" Americans are first-generation Americans, but they all came to the U.S. at an early age and generally remember little of another life. Of course, their experiences and cultural identities vary somewhat according to the age at which they reached the U.S.

Currently, about three-fourths of the U.S. Asian population were foreign-born,[15] and among the younger generation, foreign-born Asian Pacific Americans already outnumber their U.S.-born counterparts. Within this 1.5 generation, there are two distinct classes. One class is comprised of the children of wealthy investment immigrants, most of them relatively recent arrivals from Hong Kong, Taiwan, Korea, the Philippines, Thailand, Singapore, Indonesia, and Malaysia. In contrast, the second class consists of the children of refugees, or the children of fourth- and fifth-preference immigrants, most of them Southeast Asians, Pacific Islanders, or mainland Chinese nationals.

Richard is the 21-year-old son of an investment immigrant. He came from Hong Kong eight years ago with his parents.

"My father was the general manager for a large U.S. corporation in Hong Kong. Because of the 1997 situation,[16] my mother had to take my sister and me to the U.S. The company first put us on the East Coast, right near their corporate headquarters. We couldn't adjust to the cold weather and requested a move to the West Coast. We also had the difficulty of being isolated back east. Even though people were generally always nice to us and very helpful, we were the only Asian Americans in a private prep school.

"My sister is only two years older than I am, but where I adapted to the new culture right away, she still clings to the Asian culture. Even so, we were both considered very 'hip' in school; we have always attended English schools, even before we came here. Hong Kong is very cosmopolitan, you know. We listen to rap music and always carry our cellular phones in our pockets or purses. People dress very stylishly, about two years ahead of the fashions in the States. If you're young and you want to be accepted in Hong Kong, you have to wear designer clothes. My father bought me a BMW when I turned sixteen. That's cool; I never have any trouble getting dates.

"My math wasn't all that great in Hong Kong, but here in this country, I was considered among the top performers. And I kind of use that 'model minority' thing to my advantage, pretending to be 'brainy,' you know. If I need to, I can turn 'hip-hop' and make some noises to contradict the model minority image. You have to be flexible nowadays and use whatever comes your way, enjoy life, and get ahead. Hey! We're in the Space Age, man."

As a matter of fact, the term "space person" has been coined to describe the frequency with which families such as Richard's spend time in the air, jetting between Asia and the U.S. Richard's father comes to the States to visit every other month. Richard, his mother, and his sister return to Hong Kong each year during winter and spring break and over summer vacation. Now that Richard is preparing to graduate, he intends to find work in the U.S. and to be an American.

"I have a girlfriend here. My mother is mad she's not Asian, but it didn't matter to me. I plan to live here. I love America. There's so much more opportunity here."

Richard majored in business administration and wants to work either as an investment banker or a securities broker. He has already had a few very promising job interviews. "The salary," he says, "is a secondary consideration. The house and my car are already paid for by my father. I also have a nice investment income coming in each month. I just need an excuse to live in the United States. And it would also be good to get to know more investment-minded people."

Richard's sister, however, does not intend to remain in the U.S. and is planning to return to Hong Kong. In answer to the question, "What about 1997?" she replies, "It doesn't matter. We will manage. If things will not work out after 1997, I can always come back. We have American citizenship in our pockets, just as a safety measure."

Such is the *nouveau* culture: many members of this group who came to the U.S. with their upper-class or wealthy parents tend to practice the concept of capitalism to the hilt, are highly money-oriented and materialistic, and espouse living for the moment. They tend to be pragmatic in their actions and practical in both attitude and behavior. A memorable personification of this attitude is the character Chester in David Hwang's play, *Family Devotion*: "I live in Bel Air, I drive a Mercedes and I go to private school. . . . "[17]

## Coming Ashore: The First Generation

Just ten years ago, Sue was only a fourteen-year-old "fresh off the boat" newcomer when she emigrated from mainland China with her parents and two brothers. Today, Sue is a computer technician married to an "ABC"—American-born Chinese—whom she met while they were classmates at State College. "I wanted to learn English from him, and he wanted to learn Chinese from me. That's how we got together," she explains.

Sue's parents had no formal education, and both are blue-collar workers. Her uncle, an engineer, came to the U.S. in the 1950s and, later, after the U.S. established diplomatic relations with China, he applied for the rest of the family to join him here.[18]

"My parents wanted to seek a new life for us children, give us the opportunity of a better education. There has never been any doubt in our minds about how much they sacrificed for our sakes, not only coming here, but, when we first arrived, they had to work extremely hard. It was hard work for all of us. In school and everywhere else my brothers or I went, we were always ridiculed and teased for dressing poorly and not even knowing any of the fashions and the latest thing in pop culture. The language barrier also exacerbated the problem. But actually, none of these things mattered that much. We developed a 'thick skin.'

"The mean things other people can say actually mean very little compared with being labeled 'traitors' and forced to live in a rat-infested, cockroach-filled room with bunk beds stacked three tiers high. During the Cultural Revolution period in China, my parents were punished for having a relative in the United States. After we came here, there was nothing in the old culture that I still wanted to identify with but, at the same time, I felt that I would never be a real American. So, people like us, we just developed our own thing. I mix a little bit of Taiwanese karaoke, Hong Kong movies, African American soul music, California social customs—everything mixed together. We don't mind being called mixed-up kids or mixed-up Americans.

"I know that as long as I have the skills and know-how and I can make a living and be with my family, I will be content."

It is easy for young people who lived with calamity and destitution before coming to the U.S. to develop this kind of mentality after immigration. Although they still like their ethnic cuisine and the same modern entertainments as their wealthier peers, they have not had time to develop the sophistication and self-confidence needed to feel fully accepted by this society.[19] They can be characterized as the Abnegator/Pragmatist type. They are content as long as they have a steady job and a comfortable home where their family can all come together.

## The Third, Fourth, and Fifth Generations: Are We Americans Yet?

Now, let's explore the statements made by another younger generation of Asian Pacific Americans, beginning with Jeff, a 24-year-old Yonsei (fourth-generation Japanese American) law student.

"Of course I am an Asian American. The Asian part is my physical appearance, and inside, I'm as American as anyone walking down this street. My parents do not speak Japanese. We never speak Japanese at home, and my parents don't talk about the 'old country.' It's always been quite clear to me that I am an American, first and foremost. And not only that, but I'm proud of it."

Asked about Asian role models, Jeff replied, "I most admire Congressman Norman Mineta and Robert Matsui.[20] I hope to go into politics and public service some day, to make some kind of contribution, not just to the Japanese American community, but to be helpful to everyone around the nation. I think it's utterly critical and essential for young Asian Pacific Americans to get into the mainstream and dedicate themselves to improving the lives of Americans as a whole.

"In America, your sense of identity depends a lot more on your state of mind and your spirit than on your ethnic background. To be an Asian *American*, it's important to stand up and be a voice for your community. There is no room in this country for complacency. I am not so naive as to think there's no discrimination in this country. Everyone knows that the early laws in this country were enacted to prevent Asians from coming here. More than that, Asian Pacific Americans were forbidden to own property here, forbidden to intermarry, and even forbidden to testify in court. I'm sure you know what happened here in California during World War II—American citizens of Japanese ancestry were herded into concentration camps, for no other reason than their ethnicity.[21] Every single time there's an economic downswing in America, Asian Pacific Americans are the scapegoats for White politicians' mistakes or even their greed. Even today, there is heavy discrimination in our society against all sorts of groups—minorities, women, gays and lesbians. That's all the more reason why you have to speak up and fight for your rights. The reality is that no one will give you anything in this world for free. No matter what your background, you need to fight for whatever it is you believe.

"Look at the *Salazar versus Blue Shield* case.[22] As a result of that decision, they now have better training programs, more opportunities for promotion, and affirmative action for Asian American employees at Blue Shield. But no one gave those things away; someone had to take a stand.

"It's important to read about the differences between minority groups and to be familiar with the different histories, to develop a sense of understanding of different communities' perspectives on certain events—but it is more important to look for common ground. What holds this country together is not our differences, but the things we all share. I believe my generation will make major contributions to this society in terms of generating social changes and achieving economic parity, as well as individual growth, for everyone in this country. There are many problems and social ills remaining in our society, but this is still the country we live in. I am proud to be part of the process of making it even better, and I'm confident that Asian Pacific Americans will be making immense progress in the workplace."

Jeff's optimistic attitude and perceptions may not reflect the feelings of all third-, fourth-, and fifth-generation Asian Pacific Americans, but Jeff does represent a common thread. Increasingly, the younger generations of Asian Pacific Americans can be seen taking an active role in reshaping the communities in which they live. Such community- and future-oriented individuals are the Progressivists/Altruists who want to make a difference, transform the social environment, and help promote ethical values such as civility and consideration for others in our society.

## The Silent Generation

"I can communicate with the younger generation without any problems, because I take the position that I am their friend, not some 'elder' from the old country who expects special attention and demands respect, no matter if I am a good person or not."

The speaker is Emil, a 55-year-old entrepreneur who works extensively with younger professionals. "There are no doubt many differences between younger and older generations of Asian Pacific Americans. I think my generation, as a whole, is more conservative. We wanted to preserve family unity at any cost, no matter what the personal sacrifice. We also upheld our traditional codes of conduct. We stressed hard work and obedience and loyalty to our employers. For most of my generation, nothing is more important than duty and responsibility. We are responsible for creating the stereotype of Asian Pacific Americans as serious, hard-working, conscientious—and it's a very good stereotype to have.

"I have observed that the younger generations are not so duty-bound. They are freer in their choice of occupation and less loyal to employers. Who can blame them? With so much downsizing and 'right sizing,'[23] employers no longer encourage loyalty, they discourage it. Even the concept of hard work has come into question. Who values work today for its own sake? We would like to think that the value of work is based on what is received in return, a sense of satisfaction, a sense of accomplishment. Today, all of that has been changed. Even the sense of accomplishment is taken away by corporate reorganization, restructuring, or 'reengineering.' In today's environment, the chances of a worker being 'let go' have nothing to do with merit or job performance.

"It used to be that hard work was rewarded. In times of economic hardship, employers retained their hardest workers and protected them through the bad times—but not anymore. You see a whole division being closed down, a whole department laid off without exception—no survivors, only casualties.

"I have a friend who received his Ph.D. from one of the leading universities in the nation. He worked for twenty-five years as a researcher for a national company. Suddenly, at age 54, he found himself laid off, with nowhere to go and no idea what he should do. The rejection my friend experienced was absolutely devastating. He was too young to retire, but with that kind of seniority, he expected too high a salary for other firms to take much interest in him.[24] It has been nearly two years, but he is still out of work. Believe me, I know that he lies awake nights, wondering what he did wrong.

"It's no wonder if the younger generation want to have fun and enjoy life while they can. Can you blame them? The best advice I have for young Asian Pacific Americans—or any young person who wants to excel in corporate America—is to develop a flexible attitude. Learn your networking skills and focus on creativity and innovation. The younger generation of Asian Pacific Americans is, I think, much more sophisticated in that regard than we were. We were a silent generation."

Many people, regardless of their specific ethnic background, would echo Emil's characterization of the silent generation as concerned with the preservation of the family at any cost. Such individuals are often proud of having helped create the stereotype of Asian Pacific Americans as serious, conscientious, hard workers. But many are increasingly aware that achieving one's goals in the changing environment of the modern organization requires more than just hard work. One must also foster a flexible attitude. The ability to change quickly and react spontaneously to the demands of any situation that arises is invaluable, as are a willingness to seek out and seize the most promising opportunities when they arise and to take the necessary risks. Other skills for business and social success in the workplace, such as networking, creativity training, and goal achievement strategies, will be discussed in more detail in a later chapter of this book.

## The Gender Differences

"I get very angry when I hear an Asian Pacific American male saying that Asian Pacific American women have an easier time in the workplace, or even in American society in general," said Dr. Li, a 1.5-generation Asian Pacific

American as well as a family care physician who has practiced in numerous Asian American communities.

Most of the women interviewed for this study expressed similar views when specifically asked whether Asian Pacific American women are better off than Asian Pacific American men. However, some of the women were less certain of their response when status in the workplace was mentioned, but they were willing to concede that, socially, Asian Pacific American women "seem to be more acceptable" to the majority than are Asian Pacific American men.

"I think the women's movement grassroots effort has benefited Asian Pacific American women, and women all over the world," Dr. Li continued. Born in Taiwan, Li grew up in Indonesia and immigrated to the United States with her parents and siblings in 1968, when she was ten years of age. Both of her parents were highly educated engineers, and both encouraged her to speak up and to stand up for her beliefs. When her interest in medicine became apparent, they encouraged her to pursue the art of healing.

"I was very fortunate to grow up in a family environment that had experienced multiple cultural influences. As engineers, my parents were sent to work in several different countries while we were growing up. We finally settled down in the United States, and we feel right at home with the multicultural aspects of this country. We felt that we could fit right in.

"My parents were very outspoken. Sometimes, they were even accused of being too loud for Asians! Especially in my father's case; he has a completely extroverted personality and loves food and drink, too—a really jolly fellow! Some Asian-born friends actually shun him in restaurants. We used to laugh about it.

"So, the concept of being whoever and whatever I wished to be, and having the freedom to pursue my knowledge in whatever interested me, and going after whatever I wished to have—these were never restrained in my childhood upbringing. I grew up in an intellectual environment and never thought about the barriers that existed for women, and particularly Asian Pacific American women.

"The fact is, more often than not, Asian Pacific American women who express an interest in a career in health or the medical profession will be told by their college advisors to try a nursing program rather than trying to become doctors. American society tends to hold lowered expectations for Asian Pacific American women, even when their high school grades rank among the top ten percent of their class. When an Asian Pacific American woman behaves more assertively and states that her intention is to become a physician, not a nurse, she will most likely be warned of the difficulties of getting into medical school and of the rigorous nature of medical school instruction. In fact, she is likely to be told that she will fail,"[25] Dr. Li sighs.

"Relatively few women enroll in college science courses, as compared to male students. Furthermore, professors tend to ignore female students, to call first upon male students for answers, and are much more likely to engage male students in discussions. Very few college professors make eye contact with female students during the course of a lecture. In general, if a female student raises her hand to ask a question, she is far more likely to be ignored, and if she is given a chance to speak up in class, she is far more likely to be cut off in mid-sentence.[26]

"To accord with the most persistent and pernicious stereotype of Asian Pacific American women, they are expected to be frail, passive, weak individuals.[27] If an Asian Pacific American woman tries to assert herself among the male students, she will almost inevitably hear, "Where did you learn to be so pushy? You're not like the regular Asian women we used to have around here. Why can't you be normal and be more polite?" In short, an outspoken, assertive Asian Pacific American woman who has developed a commanding voice and a self-assured manner is likely to be perceived as brash, aggressive, and rude.

"This negative stereotypical image of Asian Pacific American women is not restricted to college classrooms but is also carried into the workplace.[28] The image of Asian Pacific American women as 'exotic, fragile china dolls' is so pervasive in our society that one cannot help wondering how many women have actually tried to change their personalities or demeanor to fit the image."

Dr. Li, however, was essentially oblivious to the stereotype at the time she was applying to medical schools. Certainly, her personality did not fit the stereotype, nor did she take it into account during the process of interviewing.

During her medical school interviews, Li found that eastern U.S. schools tended to be more "snobbish" than western schools, especially with regard to Asian Pacific Americans. In several of the interviews, the person conducting the interview suggested that Li looked like the "motherly type" or hinted that she might be "happier to stay home and take care of the children" rather than trying to divide her time between career and housework. She was told repeatedly that "medicine is a very competitive field" and asked if she thought herself "tough enough to handle it." Today, of course, it would be illegal to ask any such questions of a woman, regardless of the position or other opportunity for which she was applying.

"Nowadays," said Dr. Li, "there are many more female physicians. Almost fifty percent of the students in medical schools are now women, so attitudes toward us are changing. In my case, I finally did get into a medical school, and I discovered fairly quickly that there were some prejudices against female students, but I didn't really become aware of racism in America until I started my medical practice in the Asian Pacific American communities."

Statistically, Asian Pacific American women suffer a higher homicide rate than do women of any other group.[29] During her interview, Dr. Li stated that she was unaware of this fact but was not altogether surprised.

She goes on to say that "many Asian Pacific American women, especially new-comers such as today's Southeast Asians, do not yet understand American health care systems and do not have health insurance or belong to HMOs. They work hard taking care of their families and do not take time off for themselves. They are more likely to put themselves last, take care of their husbands and others first, and are unlikely to seek immediate care except in the case of an extremely severe injury.

"I often see Asian Pacific American women coming into my office with a life-threatening illness which could easily have been cured in the earlier stages. There is much more to this story than that, however. I also see women struggling to deal with mental or emotional problems, which is equally disheartening to me, if not more so. This kind of difficulty is common wherever circumstances result in a person having feelings of low self-esteem. Many of my female patients are under great pressure to carry on because they are in the position of being the central caregiver for an entire family—which may include the extended family or even an entire clan.

"Traditional Asian Pacific American women are raised to think of themselves as inferior. Unfortunately, this notion of inferiority is easily reinforced by mainstream American values and beliefs. I could cite many cases of this kind of thing. Even a woman's own children, as they begin to adapt to American cultural values, are likely to begin perceiving their traditional Asian Pacific American immigrant mother as misinformed, ignorant, and superstitious. Any normal person might break under that kind of treatment, especially if she has been raised to expect her children's esteem and obedience. And some women also have the added misfortune of living with an abusive husband. Since divorce is disgraceful and unacceptable to most traditional Asians, a woman will usually learn to endure and even to rationalize all the pain she endures as a sacrifice for her children's sake and, essentially, to see herself as the family's saving grace. Therefore, she will be more likely to remain in an abusive situation than a White or African American woman might be. And that, I think, might explain part of your homicide rate for Asian Pacific American female workers.

"But on the other hand," Dr. Li said with emphasis, "the status of women is definitely determined by the family's socioeconomic level. The more a woman is rooted in her cultural traditions, the worse off she will be in America, regardless of whether she is from Asia, a Pacific Island, Latin America, Europe, or even if she's an African American. The most important factor is willingness to accept modern values. A person's level of education and her other learning experiences therefore have more bearing than background or ethnicity. *Race is not the problem. Class is.* The hospitals, schools, community groups, and government agencies should perhaps all work together to provide training opportunities for these women, to raise their awareness, to support their continued learning, and enable them to be better, more effective Americans in our society.

"But please don't misunderstand me. Many women, not only Asian Pacific Americans, play the dual role of principal caregiver within the home, and responsible career woman or wage-earner outside the home, and we take it very seriously. We are not 'stuck' in this life; we want it, we demand it, and we excel at it."

Dr. Li does not believe that being an Asian Pacific American woman has hindered her professional development. "I was offered an administrative position, but I refused because I do not enjoy doing administrative duties. I want to spend my time with primary care, where I am most effective and most needed. I work well with my liberal, intelligent young male colleagues, occasionally have problems with the old guard, but I understand this has been a gradual educational process for them as well. They have no role model and don't know whether to treat a female colleague as a daughter or a mother, but the time for complete equality will come some day. And after all, Asian Pacific American physicians are highly regarded, so any feelings of animosity I detect in the workplace may arise from professional jealousy rather than racial bias."

Dr. Li is happily married to a U.S.-born Chinese American who is a professional artist. Her own profession has provided her with a healthy self-identity. Her observations regarding the public perception of women will be familiar to many readers and are in accord with many current research studies. One recent exploration of the stereotyping of Asian Pacific American women can be found in *Good for Business: Making Full Use of the Nation's Human Capital*, a fact-finding report issued by the federal Glass Ceiling Commission in March 1995.

Dr. Li's view that "race is not the problem. Class is" is also significant. In essence, race and ethnicity are often perceived in this society as indicators of personal power, and one cannot change one's race. However, social class is a measure of power which can be changed; and once in power, individuals can assert their ethnic identities more easily and more effectively. Thus, Dr. Li and many others like her believe that the opportunity to change one's views and educate oneself to modern values is of paramount importance. Her belief that training, teaching, and mentoring programs at all levels in governmental agencies and in community groups would bring more awareness and empowerment to the deprived members of our society deserves to be taken seriously. An effective society, like an effective organization, depends on shared effort and a common commitment by all to the excellence of the whole.

Finally, Dr. Li raises the intriguing perspective that not all mistreatment of Asian Pacific Americans is racially motivated but, for example, can stem from professional jealousy as well as other psychological factors including a self-image that depends on the rigid maintenance of distinctive roles and behaviors for male and females.

## GenerAsian: Here She Comes!

"There is no doubt that women suffer inequity both in general and in the workplace. The peculiar reality is that, even though Asian Pacific American males and females have been equally subject to subordination under White males, Asian Pacific American males regard themselves as dominant over women, especially women of their own ethnic background."

The speaker is Julie, a 29-year-old office manager. Julie was born in Hawaii, came to California to attend college, and decided to remain on the mainland. Her father is half Chinese and half Japanese. Her mother is half Hawaiian, one quarter Filipino, and one quarter Burmese. A very striking, intelligent, sensitive, and worldly woman, Julie has traveled to Europe, Asia, and other parts of the world many times.

"Recent statistics show that the number of Asian Pacific American women with college degrees or professional licenses has doubled, and yet their average salary remains low and the number of Asian Pacific American women with blue-collar jobs remains at eleven percent, the same as for other minority women. So, obviously, not every Asian Pacific American woman has a 'success story' to tell.

"We have also seen more interracial marriage among Asian Pacific American women.[30] There's always a lot of talk—especially, it seems, among Asian Pacific American men—as to why more and more Asian Pacific American women are marrying outside of their race. Actually, the reason is rather obvious, but at the same time it's pretty complicated. If a woman grows up in a male-dominated, traditional family, she can't help noticing how that culture subjects her mother to second-class status and treatment, forcing her into dependency. Wouldn't it be reasonable for her to select a mate who comes from a more liberated family, who would accept her independence and her intelligence more readily? And another factor is that, for some peculiar reason, Asian Pacific American males tend to shy away from dating intelligent, good-looking Asian Pacific American women.[31] I experienced some of that in college. I went to UCLA; there was a joke that these letters stood for 'University of Caucasians Living among Asians.' Neither I nor many of my Asian Pacific American women friends were asked out very often by Asian Pacific American males, and we used to wonder why and talk about it. In my own case, I realize I look a bit different from other Asians."

Julie has always dated non-Asians. "The interracial socialization skills we developed through dating people of different ethnicity have also helped us to build a comfort level in the workplace. I have no problem dealing with non-Asian co-workers or supervising them as subordinates.

"I had always considered myself an Asian until I moved to the mainland. My father always kept the traditional Asian customs; he was a stern disciplinarian and expected good behavior and conduct from us. We had to get the best grades in school. Education was always extremely important. My mother, on the other hand, was a lot easier on us. It provided a good balance for us. My father kept us on the straight and narrow, but if things got too unbearable, my mother was always there to provide warmth and understanding and a shoulder to cry on. Deep down, we always knew our father cared for us and loved us. He worked very hard for the family."

Julie's father is an entrepreneur who owns a retail store. Her mother, however, controls all the finances for both the household and the business.

"We all know that our father is the boss on the surface, but the real power in the family is in our mother's hands. She handles everything with enough tact that she always gets what she wants, but she gives the glory and the prestige to our father. She always told my sisters and me, 'Learn to keep the finances under your control, and no man can control you. Even if he wants to disgrace you, he needs to think twice, because he can't afford to do it.' I think that's how many Asian Pacific American women handle their lives.

"Another traditional value my parents developed in us is keeping an open mind and developing a breadth of perspective on life. My father always brought the whole family along on any business trips he took—at my mother's insistence, that is—so we have all been to all the countries of Southeast Asia, Europe, and most of the other Asian nations. When I first started working as a buyer in New York City, I was traveling to Europe every three months, so my childhood travel experiences really proved invaluable. I think our generation is much more sophisticated than the older generations in this regard. And with the changing nature of work itself, the advent of so much new technology— e-mail, faxes, telecommunications networks—compared to our parents we seem to be flying all the time, either traveling through real air space, or lost in cyberspace on our computers.

"For the older generation, the concept of 'home' as a fixed place was very important, especially the 'old country,' the place of origin where a person in some sense truly belongs. For the younger generation, there is more of a concept of 'space' than of 'home.' They don't need a fixed place to have a sense of belonging. It's amazing to realize that the world still contains some tribes living according to the most ancient traditions, and at the same time this new breed of college-educated professionals and specialists are creating the future, whether it's good or bad. Young people like my sisters and brothers— and myself—are like cultural chameleons. We know how to camouflage ourselves and move from one society to another without attracting the wrong kind of attention. We are like birds flying from one country to another, and dreaming of flying from world to world."

Reminded that the vast majority of American workers do not enjoy such advantages, and, on the contrary, the majority of jobs are more down-to-earth and that most American workers carry on a daily struggle for survival, fighting the very real problems of racism, sexism, and other inequities, Julie lights up even more:

"I know! The old systems and institutions are always slow to change. But the organizations that succeed in the future will be the ones that value individual creativity and innovation and always remain open to new technologies.

"Television, MTV, digital technologies—these things have united the 'Generation X-ers' all over the world. MTV has cut across international culture. The concept of different cultures for different lands will disappear faster than most people expect. There will be a period of vulnerability, and the organizations that don't keep looking forward will get left behind. There is going to be a new world order, and anyone who hopes to survive will have to learn to deal with it.

"European immigrants came to America hoping to establish a homogeneous White society. They saw themselves as sitting on top of the world, and for a while, the world seemed to accept it. But the winds have definitely shifted.

In the future, such narrow-mindedness won't be allowed, and the sooner the last of the old White corporate decision makers understand it, the better. It's my perception that some of the decision makers in D.C. did understand the need to change, as early as the 1960s. Otherwise, why did they liberalize the immigration laws in 1965—I should say, 'humanizing' the immigration laws—so that hard-working, enterprising people from different parts of the world who wanted to come here can be offered their chance to do so, not just any Europeans?

"To be frank, this country needs new blood and fresh ideas to revive the economy and change the course of downward trends and diminishing growth. Japan and western Europe and even so-called Third World countries are growing stronger,[32] but American workers are being laid off by the thousands, sometimes on a daily basis. It's unfortunate that so many Americans are unemployed today, and it's even sadder that some of them blame all their troubles on immigrants and 'foreigners' whom they see as 'invading' the U.S. and pushing people out of their jobs. The reality is that this situation was caused by poor planning and bad business judgment on the part of multinational corporations, headed by White executives who lack the vision to see what's best and what is correct for the future of America."

Julie is very optimistic about the role that Asian Pacific American men and women can play in corporate America. She thinks that society has evolved to the point where more and more Asian Pacific Americans will have opportunities to make managerial decisions. Younger generations of Asian nationals and Asian Pacific Americans will be more readily and fully accepted into the organizational world and will make increasingly important contributions in the workplace.

"Well-educated and culturally sophisticated Japanese, Chinese, Koreans, Filipinos, and East Indians have made great upward progress. Next, watch out for the Vietnamese, Laotians, Hmong, and Pacific Islanders to make their mark. There will always be a few ignorant, backward-thinking individuals ready to blame the current scapegoat for all their troubles, always be a few prophets of doom ready to kill all the 'foreign devils' and 'save' America for the 'Americans.' People with that kind of mentality should be educated to realize we're all in this world together.

"The whole world is moving toward unity. The United States is a microcosm of the world. The English language is becoming a global language; everyone may not speak with the same accent, but we are all communicating. There are new art forms and new musical genres that blend East and West, tribal wisdom with technology. We will have a new world literature that links up the universalities of the human experience instead of glorifying the nations.

"Generation, gender, and race will be less of a peril in the workplace. Technical ability, proven skills, and the ability to learn, combined with a keen awareness of business ethics and a commitment to civil order, will be more important—and even more significant, there will be an institutional concern for the survival of humanity. Organizational culture will go beyond the artificial national boundaries. Asian Pacific American workers will be extremely important in the global culture as agents of change."

For Julie and her generation, the future looks bright indeed—at least through Julie's eyes. Because technological advances are easily accessible, creating almost instantaneous global communication, young people living in the United States tend to consider themselves far more sophisticated than their parents were at their age. They also have a different spatial conception of the world as a global village linked by computer networks and readily available, high-speed transportation. Julie is at the forefront of this attitude, addressing social issues and future possibilities with conviction and a good deal of foresight. In fact, many of Julie's ideas about internationalism and technology in the future, and even the mistakes of American business leaders in the past, are not too different from a perspective shared today by a number of forward-thinking corporate leaders and other organizational decision makers.[33]

## Summary and Discussion

Not all Asian Pacific Americans share Julie's vision of the future. Some of the older newcomers—in particular, perhaps, those who arrived most recently from Southeast Asia—feel that they will always be "Asian," and that "Americans" will always look down on them and consider them outsiders, unequal in society and especially unequal in the workplace. Even among members of the younger generation, not everyone expects the sort of sweeping social reform that Julie depicts. As one young Asian Pacific American expressed it, "We may never be accepted entirely as American. That's okay—we're not one hundred percent Asian, either."

Most younger Asian Pacific Americans have no memory of a distant "homeland" beyond the borders of the United States. This is obviously true for the Asian Pacific Americans who were born in the U.S. Among members of the 1.5 generation, any early memories which may remain are almost inevitably concerned with war, hunger, and the deaths of relatives and friends. Such recollections cannot even be compared to the fond reminiscences of home and a peaceful, loving family life that most older immigrants treasure throughout their lives. Those who come to America as refugees are more likely to want to forget the past and to create completely new lives. Hence, for many of them, the concept of "home" does not pertain to a particular plot of land, but to the entire planet or even the cosmos.

Although the glass ceiling and a disturbing xenophobia still exist in some domestic corporations, for the most part, the "yappies"—young Asian professionals—are upbeat and optimistic about their future in the global workplace. They see a future beyond the national borders. "Career," as Julie expressed it, "is internationalized. Before long, if they're not already here, there will be a whole class of successful 'migrant' professionals whose workplace is the entire global village."

Yet other young Asian Pacific Americans are more pessimistic and feel "lost," saddened by the restless political atmosphere and by complex, changeable economic conditions into thinking that there are no opportunities left, that they will never have a fair chance to excel or even to compare favorably to the accomplishments of their parents' generation. However, they are not a generation inclined to "suffer in silence."

Few young Asian Pacific American women believe the notion that they are treated better in the workplace than their male counterparts. Rather, young Asian Pacific Americans of both genders who were interviewed for this book seemed to think, perhaps simplistically, that in the long run, what determines one's ultimate happiness in life is each individual's perceptions and sense of self. The key determinant of a successful and fulfilling work life is intrinsic, whether one enjoys the undertakings in which one is engaged. The older generation sought security in professions and were motivated by extrinsic rewards. The younger generation seem to be aware that the American social environment allows them considerable freedom to create their own culture and identity.

Furthermore, most Asian Pacific American women believe that the U.S. gives women far more latitude than do the majority of Asian countries, and that American organizations are more receptive to professional Asian Pacific American women today than they have been in the past. Some still cast doubt, suggesting that their increased role in management and the professions may be mere tokenism. Many working-class Asian Pacific American women do continue to hold very low-paying jobs, and as a group, these Asian Pacific American female workers have the least access to the societal power base. The gender gap between Asian Pacific American men and women remains highly visible.

Even so, living and working in the U.S. remains attractive to and desirable for educated, middle- and upper-class women from India, the Philippines, and other Asian and Southeast Asian countries.

◆  ◆  ◆  ◆  ◆

## CASE FOR CRITICAL THINKING

Jackie Chin was born and raised in the Chinatown of Oakland, California. "I got my business degree from San Jose State. I answered an ad from an import-export company. The owner was an Asian Pacific American in his late fifties, originally from mainland China via Taiwan, probably in the early 60s. He asked if I could speak Mandarin. I said no. To make a long story short, he implied that my kind has a 'bamboo heart' (i.e., empty inside and understanding neither the Chinese nor the American cultures). I felt insulted. I said, sarcastically, 'What are you looking for, a White dude who speaks Mandarin?' His reply was, 'Yeah, that's the ideal candidate.'"

### Discussion Questions

1. Is there a generation gap in this case?
2. Was the owner's assumption caused by ignorance? Prejudice? Could it be both?
3. Was it right for Jackie to feel insulted and angry?
4. Should Jackie try to educate the owner?
5. What course of action should Jackie take?

◆  ◆  ◆  ◆  ◆

## EXPERIENTIAL EXERCISE

*Is There a Gender and Generation Gap?*

### Objectives

To have a better understanding and awareness of the issues that managers face as the workplace becomes more diverse.

### Starting the Exercise

Ask the students to interview two people of managerial rank or higher in medium to large companies: one of the two must be a woman; the other must be at least 55 years of age (older if possible). Students should request approximately one-hour informational interviews with each person to learn more about the challenges each perceives as relevant to his or her gender or relative age in the organization. The interviewees should be guaranteed complete anonymity. Students should try to learn the participants' perceptions about their careers, the younger employees, and the organizational goals. Some questions to be included in the interviews are the following:

1. Have you ever felt that you were being given special consideration or passed over for promotion because of your gender?
2. Do you encounter communication barriers, or other barriers, in working with people younger than yourself or with members of the opposite sex?
3. Are you aware of any organizational inequity related to your gender (age), and if so, what strategies do you use to overcome them?

Students should summarize their interviews and come to class prepared to engage in group discussion, comparing their findings with those of others.

## NOTES

1. Hip-hop is a highly energetic form of popular music with strong ties to the urban GenerAsian. According to Oliver Wang, who developed a radio show on Asian Pacific American music and culture, the hip-hop community has been heavily dominated by Filipino talents since the early 1990s.

2. According to Julie Sue, a staff attorney with the Asian Pacific American Legal Center (APALC) of southern California who represents abused Thai garment workers, a 1994 study revealed that 50 percent of all licensed garment shops failed to pay their workers the federal minimum wage, then $4.25 per hour. Sixty percent did not pay overtime, and 90 percent had violated health and safety codes at one time or another. Many unlicensed, underground operations employed even more abusive practices. Recently, the coalition Sweatshop Watch—led by APALC with the Coalition for Humane Immigrant Rights, the Thai Community Development Center, the Korean Immigrant Workers Advocates, and the union of Needletraders, Industrial and Textile

Employees—was organized to force government agencies into taking more action.

3. Noting that Masters and Johnson's research for their *Sex in America* survey had included only a nominal number of Asian Pacific Americans, Jeff Yang, editor of the youth-oriented *A. Magazine: Inside Asian America,* initiated a national Asian American Sex Survey. The survey instrument was distributed at various community events and meetings of interest to Asian Pacific Americans, published via the Internet, and also reprinted in the weekly newspaper *Asian Week.* More than 700 Asian Pacific Americans completed and returned the questionnaires. For statistical and verbal summaries of the results, see *A. Magazine* (August/September 1995).

4. Everett C. Ladd, Executive Director of the Roper Center for Public Opinion Research at the University of Connecticut, defines the generational lines as follows:

Generation X-ers—born between 1965 and 1977
Baby Boomers—born between 1946 and 1964
Silent Generation—born between 1933 and 1945
Depression Generation—born prior to 1933

5. Many people are under the erroneous impression that, since Asian Pacific American women are more acceptable to the mainstream society because of media stars such as Connie Chung, they are better off in the workplace than are Asian Pacific American men. However, according to the March 1994 U.S. Bureau of the Census report by Claudette Bennett, the median income for Asian Pacific American males was $30,903 in 1993 but only $24,346 for Asian Pacific American females. Furthermore, whereas 17.7 percent of Asian Pacific American males earned $50,000 or more in 1993, only 6.8 percent of Asian Pacific American females had comparable earnings.

6. The recent actions and speeches of certain members of Congress, as reported in various news media, illustrate the unfortunate prevailing attitude toward immigrants today. For more detailed accounts of "immigrant bashing" directed toward Asian Pacific Americans, read Ronald Takaki's *Strangers from a Different Shore* (Boston: Little, Brown, 1989) and Sucheng Chan, *Asian Americans* (Boston: Twayne, 1991).

7. Due to expanding political power and a worldwide demand for U.S. products, the U.S. prospered through the 1960s, creating the best economy the nation has ever enjoyed. A recommended reading is Robert L. Heilbroner and Lester Thurow's *Economics Explained* (New York: Simon & Schuster, 1987).

8. In an informal survey conducted between 1989 and January 1997 of 150 Asian Pacific Americans aged 16-30, all but six of the participants claimed

that their Asian Pacific American parents had pressured their children to excel either verbally or nonverbally, directly or indirectly. The indirect method would include making frequent references to the successes of close relatives on the assumption that the children would endorse them as role models.

9.  Television and other mass media today have generated much of the stereotyping of Asian Pacific Americans. Perhaps the most damaging of these stereotypes was that Asian Pacific Americans are technical wizards with little interest or ability in leadership roles. For more information, see S. Sue, N. Zane, and D. Sue, "Where Are the Asian American Leaders and Executives?" *Research Review* 9 (1985): 13-15.

10.  In Romanucci-Ross and George A. De Vos' *Ethnic Identity: Creation, Conflict, and Accommodation* (Walnut Creek, CA: AltaMira, 1995), it was noted that children of parents who carried little ethnic baggage in their search for upward mobility miss the satisfaction of having the sense of ethnic belonging that their parents experienced.

11.  The acronym "FOB" stands for "fresh off the boat" and refers derisively to recently arrived newcomers as well as to individuals who are slow to "Americanize" their dress, speech, and attitudes.

12.  The high demand for professionals and a shortage of skilled workers in the U.S. in the late 1950s and early 1960s, coupled with the passing of the McCarran-Walter Act by Congress, allowed immigration from the "Asian Pacific Triangle."

13.  Professor Sucheng Chan's book *Asian Americans* (Boston: Twayne, 1991) is a scholarly text which has received more attention in Asian American studies classes than it has popularity with the general public.

14.  Larry Shinagawa and Yen Le Espiritu treat Asian Pacific American pan-ethnicity in several writings; see chap. 2, n. 19 and n. 22.

15.  Statistics reported by the U.S. Department of Commerce, issued September 1993.

16.  The "1997 situation" refers to the sovereignty of Hong Kong, which is currently a dynamic, cosmopolitan, capitalist country. Previously leased to Great Britain, Hong Kong was returned to the People's Republic of China on 1 July 1997 under the terms of a ninety-nine-year agreement.

17.  The West Coast premiere of David Hwang's *Family Devotions* was on 7 February 1987 at San Francisco State University.

18.  The establishment of diplomatic relations between the U.S. and China was not formalized by Congress until 1978, six years after President Nixon's historic visit to China.

19.  Many Southeast Asian refugees have expressed these sentiments, among them Mila's brothers and sisters, discussed in a previous chapter. For more

details, see S. Gold, *Refugee Communities: A Comparative Field Study* (Newbury Park, CA: Sage, 1992).

20. Congressmen Mineta and Matsui are both Democrats from California. Mineta has since retired.

21. For a more accurate historical account, see Roger Daniels, *Concentration Camps USA: Japanese Americans and World War II* (New York: New York University Press, 1971).

22. A 1972 class action lawsuit was filed by Emma Salazar, a Filipina, against California Blue Shield on behalf of Asian Pacific Americans.

23. The term "downsizing"—often replaced in recent years by "rightsizing"—was coined by the business community to refer to the laying off of employees as a cost-cutting measure.

24. According to 1995 statistical data from the U.S. Department of Commerce, middle managers and professionals now account for 11.3 percent of the unemployed, up from 9.4 percent five years earlier.

25. These sentiments are echoed in A. M. Morrison, K. P. White, and E. Van Velsor, *Breaking the Glass Ceiling* (Reading, MA: Addison-Wesley, 1987); and M. D. Fottler and T. Bain, "Sex Differences in Occupational Aspirations," *Academy of Management Journal* 23 (July 1980): 144-9.

26. In 1978, authors Margaret Hennig and Anne Jardin, in *Managerial Women* (New York: Simon & Schuster), reported the negative attitude toward women in colleges. Almost 20 years later, many college women still report such treatment in campus classrooms.

27. As reported by the federal Glass Ceiling Commission in its fact-finding report, *Good for Business: Making Full Use of the Nation's Human Capital* (Washington, DC: U.S. Government Printing Office, March 1995).

28. Many research studies have shown that women are interrupted more frequently than are men and are generally taken less seriously when speaking. See D. Tannen, *You Just Don't Understand: Men and Women in Conversation* (New York: William Morrow, 1990); and F. Schwartz, "Management Women and the New Facts of Life," *Harvard Business Review* (January/February 1989): 65-76.

29. According to the U.S. Department of Justice, Bureau of Justice Statistics, the homicide rate for working women (per 100,000 female workers, and including vehicular homicide) was three times higher in 1993 for Asian Pacific American female workers than for African American female workers and four times higher than for white female workers. One must take into consideration that the total number of homicides of women workers in 1993 was 5278, and

that only 2.9 percent of the labor force was composed of Asian Pacific American women.

30. For the most current statistics and analysis of this cultural phenomenon, see Larry Hajime Shinagawa and Gin Yong Pang, "Asian American Pan-Ethnicity and Intermarriage," *Amerasia Journal* 22 (1996): 3, 32.

31. No current research has been conducted in regard to Asian Pacific American men shying away from intelligent Asian Pacific American women, but in an informal survey of the women interviewed for this book, including Dr. Li, 80 percent agreed with Julie's observation.

32. This may refer to the increased foreign competition in the 1970s and throughout the 1980s. Industries disappeared, and giant corporations took over one another.

33. This is according to a *Wall Street Journal* article by Joseph White and Carol Hymowitz, "Broken Glass: Watershed Generation of Women Executives Is Rising to the Top." A growing cadre of women who launched careers in the 1970s are breaking through cracks in the glass ceiling to land top, front-line corporate jobs once monopolized by men.

# Six

# The Glass Ceiling Metaphor, and Decision-Making and Leadership Styles

## The Glass Ceiling Metaphor

Since the 1960s, American society has been portrayed—at least on the surface and in the rhetoric of American politicians—as a land of equal opportunity where all qualified workers are assured of an equal chance to achieve their highest potential in their chosen careers. However, in reality, the opportunities for advancement for women and minorities have been far less than satisfactory. In most large U.S. corporations and even government organizations, women and members of ethnic minority groups, regardless of individual talents, more often than not have been confronted by an invisible, artificial barrier to their advancement to management and decision-making positions. Hence, a decade ago, the term "glass ceiling"[1] was coined to indicate growing public consciousness of the existence of this invisible, impenetrable shield that hinders or blocks the advancement of minority men and of women in general.

Secretary of Labor Elizabeth Dole and her successor, Secretary Lynn Martin, later became involved in identifying and publicizing the glass ceiling problem. Their work resulted in the issuance of the "Report on the Glass Ceiling Initiative," which in turn prompted Senator Robert Dole to introduce the Glass Ceiling Act, enacted as Title II of the Civil Rights Act of 1991.[2]

Early in 1995, the federal Glass Ceiling Commission released a report confirming that the glass ceiling still persists in today's society; 97 percent of the senior managers of Fortune 1000 industrial and Fortune 500 companies are White males. Furthermore, although 5 percent of senior managers in Fortune 2000 industrial and service companies are women, all of these women are White.[3] This 1995 report also found that the few women and minorities who are employed in higher positions typically earn about 21 percent less than White males with the same qualifications employed in the same capacity.[4]

## Effects of the Glass Ceiling

The answers obtained to this question about the glass ceiling through interviews and surveys of Asain Pacific Americans have been highly variable. The next few pages of this chapter focus in greater detail on some perceptions, opinions, and observations of Asian Pacific American workers regarding the glass ceiling. In particular, we will see how some Asian Pacific Americans are changing their decision-making and leadership styles from the stereotypical Asian cultural passivity to that of the White-male-dominated culture without sacrificing their own principles. Several relevant research studies and statistical surveys will also be introduced and discussed.[5]

We begin with a 1994 survey of Fortune 1000 industries and Fortune 500 service industries, which discloses that only 0.3 percent of senior-level managers are Asian Pacific Americans. However, at the same time, the study reveals a gradual and steady increase in representation by Asian Pacific Americans on boards and decision-making bodies of U.S. foundations and corporations in recent years.[6]

In California's Silicon Valley, one-third of the high-tech manufacturing workforce is comprised of Asian Pacific Americans, and yet almost all of the high-ranking management positions are filled by Whites.[7] Although some experts cite the lack of role models and mentors as a primary cause of this phenomenon, others point out that the "old boys" network simply and un-equivocally excludes Asian Pacific Americans because upper-level management regards Asian Pacific American workers as hard-working and diligent, but nevertheless to be "seen but not heard, to be bossed, not bosses."[8] Such a view makes little more of Asian Pacific Americans than a pack of modern, high-tech coolies.

A broad view of the glass ceiling problem was expressed by one of the more successful Asian Americans, a senior manager with an international investment firm. As he explained frankly, "This wall of subtle discrimination has harmed the entire U.S. economy in the increasingly competitive global business environment.

"But the intriguing part," he continued, "is that, oftentimes, they [Whites] don't actually consider us a minority. They don't see us in that context, so we hear that we have such a positive image. But have you ever heard of a single major U.S. corporation being headed by an Asian? Of course not. There is definitely a ceiling. I sometimes think it's a *cement* ceiling for Asian Pacific Americans! People still have the stereotypes of mysterious Asians who can't be trusted."[9]

Another interviewee's view of the glass ceiling problem was tempered with traditional wisdom: "There is an old Chinese golden rule of patience. Never mind the ceilings. The White 'old boys' network is getting increasingly older and older, and they are dying. Organizations have to be infused with creative ideas and new vitality. Just wait, and our time will come."

There is no doubt that qualified Asian Pacific American workers today still face major forces blocking their upward mobility in the corporate hierarchies. Nevertheless, many are hopeful that the prospects for future development are more positive. In the final analysis, the reader is encouraged to make his or her own assessment and, by following up some of the suggestions for further study, to recommend his or her own solutions.

## Case #1: At Odds with the Glass Ceiling

"I think the 'glass ceiling' notion is a self-imposed and detrimental one; it introduces a negative idea to the thoughts of aspiring young managers. Instead of concentrating on their abilities and skills, and trying their best to support and build the organization, women and members of minority groups are being hampered by the fear and conflict that the glass ceiling brought on them."

The speaker was Mr. C, who came to the United States in 1947 from Shanghai, China, to pursue the study of engineering at the Massachusetts Institute of Technology. Little did he know then that, within two years time, the Chinese communist party would take over mainland China, uprooting millions of well-established, upper-crust Chinese and forcing them to flee from their own country.

After the communist regime closed China's doors to the outside world, Mr. C was stripped of financial support from his family and had to go to work to support himself and his studies. Through his working experiences came two revelations which altered his life for a second time. First, he discovered his own talent for strategic planning; second, he realized the dynamic economic force and the unlimited potential in the American business world. He abandoned his earlier plans for a Ph.D. in engineering and instead applied to and was accepted by the Harvard Business School.

After two years, he graduated from his M.B.A. program with honors and thought himself ready to apply for entry-level management positions. But no one wanted to hire him.

"I was not surprised that White managers looked indifferently upon a Chinese in a managerial position at that time, but I was saddened by the indifference of the business community in Chinatown, whose members in those days consisted mainly of Chinese who came from Canton—the southern part of China. It was inexplicably hinted about that, because I came from Shanghai—the northern part of China—I was not to be trusted.

"Meanwhile, I had many offers of engineering positions, so I decided that I would take an engineering job first, as a stepping stone, and work my way into a managerial position laterally."

Mr. C did succeed; he became the research director of an 80,000-employee organization in eight years, and three years later was its executive vice president.

"As long as you can obtain profit for the organization, keep your constituents happy, and provide for a good quality of life for your employees, I don't think it is difficult to achieve a leadership position in any organization," Mr. C proclaimed.

Mr. C never found out whether he had it in him to be the first non-White CEO of his organization; in 1974, he departed to form his own company, in partnership with his wife. Today, their company has nineteen offices spread across the globe. Mr. C's present business in Europe and the United States provides security, but his investment for the future is in business based in the People's Republic of China.

When asked about his management model, Mr. C answered, "Perhaps some traditional Chinese values with some Western practices. I emphasize innovation and use creative management techniques to encourage my employees to make a difference in this world." He adds, philosophically, "We are only passing through this world in a very short period of time. In the final analysis, fame or worldly possessions are really meaningless objectives. Nothing matters except the good work we can do to improve human conditions and contribute, no matter how minimally, to the development of humanity. Only then can we say that we have indeed made a difference in our journey through life."

One cannot help wondering what would have happened had Mr. C remained with his old employer and become its first non-White CEO. Who really lost the most when Mr. C abandoned the system to start his own business? Certainly, the employer lost the benefits of Mr. C's continued participation in its growth and development. One can only speculate as to the benefits lost to younger generations of Asian Pacific Americans.

One might also speculate that, because Mr. C was born outside of the U.S. and never experienced discrimination as a youth, he was perhaps able to build more self-confidence and a more positive self-image than did the American-born generations of Asian Pacific Americans who were potentially subject to discrimination and some measure of self-doubt all of their lives. According to the locus of control theory discussed in chapter 3, such victims would tend to develop low self-efficacy and to become externalizers.

Whether we attribute Mr. C's ability to attain the goals he established for himself to his strong inner self-concept, the high degree to which he was able to integrate his essential identity with an established social role, or his high level of self-control and ability to adapt to external demands, we can categorize him as a Progressivist/Altruist on our typology model. A mature individual such as Mr. C who possesses a highly developed personality structure that can synthesize Eastern and Western values and derive a sense of direction responsive to diverse aspects of the environment while consciously meeting commitments to others may eventually break through the glass ceiling.

## Case #2: The Loss of a Valuable Worker

Thi Nguyen is one of the 1.5-generation Asian Pacific Americans, one who was born overseas yet came to the United States as a child. Thi arrived in 1978 from Vietnam via Thailand and Hong Kong at the age of nine. She speaks fluent, unaccented English and serves as spokesperson for her non-English-speaking parents. Although she had always been an important link between her parents and the outside world, this role became absolutely crucial six years ago, when her half-brother, who was five years older, killed himself.

"I was a straight-A student in junior college. I had to quit and work as an accounting clerk to help support my parents and two younger sisters." Thi was an excellent worker, reliable and dependable, and both fast and accurate. During her six years with the company, she often helped with, or completed alone, tasks for which her boss was personally responsible. She never received a promotion, and recently she learned that an inexperienced co-worker, newly hired in her department, would receive a salary more than 50 percent higher than Thi's. She decided to leave the company.

"Money is one reason, but in the six years' time, I've had to train three supervisors. I do more and more of their work, with no recognition." Thi's boss was stunned when she gave notice of her resignation. "She said that I was so quiet, she had no idea that I was not satisfied. That's probably true; I don't want to waste time talking at work. But she treats me like a work machine anyway. To this day, she still could not even pronounce my name."

When asked why she didn't speak up and talk to her supervisor about the obviously unfair treatment she had received, Thi answered, "Where I come from, my parents taught me to respect my elders and always be loyal to the boss and the company. We were taught to be humble, never boastful of our achievements. It was up to superiors to recognize my good work and very embarrassing for me to tell them how good I am. It's not my nature.

"In the first two years, I was grateful to even have a job to support my family. This same sense of gratitude has made me overlook many other shortcomings of my supervisor and the company policies.

"I think, after so many years, I have seen and learned a lot. I finally got over the feelings of inadequacy and gained some self-esteem. If they only showed me some recognition and appreciation, it would make a world of difference.

"But it has not all been wasted. I have learned, and they actually did me a favor. My present job pays fifty percent more. By changing to a new environment, I became a new person. I began to open up. I kept telling myself that I was born in Asia, but I have a right to live in America, and I am an American!"

In Thi's case, one might argue that confronting the negative force of discrimination actually caused her to emerge as a stronger person. In our typology model, she began as a typical Abnegator, but her experiences in the workplace pushed her to the right on the typology chart, and she became better assimilated into her new environment. Had her employer been more sensitive to Thi's needs or started a diversity training program within the organization, they could have seen her performance and dedication in a different light and ultimately might not have lost such a valuable worker. In a sense, the company became a victim of its own self-imposed glass ceiling system.

## Case #3: Rights Must Prevail

Raj Singh's parents, who are both engineers, came to the United States from India via England. Raj was born and grew up in a predominantly White American suburb. "I never thought of myself as Asian Pacific American and couldn't conceive of myself being discriminated against until I left home and started college." Once at college, Raj was exposed to a most subtle form of racial discrimination.

Raj's parents wanted him to study medicine, but he developed a great research interest in biology and biotechnology. Since receiving his Ph.D., Raj has helped his employer obtain several U.S. patents on projects.

When a section chief position became available, Raj applied. He was told that he didn't stand a chance of receiving the promotion. "You don't have the looks and the style. This position requires occasional contacts with the public."

Raj was furious. Although he had been brought up under the influence of Hinduism, and his parents had taken him regularly to Hindu temples, his parents had also been highly educated in the West and had upper-middle-class professional backgrounds prior to immigration. The concept of equality has been important. Historically, there is ample evidence that Asian Indians have suffered widespread prejudice, discrimination, and barriers to equal opportunity on various levels,[10] but Raj is of a different generation.

"Although I am Indian by blood and heritage, I am an American. I was born and grew up in this country, and I would not let anyone take my rights away."

"I was humiliated, but it was the principle of the matter that I had to stand up for, and against all of the unfair practices in the American workplace. If I don't stand up for equality, then I think I would have wasted all the efforts that my parents have made for me.

"I know that filing a discrimination charge against my employer will be a hardship for everyone involved, but to be an American citizen, I have to do this. I must defend the equality that so many of us have worked so hard for so long to achieve."

Raj's lawsuit against his employer is still awaiting a court date. Prior to this incident, Raj viewed himself as an Assimilator. His encounter with the glass ceiling transformed him into a Progressivist.

It is unfortunate that the corporate managers in this case lacked the foresight to prevent this dispute. The result, for the organization, is a significant and ongoing expenditure of time and resources, not to mention emotional distress on both sides of the entanglement which will probably benefit no one. The corporation had failed to initiate training programs that could have ensured greater sensitivity toward an ethnically diverse workforce by teaching managers how to support all employees, not just those who happen to share their supervisor's culture or ethnicity.

## Case #4: Suggestions for Breaking the Glass Ceiling

"Discrimination in the workplace? There is no doubt about it. As human beings, we have an inherited discriminatory nature. And if I may be so frank, Asians are especially guilty of this. So there is nothing new under the sun.

"Sure, there are also glass ceilings in the sciences—and everywhere else, all groups. But the glass ceiling is not unbreakable. It takes know-how and a lot of energy to break it, but it can be done."

The speaker is Dr. M, who came to the United States during his teens in the 1950s. His father was an early immigrant who was stranded in the U.S. because of the Chinese civil war. It was not until the 1952 Immigration and Naturalization Act gave preferential status to relatives of immigrants to join their families that Dr. M and his mother were allowed to come to join his father. The father, because he spent many years living alone in the United States, had suffered and become somewhat indifferent to many of the difficulties.[11] However, he made certain that his children all received the best education possible.

"My father was an eccentric man. I always felt that the most effective way for me to acknowledge the lost time our family had spent without him, the only way I could truly communicate to my father my respect for him, was through educational attainment." Dr. M went to one of the best undergraduate universities and later received a Ph.D. in physics from one of the most prestigious Ivy League institutions. He is now in his late fifties and a department head for one of the most renowned research laboratories in the country.

"There are many factors contributing to the success in the workplace. Lately, we hear a lot of discussion equating genetics to the success rate; for example, attributing success of an overwhelming number of American Jews to their genes. But has anyone related all of this to the family structure, like the fact that Jewish mothers are always proud of their children, always make them feel special or superior? This kind of upbringing, in my view, has more influence than inborn ability alone.

"Now, let us consider Asian families. Most value hard work, but simply working hard in silence is a model of passivity. The traditional value of humility as a virtue acted to channel the children of traditional Asians into fields that do not stress or call for assertiveness. This makes it easy for others to see traditional Asians as docile nerds, ideal for peeking down microscopes and peering at computer screens and such. In other words, as long as Asian Americans, especially parents, continue to play the old role, fail to develop mutuality and undertake steps necessary to change, there will always be fewer Asian Pacific American managers."

When asked for some suggestions or practical steps one could take to enhance one's chances for success, Dr. M replied, "I never gave that much thought until later in life, when I came to realize the importance of developing a need for power in one's earlier life. This need for power provides energy, ambition, and motivates one to be in a position of power and to enjoy it. The first step is for parents to encourage their children to ask questions. They should empower them in every way they can and not be afraid of losing control of their children. And people such as me," he pointed to his sparse gray hair, "should serve as mentor to the young."

Reminded that there are three distinct kinds of skills one must learn before becoming a manager—technical skills, human relations skills, and conceptual skills[12]—Dr. M agrees that most Asian Pacific Americans spend too much energy on technical skills and neglect the other two areas (see Box 6.1).

"Human relations skills include knowing the proper etiquette in organizations as well as networking within one's profession or business. Quite often, not knowing the rules that govern business etiquette can cost a promotion. Understand the organizational culture and find a mentor. Learn to dress appropriately, to observe expected behavior, to speak up assertively at meetings, and to socialize comfortably."

Dr. M thinks teaching the conceptual skills, such as planning ahead, to young aspiring managers is the most difficult task of all. "I told a young engineer the other day, 'Always do things for the future.' He was perplexed. It happened that this young man likes to fish. So I asked him, 'When you fish,

---

Box 6.1
*Managerial Skills*

The successful manager must employ three different basic skills, regardless of the type and size of the organization he or she is managing. These are (1) technical skills, (2) human relations skills, and (3) conceptual skills. Generally speaking, upper-level managers will use more conceptual skills, and lower-level managers will rely more on technical skills. However, effective managers at all levels need human relations skills because all managers need to delegate tasks, to accomplish company goals by coordinating the efforts of others, and to communicate information and policy.

*Technical skills* include the ability to perform specific functions such as accounting, computer programming, or engineering. For managers, they also include administrative functions such as gathering and analyzing data, planning, organizing, and providing leadership.

*Human relations skills* are essential to an understanding of other people and effectively interacting with them to generate cooperation, productivity, and teamwork. Human relations skills include both oral and written communication skills, not only as required for formal meetings, interviews, and presentations, but also as needed to maintain positive, more informal relations with personnel at all levels through casual conversation, and so on. Similarly, managers must be able to communicate in writing for a wide range of purposes and to all constituencies of the organization. Of the three basic skill areas, experts consider human relations skills to be the most difficult to teach.

*Conceptual skills* include the ability to see "the big picture" and relate parts to the whole. They also include techniques for identifying problems and opportunities, making decisions, and generate strategic planning for the organization. Many researchers consider decision making and the ability to lead as major managerial activities that require conceptual skills.

*(Derived from multiple sources; see note 12.)*

---

do you drop in your hook right on top of a fish, or do you drop your line upstream and let the current take the bait down to the fish? This is the same principle as strategic planning. Always be thinking ahead.'

"There are many successful Asian Pacific American role models for young people to emulate. One notable individual I could name, one of the most important figures in higher education today, cannot speak English with the correct pronunciation, yet he has the drive and the human relations skills to put the right person on the right job and the foresight to plan ahead. Of course, health and opportunity also make important contributions to success. All in all, if you play your cards right, being an Asian Pacific American can actually help in the present era."

Dr. M is indomitable in his feelings and enthusiastic about his suggestions for breaking through the glass ceiling. He does not consider it constructive to view the glass ceiling as "imposed" by White males to "imprison" Asian Pacific Americans and others. At the same time, he does not believe that one should wait passively for social change or, conversely, expend all of one's energy in confrontation. Rather, Dr. M would advise Asian Pacific Americans to work both internally, to develop themselves, and externally, to change the system from within for eventual improvement of the workplace.

Having gone through the acculturation process from being an Abnegator/Pragmatist to becoming an accomplished Progressivist/Altruist, Dr. M is optimistic that, in today's society, one can indeed break through the glass ceiling. His approach to changing the system from within will not appeal to everyone, but his suggestions are nevertheless experience-based and practical. Some of them will be explored in greater detail in a later chapter.

## Decision-Making and Leadership Styles
## of Asian Pacific Americans

What are the decision-making and leadership styles of Asian Pacific American managers? This question was asked of many successful Asian Pacific American workers who have been promoted to management positions. For most of the respondents, Asian Pacific American managers were not perceived as collectively having a management style distinct from that of the mainstream culture. Few, if any, considered Asian Pacific Americans at an advantage compared to the mainstream.

"The perception that Asian Pacific Americans are only good at 'programmed decisions' and never any good at 'nonprogrammed decisions' is utterly wrong," said Leo, a midlevel manufacturing supervisor. "Because Asian Pacific Americans are associated in the minds of so many with traditional cultures and with placing a high value on obedience to custom and law, many believe that making programmed decisions is a more appropriate activity for Asian Pacific Americans than making unprogrammed ones."[13]

As explained by Herbert Simon, a pioneer researcher in the field of management decisions,[14] programmed decisions are those that are repetitive in nature and tend to recur in normal operations. Routines for solving programmed decisions can be learned in advance and are formalized in company rules, policies, and standard procedures. In contrast, nonprogrammed decisions are usually unpredictable in nature. Because they may concern moral issues or ethical positions, few, if any, procedures for resolving them can be developed in advance. Instead, to be considered skilled at making nonprogrammed decisions, decision makers must be seen as resourceful, creative, assertive, quick, and sometimes willing to take some calculated risks. Unfortunately, spontaneity of this sort is not part of the stereotype imposed on Asian Pacific American workers.

"All I can say is that this kind of cultural ignorance is staggering," Leo continued. "Look at the Pacific Rim countries! Can anyone believe that in all of Hong Kong, Taiwan, Japan, Korea, Singapore, and India, there isn't one single great business manager? Don't they think that at least one individual in at least one Pacific Rim organization is capable of providing inspirational leadership? And creating workable solutions for their organizations? These nations wouldn't be so successful if their leaders were weak or uninspired— in fact, some of them are downright aggressive!"

"What bothers me most," said Laura, a Chinese American, "is the misguided picture created by the so-called diversity experts."[15] Laura is a language instructor for a community college. "For example, I know of one woman; she and her husband speak Chinese at home and teach their children Chinese history and respect for traditional Chinese culture. She has a strong sense of pride in her family's heritage, so the experts would classify her as having 'high identity' with the Chinese American minority group and, consequently, as not being fully acculturated to mainstream America. So, she should be predictably less successful in the workforce than a Chinese American who did none of these traditional 'Chinese' things. That person would be classified as having a monocultural majority identity and assumed to be fully assimilated into the American workplace. But in reality, these classifications can be completely spurious.

"For one thing, a Chinese American supposedly having high identity with the Chinese American minority group can simultaneously have an equally high identification with the majority group within a social or work setting. In fact, the argument could be made that individuals with multicultural experience have a more dynamic perspective and will make better decisions and be better organizational leaders than those who have only one frame of reference. If I say I possess knowledge of an Asian culture, does that in some way preclude my possessing comparable knowledge about Western culture? On the contrary, the person who does not understand her own traditions seems the most likely candidate to have difficulty deciphering the values and standards of a new culture. As a matter of fact, as I think you know, some Chinese Americans use the term 'bamboo hearts'—that is, empty inside—to describe those unfortunates who are neither in tune with mainstream America, nor with their own traditions. What sort of decision maker could such a person be?

"I suppose it's always wrong to be too eager to classify or categorize people; one has to see each individual as a separate entity. However, having said that much, there are certain commonalities among Asian Pacific Americans."

Several other Asian Pacific American managers echoed Laura's observations. Many highly accomplished Asian Pacific Americans have observed that the majority of Asian Pacific Americans, especially the most recent immigrants, have a tendency to observe the cultural tradition of respect for elders and supervisors. They tend to be more formal and acquiescent with a boss and will ask their bosses to make even small decisions for them. However, this deference is not because Asian Pacific Americans are incapable of making decisions on their own; rather, it is to show respect. Such individuals may need little more than a bit of encouragement to develop decision-making styles that would be more acceptable to their employers.

Because Asian cultures stress group welfare and community harmony, some conservative and more traditional Asian Pacific Americans are more at ease making decisions based on team efforts. As one Japanese proverb expresses the value of conformity, "A nail that sticks out gets hammered down." Thus, leaders who expect individualism to be generally discouraged by society will tend to shy away from high-profile leadership positions and the public attention they bring.[16] However, when such an individual is given an opportunity to manage and make decisions, the resulting managerial style can be extremely effective. Such initially "unwilling" leaders often develop into experts at motivating subordinates to excel individually in order to work more productively as a member of an integrated team.[17]

Many Asian Pacific Americans were also raised to believe that "if you don't have anything of value to say, don't say anything." This can put them at odds with an American corporate etiquette that values outspoken speech and direct confrontation and, consequently, limits their opportunities for moving to leadership positions.[18] Therefore, corporations may find it fruitful to provide career development and leadership training programs for Asian Pacific American personnel which directly address styles of communication and related matters.[19]

Although relatively few experts might do so, one could argue that the temperament and cultural background of Asian Pacific Americans actually

---

Box 6.2
*Emerging Concepts on Leadership*

*Path-goal theory* maintains that an effective leader understands each subordinate's needs and helps fulfill those needs based on subordinates' accomplishment of specific work goals. It is also the leader's job to show subordinates the *paths* (or behaviors) best suited to goal attainment.

*Transactional leadership* uses path-goal theory as its framework. The transactional leader identifies what work must be accomplished for subordinates to receive the contingent reward. For example, if sales increase, a bonus will be paid; if quality of work improves, a raise in pay will result.

*Transformational leadership theory* maintains that a leader must be able to inspire subordinates with a higher vision and to develop beyond what they would have thought themselves able to accomplish. Transformational leadership means bringing subordinates together to work toward challenging goals to achieve results greater than expected.

*The Participative Leader* involves subordinates in decision making, encourages discussion, and seeks egalitarian solutions to problems. Participative managers recognize that because workers are directly involved with day-to-day performance, they possess knowledge and experience which can contribute greatly to the organization.

*(Condensed from multiple sources; see notes 21-24.)*

---

makes them better candidates for leadership positions than traditional western leaders. Most traditional leaders are autocratic in their use of power. They centralize authority and do not involve subordinates in their decision-making processes. These managers issue orders and augment their positions of power by keeping information and resources to themselves as a means of controlling others. Subordinates are seen as exchanging their time and labor for economic gains and as needing to be coerced into action. Subordinates are very likely to be poorly motivated and highly unlikely to be willing to give their best efforts. In a national sample of workers, 78 percent of the participants reported seeing no correlation between pay and performance.[20]

In recent years, perhaps because today's more multicultural workplace demands greater organizational improvements, researchers have revealed that the most effective managers and leaders are those who can go beyond the traditional, autocratic approach and inspire employees to improve their own performance by looking beyond their own self-interests. The more advanced leadership theories include the transactional leadership style,[21] the "path-goal theory" of leadership,[22] and the more recent—and more challenging—transformational[23] and participative leadership styles.[24] All are concerned with a leader's ability to support subordinates and to consult with them in making decisions about work-related matters.[25] Under these theories, the effective leader is one who promotes subordinates' efforts as well as achieves organizational goals[26] (see Box 6.2).

Many "old-style," autocratic organizational managers refuse to practice a participative management style for fear of losing their power and influence. However, recent evidence points to the beneficial outcomes of participative leadership: employees who have the opportunity to participate in work-related decisions have reported greater job satisfaction than those who do not.[27] Because Asian Pacific Americans will predictably perform well using participative management techniques, a trend toward more extensive use of such modern management techniques could well have a positive impact on the number of Asian Pacific Americans promoted to managerial roles.

Although no one can predict the future in a fast-changing environment of global competition and uncertainty, it is reasonable to conclude that the most effective organizational managers will be those who can cultivate a style of leadership that generates results. The future prospects for Asian Pacific Americans as decision makers look promising.

## The Asian Pacific American Power Base

On a behavioral level, Asian Pacific Americans tend to be influenced by a traditional culture which has honored expertise, knowledge, and wisdom for thousands of years.[28] Personal success is acceptable if it has been achieved through hard work and diligence, but to use other sources of power, such as some of those defined by French and Raven,[29] is not viewed favorably within the community. Furthermore, because of tumultuous wars and warlords and the unsettled social environment in Asian nations, many Asian Pacific American immigrants view *position power* as transitory and even fleeting. Seeing that so many powerful people or groups can be deposed leads to thinking that, no matter what one can establish, nothing will guarantee its permanence. Asian Pacific Americans tend to build *expert power*, which can be seen as more permanent because it is portable, easily carried wherever one goes, and used wherever needed.[30]

Asian Pacific American cultures also tend to encourage the development of *achievement need* (nACH). This is also compatible with the "self-containment"

---

Box 6.3
*The Power Variations*

Over the years, researchers have offered various concepts of power in organizational settings. In 1960, authors John French and Bertram Raven proposed five possible sources of power which could be used by individuals to influence others.

*Coercive power:*   The power of superior force, such as using fear and punishment to correct undesirable behavior. Few organizations adopt this form of power today because it works well only in temporary situations. Furthermore, coercive power sometimes backfires, and an individual may retaliate by using "negative power."

*Reward power:*   The ability to influence behavior by distributing resources as rewards. The rewards need not be material (such as money); they include promotion, new status, or a better job assignment.

*Position power:*   Also called legal or legitimate power. Position power comes from occupying a role or position in the organization which gives one access to organization functions. Those who receive position power generally also receive other sources of power as well to ensure their effectiveness.

*Expert power:*   A person with specific knowledge or special expertise is difficult for the organization to replace. Expert power is a personal characteristic; unlike reward, position, and coercive powers, expert power is not prescribed by the organization. Expert power is the most pleasant form of power.

*Personal power:*   Often called charisma, or simply popularity, personal power comes with personality. It cannot be given by the organization, although it can be enhanced using expert, position, or reward power.

These powers are not usually used independently but rather in various combinations.

*(Source: See note 29.)*

---

concept.[31] According to nACH thinking, one can only rely on one's self to excel, and the way to achieve desired goals is to focus directly on personal improvement. Specific, concrete feedback on job performance is highly valued as an indicator of progress.

However, in the large, complex organization of today's business world, no one can perform all duties alone. A good manager must be able to delegate and influence others to perform well for the organization. Managers must be willing to allow others to accomplish some of the many tasks and share in the achievements. Therefore, to be a successful manager, whether one is Asian or not, one must understand and be willing to assume *position power* (see Box 6.3).

## The Concept of Conflict in the Traditional Asian Psyche

Conflict is unavoidable in modern organizational life. As a matter of fact, it is generally accepted as a necessary part of any organization's growth and maturation process.[32] Managers sometimes even deliberately create what is called a "functional conflict" in order to stimulate and energize work team members. For example, an accounting department and a sales department who disagree about the most efficient way to lower invoicing costs may compete to develop an even better method, to the ultimate benefit of the entire organization. Thus, it is important to remember that "functional conflicts" are considered positive, and that only "dysfunctional conflict"—that is, a confrontation or dispute between groups that can ultimately harm the organization—is to be avoided.[33]

However, in traditional Asian cultures, all conflict is to be avoided at all costs. Maintaining peace and order is seen as a key part of a successful manager's duties and responsibilities; the manager is expected to generate a spirit of harmony and cooperation that is free of organizational conflict. All signs of conflict or confrontation are viewed as having a negative connotation, whereas the traditional principles of harmony and peace can be found at the heart of Asian behavioral expectations and norms.[34]

In today's corporate world, anyone taking this kind of traditional approach to organizational order is likely to be perceived as too passive, much too compliant, and not particularly desirable as managerial material.

## Summary

According to a survey commissioned by the federal Glass Ceiling Commission, most of the CEOs of major U.S. corporations think of the glass ceiling as affecting only female employees. A few mentioned minority men, but generally in a context which implied they had in mind African Americans. One CEO (of an international investment firm) said that he was actively recruiting Asian Pacific American managers. The results of this survey may help explain why less than two-tenths of one percent of Asian Pacific American men, and one one-hundredth of a percent of all Asian Pacific American women, hold corporate directorships.[35]

Asian Pacific Americans are simply nonexistent in the consciousness of corporate movers and shakers. Their attitude of "benign neglect" and even blatant ignorance of the complexity and needs of, and differences among, Asian Pacific Americans have contributed to feelings held by some Asian Pacific Americans that they face a "cement ceiling" in the corporate world.

The stereotype of Asian Pacific Americans is that they are America's "model minority." They are hard-working; highly educated; excel in science, engineering, and technology; and exact with details. Culturally, they are said to be resourceful, patient, polite, nonconfrontational, and law-abiding. In a more negative light, Asian Pacific Americans, as a group, are also considered passive, unassertive, and good with technical skills but poor at human relations. They are considered lacking in leadership qualities and, consequently, poor at issuing orders and making forceful decisions.

Many Asian Pacific Americans feel that they are not receiving equitable treatment from the establishment, and that their superior educational attainments and high job performance rates are not leading them to senior decision-making and leadership positions.

Although managerial effectiveness may demand certain human relations skills, these skills are not abstract considerations. Rather, they occur in the context of an organizational culture and exist in relation to the particular people who work within it.[36] Consequently, upward mobility can be the result of arbitrary or subjective evaluations. Where upward mobility is lacking for Asian Pacific Americans, the most likely cause is the external environment: an organizational structure and a particular organizational culture that excludes them.

However, not all Asian Pacific Americans have encountered obstacles to higher positions. A majority of Asian Pacific Americans are confident that if Asian Pacific Americans learn to accept for themselves the dominant culture that values aggression and socializing over hard work and other merits, they could gain admission to the "old boys" network. Or, if they cannot make it, the younger generation and their children will succeed. For this reason, many older, high-achieving Asian Pacific Americans are now organizing mentoring programs for younger Asian Pacific Americans.

Nevertheless, other Asian Pacific Americans feel they should not change their cultural beliefs and sacrifice their own principles to be granted management positions. The concept of being aggressive and stepping on others to get ahead is seen as especially counterproductive to a humane workplace. According to this view, times have changed, and autocratic managers are out of date. In recent years, the human rights movement and the success stories of Japanese-style participative management are beginning to make the dogmatic, autocratic managerial style obsolete.[37] If this trend continues, many believe that Asian Pacific Americans inevitably will be seen as excellent managerial material for the new era.

The final conclusion here is that an Asian Pacific American is more likely to break through the glass ceiling if he or she is equipped with all three components of managerial expertise—technical skills, human relations skills, and conceptual skills—and a willingness to assume "position power" from the current establishment. Even though Asian Pacific Americans as a group do face discrimination, it is almost inevitable that they will break through the glass ceiling, if not today, then in another generation or two.

Some theorists have suggested that Asian Pacific American families need to begin actively fostering managerial aspirations in the home, training sons and daughters to enjoy power, to love working under pressure, and to develop keen socializing skills—and not in the interest of personal gain, but in order to contribute more substantially to the American economy, make the U.S. more competitive in the global market, and make American organizations better places to work in terms of the quality of life of all employees. At the same time, others scorn such an idea and question not only the principles but the ethics of such an approach to success.

"Look, what's so great about being a manager, anyway? Just being a leader and being able to make important decisions to increase the bottom line? I'd rather teach my kids to be Michael Chang or Kristi Yamaguchi. I'll bet my children have more fun on the tennis courts and ice skating rink. And don't give me that worried look! There will always be more talented Asian Pacific Americans in every profession to break all kinds of records—whether they crash through the ceiling or not!"

◆  ◆  ◆  ◆  ◆

## RESEARCH PROJECT AND DISCUSSION

*Keeping Current with the Status of the Glass Ceiling Effect*

*Beginning the Exercise*

Ask the students to go to the library and search through recent issues of the *Wall Street Journal, Asian Week, Time, Fortune, Newsweek, Business Week,* or other popular magazines or local papers. Clip or copy an article relating to the glass ceiling or discrimination in the workplace and bring the article to class for discussion.

1. What were the events that the article described?
2. Who was involved in the case? Some possibilities include women, gays, African Americans, Latino Americans, and Asian Americans.
3. In what way(s) are they being discriminated against?
4. Do you think the organization in the story was guilty of wrongdoing, or was the individual who complained simply "lawsuit happy"?
5. As far as you can tell, what kind of decision-making approach and leadership style are used by the organization's managers?
6. How would you recommend the organization correct or improve the situation?
7. What actions might be taken to prevent similar occurrences in the future?

◆ ◆ ◆ ◆ ◆

## EXPERIENTIAL EXERCISE

### *Your Potential as a Manager*

Many young people have managerial aspirations, but how can a person be sure of having management potential? The following questions may help you discover more about your own managerial aspirations.

1. When a subordinate asks you for a half-day off as a personal favor, you will always
   a. agree to the request.
   b. refuse so as to discourage people from asking for favors.
   c. consider the specifics of the situation before deciding.
   d. feel uncomfortable saying no.
2. When there are difficult tasks to be performed, you
   a. do it yourself because you can't trust anyone else to do it as well.
   b. delegate it to someone whom you wish to discipline or punish.
   c. delegate it to anyone available at the time of need.
   d. call a departmental meeting to discuss who should perform the task under your direction, and how they should go about it.

3. If the human resources department sends you an employee whom you feel is not experienced enough to perform the job at hand, you will
   a. waste no time sending the person back to human resources.
   b. wait for the person to make a big enough mistake that they will quit.
   c. do everything you can to help the new person.
   d. let the person sit around observing things and see what happens next.
4. If your subordinate habitually make the same mistakes over and over again, you
   a. transfer the person to another task.
   b. threaten to fire the person next time the same mistake is made.
   c. try to discover the cause by going over the job process and getting more feedback from the employee.
   d. punish the person by deducting part of his or her salary.
5. If your supervisor made a completely unreasonable request, you would
   a. let her know she was being unreasonable.
   b. do what she wanted and keep your anger to yourself.
   c. keep your mouth shut and find a reasonable alternative on your own.
   d. gather information and try to convince her there are better alternatives.
6. If your supervisor invites you to attend a networking party she is hosting for clients, you
   a. would decline if you don't know any of the clients.
   b. would go and do your part to make the clients feel comfortable.
   c. would go and enjoy the party as one of the guests.
   d. would go and sit quietly by yourself, sizing up all the guests.
7. If your supervisor does not take one of your suggestions seriously, you
   a. persevere and bring the matter up again and again.
   b. make an appointment with her to discuss it in more depth.
   c. make sure all the other workers know how the boss is behaving.
   d. see if the competition might be more willing to use your ideas.
8. If a co-worker tells you that you have made a mistake, you would
   a. first find out if it was really a mistake, or not.
   b. reciprocate by trying to discover a mistake that he or she made.
   c. avoid the fault-finder's company in the future.
   d. feel guilty about your mistake.
9. If you failed to achieve a project on time, but for reasons beyond your own control, you would
   a. feel depressed anyway.
   b. quit working for the company.

     c. realize that so many things are beyond our control that it doesn't
        matter.
     d. try to figure out why and go on to the next project.

10. If you unexpectedly see the chairman of the board at an informal
    gathering, you
     a. avoid him and try to have a good time anyway.
     b. go up just to say "Hi," then leave the party.
     c. wait for an opportunity to exchange a few pleasant, private words
        with him.
     d. join the circle of guests in his vicinity and listen to the conversation.

*How Did You Do?*

Each correct answer is worth 10 points. The correct answers are:

    1. c   2. d   3. c   4. c   5. d   6. b   7. b   8. a   9. d   10. c

Your score:

80-100:    You should be an *excellent* manager.
60-70:     You missed a few, but with training you can still be a *good*
            manager.
40-60:     Take a look at what you missed and study hard. Your chances
            are still *fair*.
under 40:  Oops! With this score, you will need to acquire some new skills.

## NOTES

   1. The term "glass ceiling" was popularized by the *Wall Street Journal*'s
"Corporate Woman" column in 1986. Subsequently, President Bush appointed a twenty-one-member Glass Ceiling Commission to identify glass
ceiling barriers and recommend means of eliminating them.

   2. Documented at Public Law 102-166, 21 November 1991, Civil Rights
Act of 1991, Section 203.

   3. Further information can be found in the fact-finding report of the
federal Glass Ceiling Commission titled *Good for Business: Making Full Use*

*of the Nation's Human Capital* (Washington, DC: U.S. Government Printing Office, March 1995).

4. Ibid.

5. Many of the research studies and surveys will be cited throughout this chapter. One that is highly recommended is the research study by Deborah Woo (University of California, Santa Cruz) titled "The Glass Ceiling and Asian Americans," prepared for the Glass Ceiling Commission in July 1994. The report gives an overview of the current state of research relating to this topic. In regard to the government sector, see Henry Der and Howard Ting, *The Broken Ladder: Asian Americans in City Government* (San Francisco: CAA, 1992). Also see U.S. Commission on Civil Rights, "Civil Rights Issues Facing Asian Pacific Americans in the 1990s" (Washington, DC: U.S. Government Printing Office, 1992).

6. The survey report, prepared by Lucius S. Henderson III et al. for the Glass Ceiling Commission and titled "Report on Six Focus Groups with Asian, Black and Hispanic Executives in Three Cities on Issues Related to the Glass Ceiling in Corporate America," can be obtained from the U.S. Department of Labor, Washington, DC.

7. This was reported in "Qualified, But . . .: A Report on the Glass Ceiling Issues Facing Asian Pacific Americans in Silicon Valley," ed. E. Iwata, prepared by Asian Americans for Community Involvement (San Jose, CA: Asian Americans for Community Involvement, 1993).

8. The *San Jose Mercury News,* one of the leading newspapers in California's Silicon Valley, reported on unequal job opportunities for Asian Pacific American groups in the article "Ethnic Groups Grow But Their Jobs Don't," 24 June 1991.

9. This sort of sentiment, incidentally, has also been reported in the fact-finding report of the federal Glass Ceiling Commission.

10. This sentiment has also been reported in J. M. Jensen, *Passage from India: Asian Indian Immigrants in North America* (New Haven, CT: Yale University Press, 1988).

11. Many of these early immigrants suffered greatly during this period. Interesting accounts of that generation have found their way into novels, poetry, films, and the other expressive and literary arts; among these are Rose Hum Lee, *Chinese in the U.S.: The War Has Changed Their Lives* (San Francisco: Chinese Press, 1952); Sucheng Chan, *The Exclusion of Chinese Women* (Philadelphia: Temple University Press, 1991); Maxine Hong Kingston, *The Woman Warrior* (New York: Knopf, 1976); and Amy Tan, *The Joy Luck Club* (New York: Putnam, 1989).

12. For interested parties, many texts teach managerial skills. The more widely used texts, to name but a few, include David H. Holt, *Management: Principles and Practices,* 3d ed. (Englewood Cliffs, NJ: Prentice Hall, 1995); Richard L. Daft, *Management* (Chicago: Dryden, 1994); and D. Rachman, M. Mescon, C. Bovee, and J. Thill, *Business Today,* 8th ed. (San Francisco: McGraw-Hill, 1996).

13. Among the many recent articles on the subject of management decision making, one that stands out as particularly appropriate for inclusion here is Martha Maznevski's "Understanding Our Differences: Performance in Decision-Making Groups with Diverse Members," *Human Relations* (May 1994): 531-2.

14. Herbert Simon, *The New Science of Management Decision* (New York: Harper & Row, 1960).

15. In recent years, many companies have engaged the services of "diversity experts" because diversity programs are too complex to be handled by the company's human resources personnel or affirmative action officers. Many Fortune 500 companies have hired in-house experts under the title "diversity managers." Diversity managers provide sensitivity training for firm employees. Some also conduct research aimed at attracting a more ethnically diverse client or customer base, but increasingly, many develop their own theories on diversity and make various efforts supposed to enhance this rapidly growing field.

16. Individualism versus collectivism has been heavily researched because of its relevance to the impact of diversity in organizations. T. H. Cox, S. Lobel, and P. McLeod, in their article "Effects of Ethnic Group Cultural Differences on Cooperative Versus Competitive Behavior in a Group Task," *Academy of Management Journal* 34 (1991): 827-47, implied that individuals with a collectivist orientation are more satisfied with team-bond rewards. See also Geert Hofstede, "The Cultural Relativity of the Quality of Life Concept," *Academy of Management Review* 9 (1984): 389-98; and D. K. Tse, K. Lee, I. Vertinsky, and D. A. Wehrung, "Does Culture Matter? A Cross-Cultural Study of Executives' Choice, Decisiveness, and Risk Adjustment in International Marketing," *Journal of Marketing* 52 (1988): 81-95.

17. The video "Valuing Diversity," produced by Copeland Productions for educational training, includes a depiction of this scenario for Asian American managers. Minority members who have not had previous access to management and leadership-level positions within organizations now represent a large portion of the workforce. Organizations must use this talent pool and transform these workers to enable them to contribute at their highest level of potential.

18. In "People's Republic of China," an analysis of Chinese culture, author R. L. Chung stated that the individualism emphasized in the United States is nonexistent in the Chinese mentality. See *Comparative Management: A Regional View,* ed. R. Nath (Cambridge, MA: Ballinger, 1988).

19. Taylor Cox, Jr., in *Cultural Diversity in Organizations* (San Francisco: Berrett-Koehler, 1993), states that a number of Asian Pacific Americans for whom English is a second language have reported having their work presented to senior managers by others due to concerns that they lacked mastery of some nuances of English and would be unable to speak well enough to present their own work. This practice not only denies visibility to the authors of ideas; it also contributes to anxieties and to an atmosphere of humiliation, weakening the organization in the long run.

20. Survey details can be found in D. Yankelovich and J. Immerivoki, *Putting the Work Ethic to Work* (New York: Public Agenda Foundation, 1983).

21. Transactional leadership was derived from the path-goal concept, which relies on contingent rewards and on management by exception. Although viewed as not perfect, it is a significant advancement over the autocratic leadership style. See Bernard M. Bass, *Leadership and Performance beyond Expectations* (New York: Free Press, 1985).

22. Path-goal theory asserts that leaders need to influence followers' perception of work goals, self-development goals, and paths to goal attainment. Suggestions for further reading are Robert J. House and Terence R. Mitchell, "A Path-Goal Theory of Leadership," *Journal of Contemporary Business* (Autumn 1974): 81-98, and Robert T. Keller, "A Test of the Path-Goal Theory of Leadership with Need for Clarity as a Moderator in Research and Development Organizations," *Journal of Applied Psychology* (April 1989): 208-12.

23. In transformational leadership theory, an ideal leader motivates followers to work for transcendental rather than self-serving goals. Suggested readings in this important area include Brice J. Avolio and Bernard M. Bass, "Transformational Leadership, Charisma, and Beyond," in *Emerging Leadership Vistas,* ed. James G. Hunt, B. Hajaram Baliga, H. Peter Dachler, and Chester Schriesheim (Lexington, MA: Lexington Books, 1988); Ross Groves, *The Disney Touch* (New York: Irwin, 1991); Bernard M. Bass, *Handbook of Leadership* (New York: Free Press, 1990); and Edwin Locke, *The Essence of Leadership* (New York: Macmillan, 1991).

24. Participative leadership encourages employees' participation in decision making and teamwork to improve their jobs. See Dennis C. Kinlaw, *Developing Superior Work Teams* (Lexington, MA: Lexington Books, 1991);

Victor Vroom and Arthur Jago, *The New Leadership: Managing Participation in Organizations* (Englewood Cliffs, NJ: Prentice Hall, 1988).

25. Thomas Bateman and C. Zeithaind, *Management: Function and Strategy* (Homewood, IL: Irwin, 1990).

26. See "Notes on Transformational Leadership," prepared by Kim A. Steward for J. Gibson, J. Ivancevich, and J. Donnelly in *Organizations* (Homewood, IL: Irwin, 1997). Also see James M. Kouzes and Barry Posner, *The Leadership Challenge* (San Francisco: Jossey-Bass, 1995).

27. Brian Dumaine, "Payoff from the New Management," *Fortune* (13 December 1993): 5-9; Andrew DuBrin, *Leadership: Research Findings, Practice, and Skills* (Boston: Houghton Mifflin, 1995).

28. The value systems which influenced wealth creation in the East and West are presented in Charles Hampden-Turner and Alfons Trompenaars, *The Seven Cultures of Capitalism* (New York: Doubleday, 1993). The authors claim that those who understand how culture works can turn it to economic advantage.

29. For a more detailed work on various concepts of power, see J. French and B. Raven, *The Bases of Social Power* (Ann Arbor: University of Michigan Press, 1960).

30. This information is based on interviews for this study with professionals who have achieved economic prosperity in this country. Logically, most of these subjects tend to express such a view because most of them are immigrants. However, this view is not typical of the younger, American-born Asian Pacific Americans of "Generation X."

31. See chap. 3, n. 13, McClelland; and chap. 3, n. 17, De Vos.

32. Research indicating that conflict is a fundamental part of organizational life is documented in C. Morrill and C. K. Thomas, "Organizational Conflict Management as Disputing Process: The Problem of Social Escalation," *Human Communication Research* (March 1992): 400-28.

33. For further discussion of functional and dysfunctional conflict, see Stephen P. Robbins, *Managing Organizational Conflict* (Englewood Cliffs, NJ: Prentice Hall, 1974).

34. Traditional Asian thought holds that any kind of dispute leads toward chaos. One subject interviewed related a story involving a board game designed by Michael Madsen for assessing competitive and cooperative responses in children: when the game's reward structure was changed with mainstream American children, they would quickly shift from cooperation to competition, but Asian children continued to cooperate. The demands for

interpersonal harmony were stronger than the impulse to gain a temporary advantage.

35.  Glass Ceiling Commission, *Good for Business.* The 1992 Heidrick and Struggles study of 806 of the Fortune 1000 companies also revealed the same phenomenon.

36.  Cox, in *Cultural Diversity in Organizations,* predicts that barriers to promotion of the candidate generally assume deficiencies including group "deficits" or "cultural" traits as features of individual employees who may not be positive to a particular work context.

37.  The Japanese study is very similar to the task and relationship management style mentioned earlier in this chapter. For more information, see Mark F. Peterson, Jyuji Misumi, and Charlene Herreid, "Adapting Japanese PM Leadership Field Research for Use in Western Organizations," *Applied Psychology* (January 1994): 49-74.

SECTION III

# Strategies for Change

# Seven

# Internal Strategies

## *Organizational Culture and Corporate Manners*

### Mentoring and Socializing

"Do you know what the latest fashion sandwich is?" asked Peter, one of several workers gathering around Ann's table in the company cafeteria. Ann, an Asian American woman in her fifties, looked up at Peter, and everyone else looked at Ann, waiting to hear her answer. Peter spoke again. "I'll give you a hint. It's Newt Gingrich's favorite. Lunch counters are starting to put it on their menus as the Newt Sandwich, in honor of the Speaker."

Still, no one knew the answer to Peter's question, but Ann took out a small notepad and a pencil. "Okay, you tell us, Peter," she said. "What is a Newt Sandwich?"

"All right," said Peter, grinning broadly. "Listen carefully: you put two pieces of bread in the toaster. When they're burnt, smear one piece with a lot of cream cheese, and spread the other with mustard. Put a slice of apple pie in the middle, and you've got a Newt Sandwich."

"Aaack! Yuk!" said Maria, a Latino American in her early twenties. Don, who is White, and Solomon, who is African American, both laughed hysterically.

"Is this supposed to be funny?" asked Maria. "I don't get it. Ann, do you know what they're talking about?"

Ann wasn't laughing, but she had a mischievous smile on her face as she wrote in her little notebook. Peter, leaning over to look at Ann's notes, asked, "You're specifying Grey Poupon instead of plain old mustard?"

"Don't be silly," replied Ann. "Nothing else will suit Newt's taste."

"Now *I'm* lost," said Don.

"Remember those Grey Poupon ads on TV?" asked Solomon. "It's a special kind of Dijon mustard."

"I get it!" cried Peter.

"I don't," Maria complained.[1]

"Only yappies!" Peter said. "Ha ha! Oh, Ann, you're just great!" Ann then asked Peter to explain the joke to Maria.

"The Newt Sandwich is a racial mish-mash," Peter said. "African and Latino Americans and Asian Americans represented by brown toast and yellow mustard, and cream cheese for whites. The apple pie, of course, symbolizes Americana, nostalgia for the old ways."

"Please tell me where you heard this joke, Peter," Ann said, still writing in her notebook. "In a staff meeting? Seminar? Executive dining room?"

From her behavior in the group, Ann is obviously a person of some importance and savvy, but her appearance is likely to suggest to strangers that she is more the unassuming, pleasant, and congenial type. Her hair is worn in a short, practical, stylish fashion, and her clothing is also stylish, simple in design and subdued in colors. Her make-up has been carefully applied to give her a "natural" look. In fact, taking a close look, everything about Ann's appearance has been carefully and craftily selected and arranged to produce a faultless, simple, natural look. In addition, Ann has an air of assuredness without being arrogant. She listens to others respectfully and makes suggestions and corrections without being disdainful.

Not surprisingly, others in the company gravitate toward her. Regardless of their rank or salary, co-workers seek out Ann's advice, tell her their jokes and stories, and share their news. Ann fulfills a very important function in her organization. She is a mentor. In part, mentorship consists of helping other employees to socialize effectively within the organization.

Research done by Reid[2] indicated that the majority of managers today have had at least one mentor during their careers. Someone like Ann was able to provide them with coaching, friendship, and role modeling. As noted by

Kram,[3] the major functions of mentoring include coaching in the "career functions" and also sponsoring less experienced workers within the organization to help them gain exposure and assignments on important and challenging projects. Mentoring also provides psychosocial functions by offering counseling, friendship, and role modeling, and by reinforcing acceptance. It also serves socialization functions by teaching the proper procedures and behaviors in the organization. Socialization, in Gibson's words,[4] concerns the process of learning and working with an experienced, trusted advisor. The socialization process, as Van Maanen[5] points out, is extremely important in shaping the individuals who enter the organization, and the way in which socialization is carried out must be varied from situation to situation, depending on the uniqueness of the individuals and the organizational makeup. But before going further into a theoretical discussion of organizational culture, let's continue with Ann's story.

Ann is a third-generation Asian Pacific American with mixed parentage. "My mother was always a housewife. When I graduated from high school, I came to the city to go to a secretarial school. Six months before my graduation, I met my husband. He was thirty years older than me, a very important person. I fell in love and married him. I was twenty-one. He was a widower, already had three children, and didn't want any more. He offered me a wealthy lifestyle and marvelous experiences, things a person of my station would never be able to achieve alone. For the next fifteen years, we traveled in high society all over the world. We were always so busy planning for the next event that I had no time to think. Then one day, he had a stroke and he was gone. His children were kind enough to offer me a monthly allowance, but I wanted to try supporting myself on my own."

Ann returned to secretarial school, finished her courses, and joined the secretarial pool of a large engineering firm. Two years later, one of the chief engineers left to form an engineering consulting firm with several colleagues and he invited Ann to join the staff. Ann agreed to join them; that was eighteen years ago.

On the organizational chart, Ann is officially the Assistant to the Executive Vice President. Unofficially, she is the informal leader, the powerhouse of the entire organization, which now has about 150 employees. Ann knows all of them by their first names.

"I did not seek this position consciously; it just happened over the years. My goal in life is to help people to be successful in their careers, to facilitate their work processes.

"Fairly often, I find younger employees, especially Asian Pacific Americans, who do not understand the ropes to climb in formal organizations. I try to serve as a mentor to them. I don't have any children of my own, so I like to devote some of my energy to helping them." Ann's statement accords well with the research study of Burke and McKeen,[6] which reveals that the reward for senior mentors who work with younger and new employees can be a satisfaction of their own intrinsic needs to have influence, to make a difference in another person's career, and a noble sense of volunteerism.

Organization theorists such as Fernandez[7] noted that with the increasing diversity of the workforce, minority groups such as Asian Pacific Americans may get left out of the mentoring process. Not every organization is fortunate enough to have an informal leader and powerhouse like Ann to help teach the organizational culture to the new employees and help sustain the organization's values for the existing employees. Too often, Asian Pacific American employees are introduced during a formal orientation session to a company's formal authority structure and presented with the written company rules and regulations, but once work begins, no more is said about such matters. The task of finding out what lies behind the formal structure is left entirely for the new personnel to explore on their own. Few understand the real importance of discovering the organizational culture through someone like Ann.

In his recent book *Developing Your Company Culture*,[8] Barry Phegan compares an organizational culture to a human personality. If you were about to become deeply involved with another person and even develop interdependencies with him or her, you would certainly want to know more about that person's values and standards. Logically, the same holds true for companies. How does one go about learning more about an organization's culture?

## Understanding Organizational Culture

The most popular definition of organizational culture derives from the work of Schein, who considers organizational culture to be a set of beliefs, symbols, rituals, and myths, a system of shared meanings and practices which has evolved over time and which guides employees' behaviors.[9] Charles Hampden-Turner[10] has defined organizational culture as a set of values, a pattern of assumptions, and a circle of emblematic ideologies which serve to generalize the collective effort of working together to achieve shared advantages. Charles Handy[11] implied that organizational culture is about the way work is organized, authority is exercised, and people are rewarded and controlled. Are there defined roles and definite procedures, or do results matter more than methods? Do managers look for obedience from subordinates, or do they look for

---

Box 7.1
*The Different Organizational Cultures*

Different kinds of organizational culture will appeal to different sorts of people. Within each type of culture, there are different ways to organize work, reward employees, control subordinates, and enforce rules. Four distinct organizational cultures are recognized by experts:

*The power culture*: The traditional small organization, typically an entrepreneurial venture, where one person has all the power to decide all the functions of the organization. The few rules and regulations are set by the power figure. The successes or failures experienced by other employees depend upon the personality and qualities of the power figure.

*The role culture*: The traditional large organization, most bureaucracies will fall into this category. The organization is divided into functional specialties such as production, finance, research, marketing, and so on, and coordinated by senior management at the top. There are many rules and procedures to follow; employees are selected for their ability to fit prescribed roles, and this in turn provides the individuals with security and predictability. Rewards are based on seniority. A role culture is most successful in a stable environment.

*The task culture*: Currently fashionable among market-competitive organizations, this job- or project-centered culture emphasizes getting the job done. Employees' expertise is more highly valued than seniority. This is also a team culture; it recognizes that products and services result from team efforts. The task culture is extremely flexible and can adapt to a changed environment quickly. Top managers have little day-to-day control and concentrate decision making on resource allocation, and so on.

*The person culture*: Found in modern, individualistic organizations, a person culture is not surprisingly oriented around individuals who share a common facility, such as office space, equipment, or secretarial support. This type of culture is common among law firms and other professional partnerships and corporations.

Note: It is possible for any organization to develop several cultures simultaneously.

---

initiative? How about status, dress codes, and personal eccentricities? The work of Handy, Roger Harrison, Lawrence and Lorsh, Burns and Stalker, and Joan Woodward[12] all contribute to the classification of organizations according to four distinct organizational cultures (see Box 7.1). From an employee's point of view, understanding these four classifications and deciding which type of culture is most suitable to one's own career advancement—and, if necessary, adjusting one's behavior to fit an organizational culture—will no doubt facilitate job placement and adjustment within the workplace. However, it is also important for organizations to be aware of the changing values in our society, particularly those due to today's more culturally diverse workforce. Managers must adjust, perhaps to create a new organizational culture that more definitely cares for and respects the different value orientations of its diversified workforce.

Ann thinks that few Asian Pacific Americans understand the significance of organizational culture in relation to their future career advancement and personal growth. Asian Pacific American and other minority workers traditionally have worked in bureaucratic or governmental organizations where the organizational culture clearly spells out the rules and regulations and where a seniority system enables workers to predict their exact position and status within the organization. Today, times have changed. The type of company that used to be able to provide security and stability to obedient and loyal employees who fit into the roles prescribed by the company have been affected by the turbulent environment.

Asian Pacific Americans today must be prepared to acquire technical skills and continue to make gains in a task culture, where expertise is valued. According to Ann, "The traditional Asian value of respect for education and knowledge has served the younger Asian Pacific Americans well. The future is moving toward the direction of cyberspace. Businesses can no longer survive without knowing how to function in the rapidly advancing technological world. The workers who have the know-how and skill to navigate the Internet and to guide the organization down the information superhighway to the global village are the ones most highly valued. Modern organizations cannot afford to be prejudiced against anyone for racial, gender, or any other reasons," she concluded.

Regardless of the cultural preferences existing in different organizations, building technical competence is, unfortunately, only one part of the equation for career advancement. Individuals must also give priority to such tasks as building a positive image in the workplace, developing a set of work behaviors and a personal appearance that consistently project the most positive impression of one's worth to others' eyes, and learning corporate manners and office etiquette—if not for one's own sake, then out of respect for other individuals and groups.

In the next sections of this chapter, the discussion will center on "what counts" in organizations: the unwritten rules of good communication, personal appearance, office etiquette, and effective behavior. The essence of these perspectives may serve as useful tools for those who wish to set the right style for a positive image suggesting the intelligence, warmth, integrity, knowledge, and talents leading to openness in the workplace and, generally speaking, advancement. The following advice should in no way be taken to mean that one should be a "mindless conformist" in the business world. On the contrary, those who recognize themselves as "advocates" and "activists" in the typology model in chapter 1 can use these strategies to gain a secure standing in the organizational power base from which long-term transformations may be feasible.

A good analogy might be made to a rookie football or baseball player. No matter how much potential such players might show, they will never be asked whether they have any suggestions for changing the rules of the game. Only if an athlete proves to be a truly excellent player who has gained the confidence of managers and the loyalty of teammates and fans is there any possibility of generating change. In our capitalistic society, the right to institute change generally comes with a proven ability to generate profits.

Those who take what DeVos[13] has termed a psychocultural viewpoint on things may wish to concentrate on the internal responses of Asian Pacific Americans confronted by the necessity of changing behaviors to accommodate new values. Are these individuals in danger of losing their ethnic identities, sacrificing some of their personal uniqueness, or possibly suffering feelings of self-rejection? Such concerns do seem legitimate in the current political atmosphere, which fosters the concept of "Asian American pan-ethnicity" as depicted by Espiritu[14] and the suggestion made by Shinagawa and Pan that, when institutional influences heavily reinforce and mold the individual role, many individuals develop an "identi-factual" identity.[15] Although such responses are theoretically probable, given the pragmatic nature of Asian Pacific Americans and their historical tendency to be enterprising in their quest for upward mobility, the actual risk seems minimal. Adjusting work behavior by acquiring more proficient language skills and workplace-appropriate manners does not require anyone to abandon his or her own cultural training. In fact, such adjustments can help these individuals make more effective use of their tradition-based training, actually broadening and enhancing their bicultural experience.

Furthermore, the concept of future-oriented success is deeply ingrained. In traditional Asian cultures, an "apprenticeship" in which a person submits to a period of learning from and compliance to a mentor in anticipation of acquiring competence that can lead to future high status is a common practice. Few Asians would therefore feel socially or personally demeaned by having to accommodate or adjust behavior for the sake of future achievements. Asian

Pacific Americans, in general, also tend not to build self-identity solely through outside influences. One's early self-concept is developed through close family values and later reinforced through participation in an occupation or profession. When an individual acquires competence in a profession, he or she is likely to shift allegiance to the social class of that profession and begin to identify him- or herself as a scientist, physician, or so forth.

The 1972 research studies of Caudill and De Vos involving a group of Japanese Americans and their families[16] reinforce the above explanations. The authors found that social pressures did not prevent the Nisei—the American-born, second-generation Japanese Americans—from attaining educational and occupational goals defined by their own families. Regardless of the discrimination they encountered, their sense of a "future orientation" precipitated a willingness to postpone immediate gratifications and to endure adversity. They also avoided confrontation, importing instead an accommodating but future-oriented concept of success.

Those intellectual individualists who view autonomy as perhaps the highest goal in life should try not to view the following suggested norms and protocols as blind conformity to the corporate rules. Rather, think of these suggestions as merely mechanisms for gaining entrance to and status in the corporate world with the ultimate aim of diminishing discrimination and breaking the glass ceiling. Of course, the final judgment will remain with the practitioners themselves, but there are few sensible reasons for denying oneself the advantages which come from meeting other people's social expectations.

## Personal Appearance

How important is your appearance at work? Anyone who has been working in an office long enough will tell you that the major component of others' opinions of you will be based on how you look. Research by Deborah Then and P. C. Morrow further support the notion that an individual who is considered unattractive is at a serious disadvantage in both social and professional situations.[17] People at work or in your neighborhood may not know you well, but they all know what you look like, and based on that outer appearance, they make certain assumptions about your other characteristics. This may sound shocking and even cruel to the young idealist, but our society, perhaps due to our frequent deadlines or our quest for instant gratification through avenues such as our mass media, has not yet advanced to a point where very many people will take the time to search for your inner qualities.

In fact, research studies such as the work of Hensley and Vandushaf have shown that our society rewards people for such arbitrary qualities as being tall. Again, one may find it appalling, but tall, healthy-looking people usually receive better attention and are treated better in the workplace.[18] Very slim people do not get promoted to positions of higher power and authority. Likewise, overweight people are perceived negatively and thought of as less healthy and energetic; a recent study by Klassen, Jasper, and Harris shows that they are more likely to be passed over for management positions.[19] People who do not consistently maintain an orderly, neat appearance may be assessed by others as having trouble meeting their other responsibilities (i.e., being incompetent at their jobs) or having some kind of personal problem such as alcohol abuse or intrusive emotional difficulties. Even though discrimination based on personal appearance is just as illegal as that based on race, age, gender, or sexual orientation, generally speaking—that is, excepting a few blatant cases—the subtle nature of prejudice based on personal appearance makes it difficult to prove in a courtroom.

As one college recruiter recently explained to a group of graduates who went looking for corporate jobs wearing casual attire and with hair or beards fashionably long and unkempt, "Some day when you become the boss, you can do all those things and enjoy all the ideological freedoms. But for now, if you want to get into the business world, you better learn their way of doing things. You can't afford to generate a bad image or to let a bad image go unchanged. You don't have the leverage to set standards."

One can, of course, argue that there are certain kinds of businesses, such as entertainment, where such conformity is not required, and even certain individual corporations within the publishing, computer, software, or garment industries which are associated with more lenient standards. However, these exceptions do not disprove but rather reinforce the fact that certain image expectations are associated with certain professions in our society. For example, writers almost never wear ties, and publishers tend to wear sweaters rather than suits. In short, anyone who wants to attain a position of authority in the mainstream corporate world will need to meet that world's expectations. In this regard, seeking the help of professionals, such as image consultants and speech coaches, is quite common. Such help is readily available, and the results will usually be well worth the nominal cost paid. But let us also consider, as perhaps an extreme example, the case of "Sue."

Sue left home in Fresno, California, where her parents still live, when she was sixteen years old. Today, she is an executive with a major retail chain. Sue has the style and elegance of a classic Hollywood celebrity. Her clothing is always fashionable, and although she admits to being in her fifties, she appears twenty years younger. With her light brown hair and hazel eyes, she does not appear to be an Asian Pacific American.

> I am pure Japanese. Don't let my looks fool you. I wear color contact lenses, dye my hair, had a nose and eye job. I was a high school dropout, although in later years I went back to adult school and got a college certificate in merchandising. It was when I was waitressing that I found out 'good-looking' people receive more attention—and more pay. So I thought to myself, 'Hey, why not just simply get a nose and eye job for affirmative action?'

No offense to the supporters of affirmative action; Sue's case is no doubt a surprising one to many readers, and for a variety of reasons, her methods of "improving" her appearance will not appeal to many people. The promulgation of a standard of beauty based on the phenotype of one group is, by definition, racist. However, De Vos and Wagatsuma[20] report that cosmetic surgery, especially to alter eyelid folds and to build up the bridge of the nose, has become standard practice among Japanese movie actors, among others. These various attempts to alter physical appearance presumably can be linked to the proliferation of Western values along with mass media and technology. Researchers Jasper and Klassou[21] have found that as surgical techniques continue to advance, increasing numbers of business people, regardless of ethnicity, perceive cosmetic surgery as a useful tool for advancement in a popular culture which demands ready acceptance and conformity of appearance in the workplace or high society.

But there are far less drastic means of developing a more accepted image. One way is simply to smile more often and maintain a pleasant, cheerful demeanor in casual relations. In general, first-generation Asian Americans have been taught during childhood to keep a serious demeanor and avoid any outward displays of happiness or other emotions in public, especially when engaged in serious activities such as working. Although a stoic appearance is not typical of most Pacific Island cultures, nor does it typify the vast majority of younger and U.S.-born Asian Americans, it is quite evident in many televised diplomatic and political events involving traditional Asian leaders. They are rarely seen smiling in public because a display of emotion is considered a sign of weakness by most of their constituents. But in most European cultures and, therefore, in the American workplace, a smile most often conveys a positive impression of warmth, friendliness, and collegiality. Dickey-Bryant, Mendoza, and Lautenschlager reported the importance of a smiling face and its relationship to occupational success in their 1986 article.[22] A relaxed, friendly smile and a visage of geniality can therefore help other American workers feel more relaxed in your presence and generate a positive image. Smiling is a very inexpensive way to improve personal relations and promote one's career goals.[23]

Dressing appropriately—impeccably, if economic conditions permit—is a sure way to improve appearance. Many community agencies around the country have recently begun providing services to help job seekers, especially minorities and women who have little experience in the job market, choose appropriate business attire.

"In today's tight job market," said one personnel director, "when there are so many applicants competing for every single opening, employers will look for ways to eliminate less suitable candidates from the field. The first thing they are likely to do is eliminate any applicants who are unkempt or inappropriately dressed. How you look is probably more important than your ability to do the job. If you don't look the part, no one will give you a chance to say what you can do or to let you prove it."

Kim, a Cambodian refugee, had precisely this experience while she was applying for a clerical position: "I graduated from the government-sponsored job training class with high marks, but I was always being rejected at the interview stage. I thought that people were discriminating against me because I am Asian. I went back to the Job Corps and tried to tell the director what was happening. He took one look at me and said, 'First, we need to fix you up.'"

What had happened was that, when Kim first arrived in New York with her family, she only brought one good dress. It was a pink one with Cambodian embroidery on it. Because everyone told her how pretty the dress was, she wore it to all of her job interviews, never realizing the obvious "fresh off the boat" appearance it gave her. The Job Corps director sent her to a hair stylist and a dentist, too.[24] After that, she was directed to a clothes bank[25] called "Suited for Success."

"An image consultant at the clothes bank helped me put on a little bit of light makeup and to select a maroon-colored dress with coordinated beige scarf, simple gold earrings, and tan shoes and handbag. I couldn't believe that I could look so good—like an American professional on TV! I went on an interview and got the job that same afternoon. I felt badly that I had accused people of discriminating against me because of race!"

For many readers, the story above will seem to be exactly a case of racism on the basis of the argument that "looking more White" got Kim her job. The implicit argument is that the more "ethnic" (or ethnically "other") Kim looked, the less competent potential employers judged her to be. However, from an organizational theory perspective, the argument would be that Kim needed to show potential employers that she was capable of understanding their organization's culture. Every organization, just like every country, has its different aesthetic and cultural patterns regarding such things as work hours, dress codes, and personal eccentricities, and virtually all organizations tend to recruit people whose overall appearance suggests that they will fit in and get along well with the members of the existing workforce. Marxists will argue that such patterns are a form of class discrimination, because those who cannot afford to dress up for an interview do not get a fair shot at employment. These sorts of social problems are highly complex and take years to correct. Meanwhile, various nonprofit organizations and private concerns are helping all underprivileged people, not just minorities, to take the pragmatic step of acquiring job-winning apparel.

Kim's experience was not unique. Dale, a young man from Tonga, had an almost identical experience: "I had a tattoo on my forearm and several studs in my ear. I was applying for a mailroom job. I figured, who was going to see me, sitting in the mailroom? How could appearance matter? I was lucky in one sense: I went into the place the day before to check out the address and met one of the workers there. He took one look at me and said, 'Buddy, how bad do you want this job?' I told him, pretty bad; my parents were on my case and I was out of dough. He said, 'Go get a haircut, remove those studs from your ear, and wear a long-sleeved shirt to cover your tattoo. Mister Boss Man is pretty sensitive about these things.' I did all he said and got the job."

Chances are, if Dale proves himself to be a valuable worker, he could revert to his earlier appearance without being fired from his job in the mailroom. However, even at this relatively low level, he needed to have the "proper" image—that is, the expected image—before he could cross the threshold.

"Dressing well," said Eric, a personnel director, "not only gives a good impression of professionalism, it also shows that you are an 'in' person who understands how the game is played. If you are not sure whether to choose a modern or classic look for an interview, the quickest way to find out is to go to the company at the start of the business day or at quitting time. Stand in the lobby and watch the employees passing by. Observe how they dress and carry themselves. It doesn't hurt, either, to go to the company cafeteria and watch the employees' demeanor to get a sense of the organizational culture. Then, during the interview process, you can be sure of presenting yourself as the kind of person who everyone can see will fit in.

"If you are working toward a promotion, dress as if you already had the better position. Dress like the executives you report to, but don't out-do them. What you want to demonstrate is that you have the same style as they do, but you also respect their power and status. For example, if employees at your level are expected to wear a shirt and tie, add a sports coat. For ladies, if workers at your level wear dresses, you can add a coordinated jacket. Dark colors are preferred, and you should avoid short skirts. Whatever you do, avoid a 'Las Vegas' or 'Liberace' look, including at office parties or other business social functions."

A special piece of advice for Asian Pacific American professionals: always avoid the temptation to wear any sort of Asian native dress to a company function unless you have been specifically requested by a superior to do so in order to greet a foreign client or other visitor who will be dressing similarly. Even under those circumstances, it is best to try to include some very American accessory that will blend in well and show you are proud of being an Asian Pacific American. Learn to create a new style that bridges East and West without suggesting the old stereotypes.

## Etiquette and Protocol

Parker's family immigrated to the United States from Korea when he was a teenager. His parents operated a small business, but he had always dreamed that, someday, after he graduated from the university, he would work for a large, prestigious company. He planned a career in business management and looked forward to making his family proud to have such a successful son, a manager in a renowned company.

While still in school, Parker studied hard and majored in financial management. Every summer and during semester breaks, he helped lighten his parents' workload and tried to show his gratitude for their support by working in the family business.

During the summer of his senior year, Parker's college advisor arranged an internship for him. Parker was excited by the opportunity; however, an unexpected turn of events forced him to change plans. His grandmother in Korea suddenly fell ill, and Parker's parents had to return to Korea. As the eldest son, and because his siblings were too young to take on the responsibility, Parker had to decline the internship; instead he ran his parents' business in their absence.

As a result, Parker gained more small business experience but did not develop his workplace socialization skills or pay as much attention to his behavior as he would have done during the internship. He later explained, "I was totally unprepared when I had to enter a large American corporation and tried to deal with figuring out what kind of behavior was generally acceptable in the workplace."

Fortunately, the company that hired Parker had a diversity manager on the payroll who regularly conducted sensitivity training programs for ethnically diverse employees.[26] "I learned their organizational culture, rules and procedures, accepted behavior, and some basic office etiquette as well," said Parker. A lot of it is common sense, but for people coming from different parts of the world, American common sense is not very common at all.

"For example, we learned the proper way to shake hands, we learned about eye contact, personal space, and a lot of other little things that we do or deal with every day, but until someone asks, you never think about whether you do them in a way that is accepted in the business world or not.

"In the case of shaking hands,[27] it is a standard form of greeting in the Western world. In many parts of Asia, the standard way to greet someone you meet is with a bow. The custom of bowing has been practiced for centuries, so when I was growing up, I was naturally taught to bow when greeting someone. I had never attended any formal, Western-style functions and had never considered the question of executing a proper handshake. I did not realize that my kind of handshake would present the image of someone weak or wimpy. At the workshop, we learned the correct way to grasp the other party's hand firmly between thumb and forefinger, but not with a bone-crushing grip that won't let go! Shake up and down just slightly, two or three times. Western etiquette dictates that, traditionally, a man should wait for a lady to offer her hand, but few practice this kind of reserve anymore in the modern world. Professional women should be treated as equals first. If Americans are meeting Asian clients, it would be a nice touch to follow the handshake with a slight bow to acknowledge the Asian custom.

"I also didn't realize eye contact was so important to presenting a positive image in the business world. When we were taught to bow, we were necessarily expected to lower our eyes to show respect to older persons or those in authority. That is how we show our respect and acknowledge the other person's status. I never dreamed that Westerners considered this gesture evasive. The more I tried to show respect, the more I seemed to be saying I was not to be trusted! I suppose that is part of the reason many nineteenth-century Americans believed the Chinese miners and railroad workers were untrustworthy, and the epithet 'shifty-eyed Chinese' was derived. In the American workplace of today, you must maintain good eye contact when you talk to people. Look them right in the eye when you talk to them. And remember that a smile should be part of 'business as usual.' Keep smiling to show you are friendly, congenial, trustworthy, and dependable.

"In the old country, we used to live in close quarters. I guess that's why, when we talk to people, we are usually in very close proximity to the person. Since I was already a teen when I came to the United States, I learned in school that you don't get so close to an American when you talk to them. I have no problem in standing about three to four feet away from someone during a conversation. That is the comfort zone for personal space for most Americans. But not all new immigrants will know this. They would be mortified to discover that they have invaded someone's private space!

"While we are on this subject, I might also add that members of the older generations of Asians have a habit of saying 'Yes, yes, yes.' They were taught that it is impolite to contradict others, that using negative words conveys a negative image and negative feelings. They will almost never say 'no,' which can be very confusing to straightforward Americans. They can also carry modesty or indirectness in a conversation so far that it becomes more confusing than simply saying 'no.' My advice is, the sooner you can discard the 'virtue of modesty,' the better it will be. Also, as soon as possible, discontinue the Asian protocol of acting unworthy of praise or compliments. Americans will view a modest person as weak, lacking self-confidence and self-esteem, and unsuitable for any important project.

"I also noticed that, among my parents' friends, it is quite normal to ask each other how much they paid for things. Maybe because they are newcomers, they are very interested in comparing economies of scale. But in the United States, it is not considered polite to ask such questions as, 'How much did your home cost?' or 'How much did you pay for your new car?' Even worse, in America, is to ask someone how much money they are earning. My aunt once asked an acquaintance his salary, and he told her, 'Look, lady, obviously you have a lot to learn in this country. Never discuss money matters in this country, especially someone's pay! You have to respect people's privacy.' After the man left, my aunt, who had only been in the U.S. for a few years, had to ask, 'What is privacy?' There was no word in our language to tell her.

"In Asia, it is usual for many relatives in the family to be close. Aunts, uncles, cousins, and grandparents may all live together in close quarters. Everyone knows everyone else's business, parents brag about their children's accomplishments—in modest language, of course—to the whole community, so there really is no privacy for anyone,[28] and that is the way they are most comfortable and happy.''

Parker also mentioned that, although the diversity manager's training program was very helpful, each employee still must use his or her own judgment and develop his or her own sensitivities. The program can teach an awareness of the problems that many Asian Pacific American workers encounter, but the individual must make a constant practice of observing others' behavior and conduct.

"The program simply cannot teach everything. For example, there are some rude behaviors, such as talking loudly with a fellow countryman in your native language in a company where no one else can understand the conversation, especially in a confined space, such as an elevator. I had a co-worker who loves to speak Korean with me, always in a loud voice, whenever there is a chance. When I would answer him back in English, he got mad. 'What's the matter with you? Are you ashamed to be a Korean?' When we were speaking privately in a coffee shop, I would speak our native language but otherwise, where there were co-workers around, it was only common sense not to raise suspicions about the nature of our conversation. It is simply better manners to use English in front of other co-workers. For that matter, it is considered poor manners to talk so loud, in any language, that it disturbs others.

"The seminar did teach us to utilize the lunch hour to our advantage by networking and cultivating relationships."[29] According to Parker, Asian Pacific Americans should make the most of their breaks by going out to lunch and conversing with other co-workers. Common courtesy prohibits the consumption of strong-smelling foods in a shared workspace. Therefore, it is advisable to save pungent foods for at-home meals.

## The Grapevine Can Be Useful

Too often, people hear the news at work through the grapevine, at the water cooler, or when passing in a hallway.

"Have you heard about so-and-so losing that promotion?"

"What? You're kidding! He works so hard, and he's a nice person, too."

"Yeah, but he wears white socks, you know what I mean? I hear he wore that same old stained tie when they took him to meet the Regional Director."

"They turned Sumiko down for the supervisor's job."

"I am not surprised. She is too frail and weak looking. She always wears the same gray dress, and it's two sizes too big. And she covers her mouth when she smiles."[30]

"And she never stands up straight or looks people in the eye either. She's kind of annoying."

"Chuck, what do you think of promoting Chin upstairs?"

"Hmmm. Well, technically he's good. He is very intelligent. He helped us solve that mystery with the machinery in the number two plant, after all. But you have to wonder about temperament."

"Are you sure you're talking about Chin? What's wrong with his disposition?"

"Usually, nothing. However, he may have a fight-or-flight syndrome. You normally see him sitting at his desk working quietly for hours at a time, sometimes for days. But have you seen what happens when something suddenly annoys him? All of a sudden, he's barking, yelling, carrying on . . . "

"Yeah, I guess you're right. I guess he wouldn't work out."[31]

## Managerial Perspectives

Matt, a Sansei (third-generation Japanese American) and a retired management consultant, agrees that first-generation Asian Americans, and second generation to a lesser extent, have an unfortunate tendency to demonstrate attitudes and behavior that are known as "passive-aggressive."[32] As demonstrated previously in this chapter, many of these behaviors are conditioned by the experience of being constantly perceived as a member of a minority group within society. Taking this fact into consideration, Matt still feels there is hope for individuals to break through.

"Asians and individuals from many other traditional cultures have been trained at home not to express their feelings. So the psychological defense mechanism is either to run away and hide or to bottle their feelings up until things escalate to a point where they can't contain them any longer. Then comes the sudden outburst or explosion, completely out of proportion to the issue at hand. Suddenly, this normally subdued person is being contradictory and voicing opposition for reasons that management cannot comprehend. Many Asians also internalize their feelings of rage and try to hide them away, but they end up with an attitude that suggests they think the whole world is at fault. This kind of attitude problem will inevitably work against them and hurt any chances they might have had of getting promoted.

"One must understand that the Euro-American manager will probably feel that Asians are trying to impose different cultural and communicative styles upon them. In turn, they must expend extra time and energy to deal with it. Managers may actually experience feelings of being excluded, especially if they feel that the rules of the game are being changed without their knowledge. They will become angry themselves, if they feel threatened by the idea of a new style of communication, especially if they feel this new style has been imposed by the latest wave of fashionable 'political correctness.' Perhaps, the next thing they know, they, themselves, will be passed over for a promotion in favor of an Asian Pacific American.

"Many White managers view the inclusion of Asian Pacific Americans in management as a definite threat to their own advancement. They fear a loss of control." This phenomenon was also found by the federal Glass Ceiling Commission in 1995.[33]

Fortunately, many top managers in corporate America are aware of this situation. Organization leaders have begun to realize that hiring and promoting broadly qualified and highly talented employees from different segments of society can increase their competitive advantage, as termed by Foster, Jackson, Cross, Jackson, and Hardiman.[34] With the increasing diversity of the American workforce and the technical advancement and global restructuring that contribute to strategic alliances and foreign ownership, managers will have to work across national boundaries. As related by Cox, Lobel, and McLeod,[35] organizations must fully embrace equal employment opportunity and recognize the higher overall level of talent available to them.

Catherine and Cindy, two exceptionally bright, young second-generation Asians, have both succeeded in attaining managerial positions. Both of them fully support the notion that the kind of face you present at work will determine your career path.

"It shouldn't be, but most careers and promotions are still made on the basis of one's looks, physical appearance, the shape of the body, the image one projects. No one would want to associate with someone who threatens their comfort level, that's for sure."

Many would assert that "comfort level" is a two-way street: whereas employees must learn the rituals, customs, and values of the organization or their work unit, the manager must also learn about the employees' cultural background and provide advancement opportunities that fit the skills, needs, and values of the ethnic group.[36] A more detailed discussion of what organizations and management can

do to meet the challenge of integrating the increasing numbers of the ethnically diverse workforce will be presented in the next chapter.

Joe, another young, second-generation Asian who made it to the executive suite,
claimed that there are no set formulas for success in corporate America. "Being
sensitive, observant, and keeping your intuitive antennae up. For beginners, put the
dream of being super-successful on hold for a while, and use the time to figure out
the workings of the organization. The first thing to do is be sure you can survive.
Then try to gain more acceptance. If you jump headlong into the arena immediately
and you're too aggressive about it, your plans are likely to backfire."

It seems that minority and female workers must first gain a thorough understanding of the rules laid down by the old guard—the senior managers who
control the corporate world and, therefore, the destinies of corporate personnel.
"It doesn't matter how strong you are technically, you've got to have the image
that they can picture in the boardroom before you can hope to be promoted into
management circles."

"As the client base widens and the bottom line improves, women and
minorities may begin to influence decision making at the very highest levels.
But until that day arrives, women and minorities must continue diligently to
learn the ropes if they want to succeed in a large American corporation."

A compilation of useful tips that executives and management consultants
deemed worthwhile during interviews is listed on the following pages.[37] It is
hoped that the tips can serve as valuable guidelines for younger employees,
whether Asian Pacific American or any other cultural background, who have
the aspiration to climb the corporate ladder, achieve a greater measure of their
full potential in business, and make their environment a little more pleasant
and their lives a little more interesting.

However, readers must exercise caution and reflect thoughtfully. Trust
your own judgment in sorting through the rules; most of them entail generalizations which may or may not apply to particular circumstances. Remember
that each person is a unique individual, and no two situations are identical. If
you are one of the many individuals who finds the managerial challenge and
current corporate culture poorly matched to your own personal outlook and
developmental plans, feel free to skip the next section.

## Advancement Strategies

*Be Alert*—Keep your eyes and ears open. Find out who's who in the organization,
not only who has the formal titles and where they stand on the organizational

chart, but also the informal leaders. Seek out and join the informal networking in the organization. Volunteer to participate when opportunities arise. Observe what others do and what expectations they have regarding your behavior. What organizational culture(s) and value systems are in place? What beliefs do employees share? If company practices are contradictory to any of your beliefs and values, look for another job as soon as possible. Don't waste time thinking things may change. In today's complex environment, an individual without a strong power base is unlikely to be able to exert enough influence to bring change.[38]

On the other hand, you may feel comfortable with the organization's culture, beliefs, and value systems and feel ready to play a part within the organization and to emulate the behavior of the executives. Many studies, among them the 1988 Center for Creative Leadership report, show that people tend to promote only those individuals whom they perceive to be like themselves.[39] Therefore, if you sincerely aspire to be an executive, find yourself a mentor who will serve as your role model.[40] Sign up for a training program immediately. And get started *now!* Develop a self-improvement plan and set tentative career goals. Avoid the temptation to accept a dead-end staff position or highly technical professional job that may pay well. Seek out the challenges and opportunities in your workplace. Recognize and grab them, and meet the challenges. Do not accept jobs which will not provide opportunities leading to future executive positions. Always position yourself further ahead, and keep taking one step at a time.[41]

Among your daily practices, remember to always be on time for business functions and meetings. Generally, people in the United States have a preconceived notion that Asian Pacific Americans do not have a strict concept of punctuality.[42] Although this may be true in Asia, as well as many other parts of the world, it is important in America to be habitually "on time" and never to compromise official work hours. It can also be a strategic advantage to come in a few minutes before starting time or to continue working at the end of the day for a few minutes after others have quit.

Learn to pronounce people's names and use them; people like to be recognized whether they are janitors or executives. If you recognize and greet people by their names, they feel good about you. If you can't remember someone's name on occasion, don't try to avoid the encounter, but greet them with a smile and say "Good morning" or "Good afternoon" or ask "How are things going?" Never ask a subordinate to perform a personal chore for you unless it is clearly arranged in advance and paid for. Too many managers have ruined their reputations by asking subordinates to pick up laundry, kids, or minor purchases.

One thing an aspiring executive should *never* do is date someone from the same office. Romantic involvements in the workplace still invite negative reactions and derogatory comments from others. Do not be misled into thinking that "times have changed," or that discretion will make a difference. In today's workplace, one of the greatest dangers is that if a relationship doesn't work out, there may be embarrassing consequences that prove highly disruptive to business. As one executive put it, "The kiss you get at the workplace may be the kiss of death to your career!"

"Learn to be assertive and go against the stereotype," emphasized a recruiter from a management consulting firm. "Assertiveness doesn't mean being too loud or overbearing. It means being aware that extreme humility is not a virtue in the American workplace. In fact, people are most likely to perceive a humble worker as insecure and lacking self confidence. At the same time, do not show off your expertise at another's expense—especially if the other person has more seniority than you."

For example, take the case of Gin. Gin was an honors student in financial services at Saint Mary's College. Equipped with the latest theories and technical know-how, almost immediately after graduation she found a job in a major company's financial services department. One of her team members on the job was John. John had been with the company for twenty years and sat on practically every committee and task force the company had. After a staff meeting one day, the district manager asked John and Gin to remain for a minute:

| | |
|---|---|
| **Manager:** | Well, Gin, how was your first week here? |
| **Gin:** | Very good, sir. I am nearly finished putting all the current year financial records in order. |
| **Manager:** | Well, John, have you calculated the ROI in current dollars for the past years yet? |
| **John:** | No, sir; I'm not sure how. I won't be ready until I do some further cost analysis. |
| **Gin:** | Oh, I can do it. It's really simple. I learned it from Professor Thompson at Saint Mary's. Anyone who has taken a modern college financial management course would know how. |

Gin has made a mistake by hurting John's feelings. Not only is he unlikely ever to take Gin's side in a controversy, but should she make a mistake on the job, John might make sure everyone in the organization finds out about it. A better final response from Gin would have been something like this:

**Gin:**     Oh, I may be able to help you with that, John. You know what they say, two heads are better than one. I'm sure John is more experienced than I am, but I did learn something about that in college and I'm anxious to try it out.

In this case, not only has Gin saved John from embarrassment, she has also shown the district manager that she is a good team player who can be highly valuable to the organization.

The same principle applies during more formal business meetings. You want to be heard, but you don't want to appear to be showing off. Be sure to choose the right time to speak up; if you cut others off before they have finished speaking, you will be perceived as rude or obnoxious. At the same time, don't hesitate when your turn arrives. Be well prepared to make your point.

"But beware of 'overkill,' " cautioned another executive. "Sometimes, seeming 'too smart' can be just as intimidating to higher-ups."

*Be Broadminded*—Broaden your perspectives on everything you can. Do not join cliques, and do not let it be said that you refuse to socialize with anyone outside of your own ethnic group. You can't afford to be stereotyped with any one group exclusively, because people will lose sight of your individual strengths and abilities. You want to be perceived as an individual with a definite personality. Try to blend in with all of the people in the organization. Don't isolate yourself from others, but learn as much as you can about other people and their cultures. Interact with others courteously and respectfully, regardless of their positions in the organization. Whenever someone does something to help you, be sure to say "thank you" and to show your appreciation. The effort to treat people with dignity and respect must be sincere and must never seem condescending.

Educate yourself with common sense. Read and pay attention to what is going on in the world. Many women and Asian Pacific Americans have a tendency to skip over sporting events and to turn down the occasional invitations to "go out and grab a beer after work" or even to more formal cocktail parties. Several Asian Pacific Americans interviewed for this study agreed that, although watching a football game may be tolerable, "standing around at a party holding a glass in your hand is a terrible waste of time."

The fact is, a good deal of "male bonding" centers around sports, including ball games, hunting, and fishing. If Asian Pacific Americans are willing to broaden their expertise beyond their own field, they may find the exchange of ideas and experiences among colleagues, the opportunity to learn new things, and the practice of the art of conversation all quite enjoyable. This should in no way suggest that women and minorities *must* watch sports or drink beer with White males. On the other hand, deliberate socializing may eventually result in a trade off: majority members may become more willing to participate in minority events, thereby gaining greater exposure to and awareness of Asian cultural developments.

"I was at a business conference, staying at the university dormitory," recalled an Asian Pacific American executive banker. "It was during the semester break. Students had vacated their rooms, but many books of classical reading were still on the shelves. I saw familiar names like Socrates, Aristotle, Plato, Sophocles, Homer's *Iliad* and *The Odyssey*, Virgil's *Aeneid*, Dante's *Divine Comedy*, Cervantes's *Don Quixote*, Swift's *Gulliver's Travels*, Rousseau's *Social Contract*, Machiavelli's *The Prince*, Voltaire's *Candide*, and the writings of St. Augustine and Martin Luther, among others I can't recall just now. I thought I would brush up on my knowledge of Western thought so that I could talk about it with people. I stayed up all night reading. It was really exciting and enjoyable."

Every college-educated Asian Pacific American has studied world history, philosophy, the arts and music, and other humanities at some point in his or her life. They may have since concentrated almost exclusively upon family and profession and fallen behind in this kind of reading; however, many would be surprised to find out that they were, in fact, quite well-rounded, thoughtful, cosmopolitan individuals familiar with both Eastern and Western cultures and capable of building rapport with just about everyone—not just with fellow Asian technicians. In most cases, spending a little free time reviewing the classics and organizing some of the material into a presentable (although informal) manner will yield an extremely valuable asset for public speaking. As one executive expressed it, "Memorize a few passages of Shakespeare, too, and bring in some lines from the Bible. You can't help but make a favorable impression."

"But be forewarned: there are certain drawbacks. At very least, you must be prepared to stand accused of 'turning into a White boy.' If you know who you really are and you can handle a little well-intentioned ignorance, the reward is worth the pain. Always look beyond the immediate and build for the future."

Another way to broaden one's mind and continue learning—besides reading on one's own and socializing with colleagues—is to participate in professional conferences. Join professional associations in your field and attend extracurricular functions. Do voluntary and charitable work: not only will you be providing valuable services to needy organizations, you will also be contributing to the betterment of humanity and, at the same time, getting to know people outside of your work organization. This can provide you with useful information, informal networking, and worthwhile social relationships.

There is no substitute for speaking well in public. Even if they have developed the art of casual conversation and making "small talk," many Asian Pacific Americans become bashful and self-conscious when asked to make a presentation before a group. Fortunately, there are many techniques one can use to get rid of or lessen inhibitions. There are professionals who can help you to overcome your fear, to help you minimize or lose an Asian accent, or to help you organize your thoughts and ideas clearly and take command of a group conversation. Joining a local Toastmasters group can be a simple way of improving public speaking skills.

Continuing your education in all areas of your professional life can help avoid becoming "outdated" by newer technologies or the latest theories, innovations, or skills. Continuing education takes extra time and energy, but the rewards will be substantial.

*Be Credible*—Building credibility is a must for any minority or woman who aspires to a top-level management position. One way to achieve credibility is through formal educational credentials from a highly reputable university. If your M.B.A. is not from an Ivy League institution, consider attending a few summer executive programs at MIT, Harvard, or the Wharton School. Because completing such programs requires fortitude as well as high intelligence, your success can reflect extremely well upon your credibility.

Another approach is to join as many important committees and task forces as possible. This can easily give you opportunities to work with top management personnel and let them see you and your competence and energy in action. Taking a highly visible position with a trade association or a community organization can also be effective. Get into the right social circles and develop your professional reputation outside of your own workplace. The basic idea is to get as much positive, constructive exposure as possible. Inevitably, higher-level executives will become increasingly aware of your good reputation.

Always show enthusiasm for your organization. Be positive in your attitude at all times, taking care not to display the negative emotions through sarcasm or inappropriate public complaining. These can lead to misunderstandings which undermine your credibility with the organization. In addition, avoid bringing problems you are working on to the attention of higher-ups.

Although it might seem reasonable to expect executives to take an interest in whatever happens to be going on, explaining a problem is unlikely to do anything other than draw attention to the fact that, so far, you have been unable to solve it. Even if asked how things are going, don't feel trapped into revealing your day-to-day miseries.

Luu, an accounting supervisor, had trouble getting her company's sales department to provide the records she needed to prepare the state franchise sales tax report. She had made an appointment to meet with the sales manager and was on her way when she met Eric, the general manager, on his way to a board meeting.

| | |
|---|---|
| **Eric:** | How are things going, Luu? Any problems lately? |
| **Luu:** | Well, not too good, to tell you the truth. As you know, Bill (the accounting manager) is on vacation. I've got to get the state franchise sales tax report done tomorrow to avoid paying a penalty, but the sales department is unable to provide the sales records. Maybe you could give them a call? I am worried about having to pay the penalty. I'm on my way over there right now. |
| **Eric:** | I'm sure it's an oversight, Luu. Sales is very busy just now with several key projects. Why don't you let me know what you can do first. |

In the example above, Luu mistook Eric's polite question for a much deeper concern. She might even come away from this conversation thinking, "I can always rely on Eric to step in for me, if things become any worse." But Eric is thinking, "What's wrong with Luu? She has a lot of nerve, asking me to do her job!" As a general manager, Eric is concerned with larger issues and larger sums of money than the tax penalty. This doesn't mean he doesn't care about the tax penalty; it means he has delegated the state franchise sales tax report to Luu and expects to be able to rely on his accounting supervisor's professional competence and credibility. Luu could have handled this chance meeting with Eric in a much more effective manner:

| | |
|---|---|
| **Luu:** | Very well, sir. Everything is fine. By the way, I want to compliment you on the excellent speech you gave at the Merchants' Association annual dinner and to congratulate you on the Outstanding Community Service award you received. We are all very proud of you! Nice talking to you. Good-bye! |

Eric is left thinking well of Luu and feeling positive about her potential as good managerial material with the potential to step in and be the next accounting manager, when Bill is ready to retire.

It is equally important to build credibility with subordinates and co-workers. Do not promise things that you will have a problem delivering. Always try to foster a positive image throughout all levels and departments of the organization. Deal honestly with everyone, because people can see right through hypocrisy, and being a hypocrite is the worst kind of image a manager can have. Employees will soon show low morale and begin to talk behind management's back. Once a person has truly lost credibility, there will be no chance for him or her to climb the executive ladder.

Finally, as one Asian Pacific American executive put it, "Never cast aspersions on someone's favorite subject, but do talk up the subjects you admire. Life is in the arena; you must step up and try."

## Summary and Discussion

This chapter discussed the importance of understanding organizational culture and striking a balance between individual aspirations and organizational demands. Many key concepts for managerial success have been introduced and also extended toward new possibilities and strategies for managerial agendas for both thought and action.

Suggestions are provided for keeping a positive image, which include observing the rules of expected and appropriate workplace appearance, etiquette, and behavior. These suggestions are intended to provide practical guidance for students who wish to enter the corporate world as well as to offer encouragement to those who have emerged from a culture which did not promote activism in the workplace. Reflections on a rationale for adapting to corporate norms are included.

Those who most highly value individuality may prefer to join an organization with either a "person culture" or a "task culture." In the former, individuals may set their own rules and are afforded the freedom to determine their own agenda. In a task culture, typically an academic or research setting or high-tech industry, the emphasis is on personal expertise with a corresponding greater tolerance for individual differences.

Corporate America is evolving continuously toward unqualified acceptance of a diverse workforce, but today, many rules and behavioral expectations of the traditional corporate "mold" remain in place. By understanding these expectations, one can give one's career a "jump start."

For Advocates, this approach may sound like too great a sacrifice for conformity's sake, but even with the need for change becoming increasingly urgent, it is important to realize that the most effective and lasting forms of social and cultural change are effected from within by individuals who have attained positions of confidence and trust, rather than imposed from the outside in a coercive manner that threatens those in power. Thus, the most effective advocates will be those who are willing to spread their messages of raising corporate awareness of the plight and needs of the multicultural workforce from within the corporations.

◆ ◆ ◆ ◆ ◆

## DISCUSSION QUESTIONS

1. What is the nature of the organizational culture in your workplace? Are there any informal cultures like the ones described in this chapter?
2. In your opinion, which one of the four organizational cultures described comes closest to providing an ideal work setting?
3. Why is it necessary for Asian Pacific Americans to go against the stereotype in the work setting? Is it unnatural to change one's character or appearance for the sake of career advancement? Why is it important for Asian Pacific Americans to climb the corporate ladder and work themselves into decision-making positions?
4. What is networking? How important is it to your overall career planning? Who should practice networking?
5. Discuss the advice given by experts in this chapter. Which tips do you think are workable? Is there some advice that you don't think is practical or necessary?

◆ ◆ ◆ ◆ ◆

## EXPERIENTIAL EXERCISE

*Executive Etiquette*

*Objectives*

1. To test your knowledge of proper working etiquette.
2. To compare your understanding of work etiquette with that of others.

*Procedure*

1. Read the following statements.
2. Put a check mark next to each statement that you believe represents appropriate workplace behavior for executives and potential executives. Put an "X" next to each answer which you feel represents inappropriate behavior.
3. After completing step 2, turn the page to add up your score and compare your answers to the correct ones.

*Statements*

1. I like to personalize my e-mail by making the text a little bit unusual and using some emotional terms to make my point stronger—just as I do when I write to my friends.
2. If I am invited to an office party which includes spouses, and I am single, I would R.S.V.P. with the name of my date.
3. At a stand-up cocktail party with drinks and hors d'oeuvres, I would hold my plate in the left hand and my glass with napkin in the right hand.
4. If alcohol is served at the party and I don't drink, I would turn down the drinks and be glad that I don't have the burden of holding a glass all night.
5. If I were to host an office party with many Asian Pacific American guests, my most important concern should be whether I have ordered enough nonalcoholic beverages.
6. During the weekly meeting with my staff in my office, the telephones started to ring. When I answered, it was my boss, with whom I have been playing "phone tag." Should I excuse myself to talk to my boss?
7. A subordinate asked you to lunch to discuss a client's account. Because he arranged the lunch, he offered to pay or at least split the bill, but as manager, you paid the bill.
8. At a meeting, someone asked your boss a question he couldn't answer. You have an idea and would like to offer it immediately, but you wait and, a few moments later, pass your boss a note containing a brief outline of your thoughts. Did you do the right thing?

*Answers*

1. No. Although cheerfulness is prized in the office, office informality is unlike social informality. Besides, you never know who might see your message. Preserve basic professionalism.

2. Yes. This way, your date will be expected, and your host will be able to provide for the proper number of guests.
3. No. Hold everything in your left hand so your right hand is free to shake hands. Leave space on your plate for the glass, and place the napkin underneath the plate. You can always go back for seconds!
4. No. Politely ask for a glass of water or nonalcoholic soda with a slice of lime, and carry it in your hand during the event the same way everyone else does.
5. No. According to many experts, more than two-thirds of us have social anxieties, so the most important thing to do is make sure that everyone feels at ease and comfortable. As host, I should make an extra effort to ensure that none of my guests winds up as a "wallflower"; I can be sure to welcome them when they arrive and can introduce them to other guests with whom I know they share common interests (e.g., parents of young children can always find common ground). I can even plan ahead and invite an extra guest or two specifically for this purpose, especially if I do enough home-work to discover whether my guests have any special interests—perhaps classical music, travel, or gardening. If there is a sit-down dinner, I can use place cards to ensure that my Asian Pacific American guests don't all end up sitting together at the far end of the table.
6. No. It is more important to show your respect to the staff and demonstrate the importance of the meeting. Answer the phone, tell your boss you are in a meeting and can't talk, and promise to get back to her as soon as the meeting ends. You will gain her respect as a considerate and conscientious manager.
7. Yes. The proper etiquette is for the person in a higher position to pay business-related expenses, even if invited out by a subordinate.
8. Yes. Always try to keep your superiors looking their best in public meetings. Your boss will appreciate your loyalty and reward you later.

Scoring: If you answer half of these questions correctly, congratulations on a job well done!

## NOTES

1. Ann's inclusion of Grey Poupon, a more expensive brand of mustard, suggest that only the "best" Asian Americans can be included—an odd,

satirical twist to exemplify the current political climate surrounding racial issues.

2. Barbara A. Reid, "Mentorships Ensure Equal Opportunity," *Personnel* (November 1994): 122-3.

3. Kathy E. Kram, "Phases of the Mentor Relationship," *Academy of Management Journal* 36 (1993): 608-25.

4. J. Gibson, J. Ivancevich, and J. Donnelly, *Organizations: Behavior, Structure, and Processes,* 8th ed. (Homewood, IL: Irwin, 1994).

5. J. Van Maanen, "People Processing: Strategies for Organizational Socialization," *Organizational Dynamics* (Summer 1978): 18-36.

6. R. J. Burke and C. A. McKeen, "Mentoring in Organizations," *Journal of Ethics* (April 1990): 322.

7. John P. Fernandez, *The Diversity Advantage* (New York: Lexington Books, 1993).

8. Barry Phegan, *Developing Your Company Culture* (Berkeley, CA: Context Press, 1995). Dr. Phegan and his colleague, Dr. Royal Foote, are both management consultants who have successfully used the techniques described in this chapter in numerous organizations.

9. This definition of organizational culture has been cited by Edgar H. Schein in his book *Organizational Culture and Leadership* (San Francisco: Jossey-Bass, 1985).

10. Charles Hampden-Turner is senior research fellow at the London Business School and Visiting Scholar at MIT. He is the author of seven books, including *Corporate Culture and Leadership Effectiveness* (New York: McGraw-Hill, 1989) and *Charting the Corporate Mind* (London: Macmillan, 1990). He is well-versed in the culture and strategy of Pacific Rim countries and very much influenced by the late Rollo May and Gregory Bateson.

11. Charles B. Handy, *Understanding Organizations* (Hammondsworth, Middlesex, UK: Penguin, 1986).

12. Roger Harrison, "How to Describe Your Organization," *Harvard Business Review* (September/October 1972): 77-85; P. R. Lawrence and J. W. Lorsch, *Organization and Environment* (Cambridge, MA: Harvard University Press, 1967); T. Burns and G. H. Stalker, *The Management of Innovation* (London: Tavistock, 1966); Joan Woodward, *Industrial Organization: Theory and Practice* (London: Oxford University Press, 1965).

13. George A. De Vos, "Ethnic Pluralism: Conflict and Accommodation," in *Ethnic Identity,* ed. Lola Romanucci-Ross and George A. De Vos (Walnut Creek, CA: AltaMira, 1995).

14. Yen Le Espiritu, *Asian American Panethnicity* (Philadelphia: Temple University Press, 1992).

15. Larry Hajime Shinagawa and Gin Yong Pang, "Asian American Pan-Ethnicity and Intermarriage" *Amerasia Journal* 22 (1996):32.

16. William Caudill and George De Vos, "Achievement, Culture, and Personality: The Case of the Japanese Americans," in *Socialization for Achievement: The Cultural Psychology of the Japanese* (Berkeley: University of California Press, 1972): 220-50.

17. See Deborah Then, *The Impact of Physical Attraction* (Palo Alto, CA: Stanford University Press, 1986); and P. C. Morrow, "Physical Attractiveness and Selective Decision Making," *Journal of Management* 16 (1990): 46-60.

18. See Wayne Hensley, "Height and Occupational Success," *Psychological Reports* (June 1987): 163; and Sarah Vandushaf, "The Prejudice of Height," *Psychology Today* (March 1987): 110.

19. Michael L. Klassen, Cynthia R. Jasper, and Richard J. Harris, "The Role of Physical Appearance in Managerial Decisions," *Journal of Business and Psychology* 8 (Winter 1993): 181-98.

20. George De Vos and Hiroshi Wagatsuma, "Culture Identity in Japan," in *Ethnic Identity,* ed. Lola Romanucci-Ross and George A. De Vos (Walnut Creek, CA: AltaMira, 1995).

21. Two of the many researchers whose results support the notion that Sue's actions should not be considered unusual are C. R. Jasper, "Perceptions of Salespersons' Appearance and Evaluation of Job Performance," *Perceptual and Motor Skills* 71 (1990): 563-6; and M. L. Klassen, "Stereotypical Beliefs about Appearance: Implications for Retailing and Consumer Issues," *Perceptual and Motor Skills* 71 (1990): 519-28.

22. For more on the importance of a smiling face, see L. Dickey-Bryant, J. L. Mendoza, and L. Lautenschlager, "Facial Attractiveness and Its Relation to Occupational Success," *Journal of Applied Psychology* (1986); R. Bull and N. Rumsey, *The Social Psychology of Facial Appearance* (London: Springer-Verlag, 1988).

23. A note must be added here that many Southeast Asian refugees and recent immigrants from China tend to neglect dental care despite having serious problems that warrant attention. This can also affect their appearance, rendering their smiles less appealing.

24. The American Association of Women Dentists is providing free dental care for poor women in New York. Many other organizations are providing free hair cutting and shampoos for needy men and women.

25. In many large American cities, nonprofit organizations have begun helping low-income people get ready for the job market by providing them with job-winning apparel that will give them a boost on the career ladder. For more information on attire, see S. M. Forsythe, "Effect of Applicants' Clothing on Interviewers' Decision to Hire," *Journal of Applied Social Psychology* 20 (1990): 1579-95; M. C. Jenkins and T. V. Atkins, "Perceptions of Acceptable Dress by Corporate and Noncorporate Recruiters," *Journal of Human Behavior and Learning* 7 (1990): 38-46.

26. "Diversity manager" was an unheard-of term as recently as 1988. By 1995, more than half of the Fortune 500 management teams had included diversity managers, and they often reported directly to the CEO. According to a survey cited in Julie Amparano Lopez's article, "Firms Elevate Heads of Diversity Programs" (*Wall Street Journal,* 5 August 1992), the average diversity manager's annual salary was between $75,000 and $130,000. Managers' duties are broader than those of affirmative action managers. Through diversity managers' programs, employees become more productive and work better in organizations; thus, diversity managers help improve the company's bottom line.

27. An interesting piece of historical lore on handshaking: according to Angi Ma Wong, President of Wong's Executive Consultation Services and a leader of intercultural workshops in California, the practice of handshaking can be traced to origins in Europe during the Middle Ages. Men extended their empty right hands in greeting to show that they were unarmed.

28. Even in the layout of Asian offices, one will not find private offices of the sort Westerners expect. Instead, a space the size of a half-city block or even a whole block will be used without any dividers or panels so that everyone in the company can see and hear everyone else's conversations and activities.

29. It is believed that eating lunch alone in one's office is counterproductive to one's career if not one's health. One should always use lunch time to cultivate relationships, network, and pick up the latest useful gossip and information. Grapevine information can include company news which, for some reason, never reached you through official channels.

30. Most Asians, especially most Japanese, consider exposing the inside of the mouth very unpleasant and impolite to others. Therefore, many develop the habit of covering their mouths during laughter.

31. Perhaps due to the traditional respect for elders and authority experienced during their childhoods, some individuals develop an unconscious need to avoid conflict, manifested through a suppression of their true feelings and natural expressions (flight). If, however, the mechanism for aggression avoidance

fails even momentarily, the suppressed emotions can break through suddenly in an uncontrolled manner (fight), with results that are emotionally damaging both to the self and to others, and often destructive to the relationship between them. See Nevitt Sanford, *Family Impact on Personality: The Point of View of a Psychoanalyst* (University of Illinois Press, 1964).

32. Self-negation through fearful submission to one's parents and the guilt resulting from an expression of forbidden feelings of aggression both can be powerful sources of inner frustration. Certainly, the external social environment also plays a large part in the development of passive-aggressive behavior within organizations. See Nevitt Sanford, *Self and Society: Social Change and Individual Development* (New York: Atherton, 1967); and Stephen Chang, *The Integral Management of Tao* (San Francisco: Tao Publishing, 1986).

33. According to CEOs interviewed by the federal Glass Ceiling Commission in 1995, there are no special problems associated with recruiting Asian Pacific American women and men for professional positions. It is when Asian Pacific Americans are slated for managerial positions that they are most likely to face challenges.

34. B. Foster, G. Jackson, W. Cross, B. Jackson, and R. Hardiman, "Workforce Diversity and Business," *Training and Development Journal* (April 1988): 38-42.

35. T. H. Cox, S. Lobel, and P. McLeod, "Effects of Ethnic Group Culture Differences on Cooperative and Competitive Behavior in a Group Task," *Academy of Management Journal* 34 (December 1991): 827-47.

36. Taylor H. Cox, "The Multicultural Organization," *Academy of Management Executive* 34 (May 1991): 34-7.

37. Five of the executives and management consultants interviewed are Asians who have succeeded in the business world. The other two, although not Asians or Pacific Islanders, have worked with people from those cultures and are familiar with the problems facing Asian Pacific Americans in the workplace. For the sake of easy reading, several conversations have been consolidated into this section of the text.

38. Gerald Andrews, "Mistrust, the Hidden Obstacle to Empowerment," *HR* Magazine (November 1993): 66-74.

39. All of the executives interviewed for this book more or less agreed on this point. The Center for Creative Leadership, a nonprofit educational organization founded in 1970 in Greensboro, North Carolina, focuses on research and training in management. In 1988, the Center interviewed seventy-five women executives and reached the same conclusion.

40. Kathy E. Kram, *Mentoring at Work: Developmental Relationships in Organizational Life* (Glenview, IL: Scott, Foresman, 1985).

41. Kenneth Labich, "Take Control of Your Career," *Fortune* (18 November 1991): 87-96.

42. Michael Harrison Bond, in his *Beyond the Chinese Face: Insights from Psychology* (Hong Kong: Oxford University Press, 1994), describes the construction of time by Europeans and Asians. He defines the northern European system of "doing one thing at a time" as monochronic, or M-time. Asians tend to do many things at once and so are polychronic and use P-time. The approach under M-time is to put each event into a compartment and focus all energies on the completion of one event before proceeding to the next. P-time stresses involvement of people and completion of transactions (however long this takes) rather than adherence to preset schedules. If a particular interaction is not completed, a longer time perspective and a cyclical view of time will reduce any sense of panic. Everything will happen "in its own time."

# Eight

# External Strategies

*Globalization, Family Unity,
and Organizational Development*

## The Effect of Globalization

"Everything in America is imported," said Zack. "Our strength and our ability to generate continuous progress in this country are based on outside capital and resources, which include human resources." Zack is a history major in college. He is also a native Californian who proudly traces his ancestry to at least a half-dozen cultures on several continents.

"Yeah, I know what you mean," replied April. April is a business major and a second-generation Asian Pacific American. "Burger King is owned by a British company, A&P is controlled by German capital, Columbia Pictures is Japanese-owned, and a Hong Kong corporation just bought the posh Regent Beverly Wilshire Hotel, which is pampering celebrities from around the world. Nowadays, almost any product weighing more than ten pounds and costing more than ten dollars is a global product combining parts or processes from different nations.[1] We also import human resources from abroad, from personnel for high-tech industries to farm laborers. This has been going on for ages.''

"As a matter of fact," said Zack, "this whole population is imported except, of course, the small percent who are Native Americans. When Christopher Columbus stepped ashore in Hispañola in 1492, he claimed the land as Spanish territory, despite the obvious fact that the place already belonged to someone else—the native Indians. He gave no thought to the rights of the local inhabitants; and those who followed Columbus didn't either. Initially, the French were more considerate, but the English, Dutch, Portuguese, and so on apparently felt justified in going wherever they could and taking whatever they found.[2] Don't you find it hypocritical for their descendants today to have anti-immigrant sentiments like 'Newcomer go home, hands off America'?''

"I think some people are running scared," April said. "They want America to return to an earlier time, when certain classes and ethnicities owned everything. But there is no turning back against a global movement! Some of our politicians call for sealing our borders, pulling the U.S. out of NAFTA and GATT,[3] imposing tariffs on each and every foreign-made product. This would be absolutely suicidal. What is an American product anyway? One where the raw material is domestic? Or one that is processed here? One where the parts are made here, or one where the parts are assembled here? It's not unusual for an 'American' car—a car assembled in America, that is—to have parts from Japan, Korea, and Mexico. A 'Japanese' car may contain American-made parts. How far back do you have to trace the origins of these things? And by the way, did you know that Jaguar is owned by Ford, and Chrysler owns Lamborghini?''[4]

"If it's difficult to sort out products and product lines," asked Zack, "how do you sort out the people whose ideas have contributed to American society? Assimilation is a lifelong process. Do the 'legitimate and rightful heirs' of the founding fathers really have more rights than the rest of us to sovereignty? Believe it or not, that's what one political candidate recently claimed!''

"No way! Hasn't he heard about the global village? Anybody who wants to be a leader today better realize that the global village is already here," said April. "Just think about the products you use, the clothes you wear, the food you eat, and all the people whom you met today. Everything and everyone comes from all over the world. I was vacationing with my folks in Sydney three years ago, in Vancouver two years ago, in London and Hong Kong last year. The products we use and the people we meet are the same rainbow coalition; the whole planet is going global. How could America go back to the days of the founding fathers? The human spirit is intermingling. Music has already been fused."

"Yes, MTV International—not to mention CNN, hamburgers, pizza, disco, and karaoke."

"It's the ease of transportation, too," said April, "the fact that values and ideas and communication can travel throughout the world in seconds via telephone, fax, e-mail, the World Wide Web. Actual products travel more slowly, but they still arrive within days."

"Any country that fights against the trend and tries to be isolationist instead of globalized will be left out.[5] America's main role in the future won't be as a military superpower, but as a multicultural superpower.[6] That's America's greatest strength. Asian Pacific Americans can serve a pivotal role in the process."

"Did you read about the Association of Computing Machinery's chess tournament?" April asked. "They pitted reigning World Champion Gary Kasparov against IBM's chess-playing computer, Deep Blue,[7] for a week-long, six-game match. The human champion lost the first game, but beat the silicon challenger in the next two rounds. This type of technology is really exciting. We're on our way to solving complex, intricate, real-world problems like data mining in financial markets, traffic and cargo scheduling at busy international airports. The project manager for Deep Blue is C.J. Tan. The chief designer is an IBM research scientist named Fen-Hsiung Hsu. Both Tan and Hsu are Asian Pacific Americans."[8]

"So I guess we chalk up another victory for the model minority?" asked Zack. "I suppose this may be an important victory. You know, April, I've taken Asian Pacific American history, and I've read Dr. Wu's book. I think the individual cases she presented really show the significance of the individual personality. Each of us is a unique human being with unique experiences. Yet a significant commonality among us is the determination to create a better life for ourselves and for our families."

"Yes, I agree," said April. "When I read Dr. Wu's book, I identified with Nevin. His background is very similar to mine.[9] Sometimes, I don't fit in quite right with White Americans, but I'm not entirely Asian either. The family does load a lot of expectations on us ABCs. Just because we learned English as children, they think we've got it made and they expect us to do better than they did. You know what I mean?"

"Unfortunately, I am on my own and do not have a close family," said Zack. "But I am inclined to think that the model minority phenomenon is partly a political strategy. It wasn't America that transformed the Asians in this country from 'lowly coolies' to 'model minority' citizens."

"I know that! When my parents came here in the 60s, they were already educated, civic-minded, high-principled. Is that what you mean?" exclaimed April.

"This is what I mean: according to historical accounts, the first wave of Asian Pacific American immigrants to this country had been laborers in the old country. In those days, the kind of Asians and Pacific Islanders who would leave their homeland and venture into North and South America were the ones forced to change by economic necessity. Their family's livelihood depended on their taking a risk and going abroad to earn extra money. They expected ultimately to return home, and they expected to be able to provide a better living for their families. That's one of the reasons women were left behind: the husbands were only supposed to be gone temporarily."

"I remember Professor Takaki explained it according to a 'hostage theory,'" said April. "Women were kept home in order to ensure that their absent husbands would not become prodigal sons in America.[10] They had to send remittances home to fulfill their filial obligations."

"Right," continued Zack. "Those people were peasants back home, and some were even outcasts. They were from the lowest echelons of society. But the descendants of those who remained [and] grew up in this country had begun developing a whole new mind-set. After World War II, upper-middle class, better educated Asians began to come here and found rampant discrimination against Asian Pacific Americans. However, the children of some of those peasants were already making changes and becoming stronger. If it hadn't been for the Chinese civil war and the Korean War, most of those upper-class people would never have come here. They might come here as tourists today and stay at the Regent Beverly Wilshire Hotel!"[11]

"My parents said that prior to the changes in the immigration law in 1965, the only opportunity to enter this country was in the pursuit of a higher education. Later, investors who could afford to invest a million dollars or more were also welcome to step on American soil," said April.

"Yes, but it was under precisely those conditions that the whole transformation of the Asian Pacific American population occurred. The transformation was in the type of employment, a change from busboys and laundry ladies to high-demand professionals and venture capitalists. It is the professionals and venture capitalists who are behind the success statistics. They are highly educated and often extremely wealthy. Their children are highly unlikely to disappoint their parents."

"I'm sure you're right about that. Not only do the parents pressure the kids to do well, but there's the 'saving face' factor too. Parents want desperately to brag about their children's accomplishments. They don't want to feel that they 'lose face' to the other relatives or to friends. If the children stray away from tradition, the parents are guilty of not fulfilling their responsibilities. There are a lot of psychological ramifications. I know my brothers and I are all stressed out over it," April sighed.

"So," said Zack, "what you're really saying is that Asian Pacific Americans are 'imported' high achievers. If it hadn't been for the Vietnam War, sixty percent of Asian Pacific Americans today would probably be college graduates—compared to only twenty-four percent for Whites! How would they like that kind of model minority? A bit out of proportion? And the best thing is that the U.S. federal government didn't have to pay a dime to educate them; these were the new, improved model, completely pre-educated immigrants. The minute they arrived, they started paying taxes and contributing to Social Security. How come no one says anything about that fact? Most of the media attention goes to the underprivileged. The war in Vietnam brought many new refugees during the 70s and 80s. The Cambodians, Laotians, and Hmongs may just be making the most difficult adjustment in all of human history! Imagine going from a peaceful, rural life to the turmoil in the inner cities of modern society! They have the highest poverty level, and the highest welfare-dependency rate.[12] Nevertheless, quite a few are now making it as entrepreneurs, and their children are starting to perform very well in school."

"I know the reason for that," said April. "The ones who had made it to this country in the first wave, around 1976, generally came from the educated classes. A majority of them actually spoke English quite well. Those of the second wave barely escaped with their lives and survived enormous hardships just to come here. They had to have the kind of spirit that takes risks. They had to be persistent and tenacious. That sets them apart from the ones who remained behind."[13]

"Yes. So, everything in America is imported—even the model minority!"

\*     \*     \*     \*     \*

April and Zack's conversation reflects the changing world around us. With the increases in global products and multinational corporations, organizations are now able to cross national borders quite easily. A search for product components, raw materials, or human resources can be carried out across the world. Communications, transportation, and the exchange of information have never before been so accessible. Changing technology has also played a very important part in globalization. Against a backdrop of all these changes, Asian Pacific Americans, including various recent immigrants and refugee groups, still place a high value on family unity. These individuals are determined to improve their families' lives despite challenging conditions. It is also suggested above that if there is a "model minority," it is imported as well.

Regardless, Asian Pacific Americans serve as an important link between the United States, Asia, and the rest of the world. This is a symbiotic relationship in which the role played by Asian Pacific Americans must not be ignored. The American economy depends on the contributions of its Asian Pacific component. Behind U.S. technological achievement, which serves as a model for the world, are the talents of thousands of Asian Pacific Americans.

## Family Values

Fifteen years ago, a research study was conducted to try to determine why so many Asian Pacific American women have been successful in traditionally male-dominated professions.[14] How did they manage to cope with not only meeting the demands of a changing work environment while developing professional competence, but also successfully blending work with family responsibilities and integrating their traditional values with the values of American society?

A recent attempt to locate the subjects of the original study turned up nine of them. Seven of these nine had retired, but all nine continued to lead well-adjusted lives within the American culture. Over the years, they had become more "fashionable" and "modern" both in their appearances and thinking, more outgoing and sociable, more flexible in their attitudes, and they seemed to have comfortably (if not completely) resolved all East-West value conflicts, synthesizing their Asian cultural traditions with the norms of modern Western society and the demands of the workplace.

Although two of the women did not have daughters, there were eight daughters among the other seven. All of the daughters had become professionals (one physician, three attorneys, one news reporter, a financial analyst, an accountant, and one computer firm manager), and all were successful in their chosen fields. All of the daughters were extroverted, forward-looking, assertive, ambitious, quick, spontaneous, and communicative. A decade

---

Box 8.1
*Summary of the Professional Immigrant Women Study*

First, in comparison with European American professional women, Asian Pacific American women were found to be less aggressive, less ambitious, and not so quick, spontaneous, or versatile, possibly as a result of the rigid nature of their traditional cultural influences. As children, under the influence of their fathers, most of them also developed a tendency to be obedient and, moreover, to do whatever they have been told to do as well as they can possibly do it. Growing up in this highly disciplined and organized environment, they chose fields of endeavor that matched up with their needs for structured situations, such as science and mathematics.

Second, the cultural changes and new social environment that the subjects had experienced required them to learn coping techniques and put them into practice. Studying disciplines such as the physical sciences helped the subjects to develop a realistic, practical, and highly contemporary worldview that provided them not only with economic stability and social mobility but also accomplished these things without completely sacrificing their original cultural values. By directing their focused energy toward their work, the subjects were able to increase self-esteem and to build self-confidence through a job well done.

Third, the bilingual nature of the subjects' backgrounds may also have contributed to their choice of careers in the erstwhile male-dominated physical sciences because of the perception that linguistic ability is of relatively little importance in the "hard" sciences as an indicator of technical competence and ability.

*Study conducted by Diana T. L. Wu, 1981.*

---

earlier, virtually none of these qualities had been strong in their mothers' profiles (see Box 8.1).

Were the changes in the personalities of the younger generation of Asian Pacific American women due to conscious, deliberate training by the mothers and other family members? Or were the changes influenced by peers and the American social environment in which the daughters grew up? The answers to these questions at first seemed inconsistent.

"Maybe it's in the genes or the American diet, or something in the air."

"I definitely have developed my *own* personality," one person replied succinctly. "I think the formula is one part inner traits, one part external attributes, and one part good luck to be born into the right kind of family."

When the various answers were sorted out, a unified theme emerged: all seven of the families maintained a network of kinship relations. Their family circles included grandparents, uncles, aunts, and cousins. Some of these relatives may have been seen only infrequently, but they remained in contact by phone and other means and knew they could always count on one another's support. The sense of belonging was unmistakably present. At least two or three times a year, family reunions had been held, and, during the rest of the year, news of the extended family was constantly exchanged at the dinner table: "Auntie May just received a big promotion, and Cousin Tina was just admitted to Harvard."

In addition to sharing good news with their children, parents also compared the fortunes of various family members: "Cousin William now manages the Asian division. Poor Tom is still an engineer."

Because of these conversations, the children were constantly aware of the high expectations their families held for them as well as the avenues by which they were expected to achieve their goals.

As a consequence of maintaining kinship bonds, every one of the families in the study had taken one or more of their relatives into the family home for a period of time. Cross-cultural studies show that when a household includes family members beyond the immediate parents and their offspring, the children tend to be better behaved, yet less harshly disciplined.[15] Unacceptable behavior is prohibited, but spanking and yelling at the children are less frequent. The parents are more relaxed and at ease in their attitudes toward the children, especially when another female relative such as a grandmother or aunt is available to help minister to the needs of the younger children. The emotional tension between children and the biological parents is likely to be buffered. The parents do not have monopolistic control over the children's sense of security and satisfaction, and this in turn may give greater freedom to their development.[16]

The influence of the environment in which one lives has significant effects on one's life, but the urge to attain competence in dealing with the environment stems from one's personality and childhood upbringing.[17] Having close adult relatives under the family roof would also contribute to the development of interpersonal skills and role competence. It would also help provide a substantial foundation for self-confidence which may have contributed much to their successes later in adult life.[18] On the other hand, none of the daughters openly contributed her successes entirely to her relatives' influences (see Box 8.2).

"My mother and father encouraged me to do whatever I wanted," said Paula. "But it was clear that whatever project I pursued, I was expected to

---

Box 8.2

*Role Expectations and the Self-Fulfilling Prophecy*

The self-fulfilling prophecy theory states that if children are predicted by teachers or other influential adults to improve academically, they will tend to improve in fact. Social psychologists Robert Rosenthal and Lenora Jacobson of Harvard University conducted the following experiment at an elementary school to test the self-fulfilling prophecy theory.

First- and second-grade students were given a standard IQ test but were told they were taking the "Harvard Test." Their teachers were told that this test would identify high academic achievers.

The investigators then chose 20% of the students at random and informed the teachers that these were the high achievers. The teachers were also told that a second test would be administered after one year and that nothing needed to be done until then. After a year, the students were retested, and the supposed "high achievers" were found to have made larger gains in their test scores than the "regular" students. In addition, teachers assessed the "high achievers" as having made marked gains in reading ability compared to the other students.

These results support the self-fulfilling prophecy theory and suggest that children will try to meet the expectations held for them. On the other hand, if teachers believe the prophecies themselves, they might influence events accordingly and help the predictions come true.

---

commit myself to it one hundred percent until it was completed. I discovered that I am good with computers during a school science fair, so I majored in computer science at college. Because I also have good interpersonal skills, I am now a department head managing a staff of eight computer scientists— and enjoying it! I really don't think the fact that I'm an Asian woman made a difference in the workplace. I am competent at what I do, I know it, and everyone at work knows it, and that's that."

"Dealing with clients," said Lily, "you may meet some people sometimes who are unkind, but they're just jerks and they come in all colors—black, white, brown, yellow, whatever."

Wendy agreed. "There will always be unruly people on this earth, and you can't let them get to you. I usually handle people well, so there's never been a big issue about my being an Asian Pacific American woman."

Two of the women who participated in the original study did not have daughters. One of them, an educational administrator, has three sons; the other one, a physical scientist, has one son. All four of the sons are working professionals: one is a medical researcher with both Ph.D. and M.D. degrees; one is an oncologist; one is an attorney; one is an engineer. All are happily married and lead constructive lives.

As the sons were growing up, they, like the daughters, experienced a network of kinship relationships. However, their fathers seem to have played a much stronger role in their development than was generally the case with daughters. An interesting observation here is that the sons perceive themselves as being mellow like their fathers and less aggressive than their mothers. The most valuable gift these young men received from their parents, aside from the various intellectual skills imparted during childhood, was a sense of being cherished and valued unconditionally, no matter what. "We always knew there was someone there to listen, to work things through with, and to share our feelings of joy and pride."

The experiences of the son of the research scientist were unique in several ways. Identified as a gifted child at an early age, this boy was reading medical journals at the age of six. He entered college at age fifteen and began medical school at eighteen. His parents also enrolled him in music classes, and one year he won a state-wide competition for young pianists. Obviously he was not only gifted but highly motivated toward achievement.

"I received a lot of structure and support from my parents. My mother was always there for me to ask questions, and if she couldn't answer me right then, she always took time to find out, no matter how busy she was. I remember being really bored in kindergarten. I behaved very destructively toward school property and other children as well. The teacher told my mother that I was very bad and on my way to becoming a delinquent, but my parents refused to believe any such thing. They took me to a psychologist and had me tested. Then they placed me in third grade as a teacher's aid, teaching other kids to read and do math homework. That's how I went through the school system: as a teacher's aid, and bringing my own books to school to read at my own level. I am grateful that I was born into the right family. I shudder to think what would have become of me if I had been born into a different family situation."

So, the support and commitment of family to children seem to be the most important ingredients in bringing up resilient, happy, healthy, and achievement-oriented children. One participant expressed it this way: "I grew up among many close relatives. We always enjoyed the extended family; the sense of belonging was always there. My father was strict by today's standards, but it served us well. He exerted authority and set standards, so we knew what's wrong and what's right. There was a definite expectation to do well in school, and we were disciplined if we strayed away from his instruction. There were always other people around to give us additional support.

"I feel sorry for the young American mothers of today. The nuclear family structure leaves them without any help. It's awfully lonely and difficult to struggle alone. The schools are in very sad shape in large cities. There are violent TV programs, drug problems; the whole culture is not conducive to the proper development of young kids into responsible members of society.

"I think young Asian Pacific Americans can contribute a lot to society by forming community support groups outside of their own families to help improve values and relationships in our society."

In summary, it seems that not only the second generation of Asian Pacific American women, those whose mothers found success in traditionally male-dominated fields, have continued the quest for self-actualization and further advanced their own positions in American society; the second generation of Asian Pacific American sons are equally well situated, and again because of the traditional respect for family values, a reverence for knowledge, and an unwavering determination to make tomorrow better than today.[19]

As an added note of interest, nine out of the twelve Asian Pacific American sons and daughters married outside of their own ethnicity. This may be too small a sample to be deemed significant, but it is still interesting and may suggest that factors such as external appearance and ethnic identity are giving way to factors such as inner feelings and personal values and beliefs. One's identity is becoming less determined by outward form and more determined by inner qualities and value systems. We are also witnessing the development of a pan-ethnic identity. Perhaps such changes are a natural part of the process of human development. Because of globalization, we are seeing the beginning of a true unification of humanity, a harmonizing of cultures within a borderless world.

The following pages consider some steps that can be taken and some policies that organizations, public and private, can adopt to help bring people together cooperatively to work toward common goals, to encourage family unity, and to bring up the next generation of Americans as more responsible human beings freed of the constraints of prejudice and divisiveness.

## Organizational Responsibilities

Corporate America has been, in many ways, several steps ahead of the debates over multicultural issues that are still ongoing in many facets of our society.

Robert Reich points out, as stated at the beginning of this chapter, that we are living through a transformation. To ensure global competitiveness, a nation's commitment to developing its people at all organizational levels is essential.[20] In 1980, organizations placed almost no emphasis on promoting members of ethnic or minority groups. Today, more than half of the Fortune 1000 companies have some sort of program aimed at advancing minority personnel.[21] Most of these programs are related to marketing strategies and intended to increase corporate profits; any humanitarian benefits are essentially "positive spillover."

Corporations have learned some facts about Asian Pacific Americans. In 1992, this group spent 120 billion dollars on goods and services within the U.S.[22] Corporations know that Asian Americans place three times as many overseas telephone calls as the average American, so it should be no surprise that television ads for long-distance services feature happy Asian faces.[23] Chinese Americans drink nearly twice as much cognac as the average American.[24] Koreans consume more Spam than does any other ethnic group.

As the Asian Pacific American consumer base increases and corporate America consequently earns greater profits, companies have recruited increasing numbers of Asian Pacific American workers to help target Asian Pacific American consumers. However, few personnel programs have been established specifically to train the new Asian Pacific American workers in getting along in a multicultural organization. Most existing diversity programs were designed and implemented entirely within a "Black versus White" context.

In recent years, as corporations have confronted an increasingly complex social environment, diversity managers have been positioned to deal with all segments of the workforce. Typically, the diversity of the human spectrum is represented in programs by a series of polarities: "age" becomes young versus old, "gender" becomes men or women, the "physically challenged" oppose the "able-bodied," gays and lesbians oppose "straights," and ethnics are opposed to Whites.[25] In theory, every Asian Pacific American will fall on one side or the other of each of these categories or divisions; however, this does not mean that he or she will identify with each of the categorizations that apply.

The success of a diversity program will depend in large part upon a diversity manager's ability to identify specific problems and their underlying causes correctly.[26] Although some diversity managers do take a specific interest in the problems facing Asian Pacific Americans in particular, the majority of them undoubtedly do not. In effect, there are few corporate

Box 8.3
*Individual Challenges and the Ethnically Diverse Workforce*

The diversity management training programs for White individuals in organizations deal mostly with attitude. The programs strive to achieve the following:

1. Understanding that people must be treated fairly and equitably, but there are cultural differences among them that can cause them to behave differently and hold different norms and values.

2. Building awareness about the different cultures. People from certain cultures may view certain tasks differently, have different feelings with regard to some practices, and may use different mental processes and learning styles.

3. Developing tolerance toward people who do not share one's sense of self and space, conception of time, command of the English language, or eating habits, yet they are productive workers.

4. Maintaining open communication and a nonthreatening atmosphere for open discussion. If certain behaviors or work habits seem unusual, request an explanation. If good-natured kidding seems offensive to others, realize that it may be interpreted as sexist or racist. Only with continued open discussion and communication can we achieve mutual understanding and empathy in organizations.

*(See note 28 for further information.)*

programs in place designed specifically to recruit, promote, and train Asian Pacific Americans. Generally speaking, companies located in metropolitan areas where large numbers of Asian Pacific Americans reside are far more sensitive and current in their diversity training programs for Asian Pacific American workers. As stated in earlier chapters, the learning and socialization process is a two-way proposition. More organizations today also have programs to challenge old assumptions and help White managers learn to relate to a diverse workforce and the multicultural workplace[27] (see Box 8.3).

What can companies do specifically to attract and promote Asian Pacific American managers? The following ten suggestions are derived from the Asian Pacific Americans interviewed for this book[29]:

*1. Identify and recruit qualified Asian Pacific American employees.* "Often, the recruitment efforts directed at Asian Pacific Americans are limited to the big-name schools only," complained Lara, who is Samoan. "We feel that the Pacific Islanders are completely left out and would like to see companies expanding their efforts to include us and the less privileged, who may not have the credentials but do have the ability to do the job required." Similar sentiments have been echoed by the Southeast Asian Americans, who are the newest arrivals.

2. *Devise diversity training programs for all employees.* "We appreciated and benefited from the company diversity training programs, but sometimes felt that too much time was spent addressing differences. We'd like to hear more about the commonalities; the company goals and objectives should bring out more of the things that unify us as employees." Many would definitely like to see language and communication included among the training program components.

3. *Facilitate coaching and mentoring for all employees.* "We would like to have constant coaching and mentoring to ease the tension and fear among new employees. It's also a good way to pass on organizational values and culture and to ensure consistent understanding among Asian Pacific American workers." This socialization process will have enormous benefits for new arrivals and immigrant workers who have spent their prior working lives in other countries.

4. *Establish job enrichment and enlargement programs.* "It has been shown in many studies that such programs really work to everyone's advantage. Companies that implement them also have successful track records which show that broadening the range of experiences available to employees will increase their overall effectiveness." The practice of increasing the job range and job depth for individuals has been found to have a positive correlation with job satisfaction.[30]

5. *Create a positive organizational culture.* "An organization where everyone feels that they are part of the organization and are making contributions to the workplace has the strongest basis for a high-quality working life. Committed workers will reduce waste, absenteeism, and the turnover rate, and increase the bottom line." To ensure its competitive advantage, an organization must further the course of multiculturalism and promote workforce diversity.

*6. Conduct well-constructed performance appraisal and feedback.* "Employees need to know where they stand, need to understand how they can improve themselves to achieve common goals, and need to know how others view them in the organizational setting. The kind of performance appraisal and feedback system used, and any testing employed, should be designed with fairness in mind for minorities and Asian Pacific American workers." Feedback about performance should always be given in a private setting and in a nonthreatening manner. "Saving face" is a very important factor for most Asian Pacific Americans.

*7. Ensure fairness for both managers and subordinates.* "There should be a uniform system and procedures for the selection and promotion of personnel. Merit and effective performance must remain as the basis for selecting potential senior managers, whether they are Asian Pacific Americans or not." At the same time, senior managers should understand and be aware of cultural differences. In particular, it is critical for managers to realize that not all rewards are equally desired by or able to motivate all individuals.

*8. Initiate a leadership and career development training program.* "We would like to see high-potential Asian Pacific Americans being identified and given opportunities for more exposure at the senior leadership level, and encouraged by top management to participate in decision-making functions." Allow Asian Pacific Americans to have visibility by presenting their own work and demonstrating their competence. Encourage them to overcome anxiety about their accented English.

*9. Offer opportunities for continuous learning.* "Companies need to offer tuition credits and reimbursements for college courses to upgrade skills. With the continuous introduction of newer and faster business technologies, employers need to ensure that personnel are always learning new skills to keep pace with the rapidly changing world." Most Asian Pacific Americans would rather sacrifice pay increases and bonuses for an opportunity to become better educated and increase their skills.

*10. Support the family!* Last but not least, it is extremely important for organizations to support workers' commitments to family values. The general population, and many Asian Pacific American men and women alike, would like to see companies lighten workers' burdens through such measures as providing on-site child care where children can be close to working parents.

Several subjects in this study believe that the majority of Asian Pacific Americans would be willing to receive a salary cut in exchange for a company-sponsored child care center.

A general consensus is that maternity leave could be extended up to six months, and new fathers could be given up to six weeks off as well. At present, standard practice in this regard is to provide six weeks' leave for new mothers and up to one week for new fathers. In addition to having a positive effect on worker morale, many people also believe that extending these periods is important for early childhood development.

For families with older children, organizations can provide flexible work hours so that parents can spend time with their children, attend to other family matters, and provide more responsible parenting. A recent phenomenon is that many middle-aged women are now facing the problem of providing "elder care" for their parents. It would be an added incentive for Asian Pacific American workers to receive assistance in this area.

Companies can also allow more job sharing. In some organizations, husband-and-wife teams have been allowed to share single jobs. More commonly, two women employees will share a single job, allowing each to spend the other half of her time with her children and her family.

As one subject expressed it, "No country can develop a strong economy if business is going to be undermined by family. We are all connected, all in this together. Family and business should go hand in hand."

On a macro level, organizations, regardless of whether they are in the private or public sector, must make a commitment *not* to view their employees as disposable commodities. CEOs and other higher-up executives in decision-making and leadership positions must ensure that the ethical concerns within their organizations are given the highest priority; support the establishment and implementation of viable programs to develop all employees' potential to develop and contribute, regardless of their ethnicity; devise company rules and policies that encourage and foster family unity; and create a positive atmosphere and business climate of cooperation that values human resources. Only then can corporate America remain a strong enough economic force to lead the rest of the world.

## One Final Note

In today's diverse workforce, Asian Pacific Americans may provide the sort of "new blood" that organizations will need to manage diversity to company advantage and to revitalize American industry for continued economic growth. Higher education continues to be identified as a "lightning rod" for Asian Pacific Americans to achieve upward mobility and a first step on the American corporate ladder. Asian Pacific American workers, men and women alike, are also endorsing the benefits of being assertive and more aggressive in their thinking and behavior. They have come to understand that being more assertive need not entail a compromise of their principles.

Asian Pacific American workers—men and women alike—should not be content to limit their energy and intelligence to enhancing their own job training and professional development but should involve themselves in the process of creating a better working environment for all Americans. They should support the growth and development of their communities to help enrich the lives of others. Whether for the sake of the economy or humanity, Asian Pacific Americans must work together with all other groups to better educate themselves and others. They should be creative and support the realm of the arts, and they should promote the health and welfare of all peoples. Only then can the quality of Americans' working lives be truly equitable and the working environment be enjoyed by all.

In our pluralistic society, we are learning to respect each group, but we must also work as a whole toward common goals. No one group should outshine the rest or serve as the "model" for all others. Our nation must pull together for continuing development and growth. For the U.S. to remain an economic superpower into the next century, American business and political leaders must also endeavor to become the "model" for the rest of the world to emulate. The challenge for the future, for all nations and cultures, will be to produce inspirational leaders who are globally oriented, ethically grounded, and enthusiastic about diversity.

◆ ◆ ◆ ◆ ◆

## SUGGESTED RESEARCH PAPER/FINAL REPORT TOPICS

1. Past and present contributions of Asian Pacific Americans to America.
2. A look at the future prospects of Asian Pacific American development.
3. Asian Pacific American influences on the organization of the future.
4. An overview of the Asian Pacific American motivational profile.
5. The role of family among different Asian Pacific American ethnicities.

6. Compare and contrast two Asian Pacific American families with different ethnic backgrounds.
7. Appropriate workplace behavior for Asian Pacific Americans.
8. Breaking through the glass ceiling.
9. The underprivileged Asian Pacific Americans.
10. Economic diversity among Asian Pacific Americans.
11. Asian Pacific American professionals (choose scientists, artists, etc.)
12. Asian Pacific American influences on high technology.
13. Expected spousal behavior within upper-level American management.
14. The best future careers for Asian Pacific Americans.
15. Assistance and support available to Asian Pacific Americans.
16. The proper forms of behavior and protocol for international business functions.
17. Effective communication in organizations.
18. The dos and don'ts in the office setting.
19. Providing effective leadership for diversity in organizations.
20. A study of Asian Pacific American entrepreneurs.

## NOTES

1. The remark, reported in the *Houston Post* for 2 February 1992, was made by Robert B. Reich, a Harvard political economist and U.S. Secretary of Labor in the first term of the Clinton administration.

2. Recommended readings for students interested in ethnic studies and history are Christopher Columbus's letter of 14 March 1493 to Gabriel Sanchez, Treasurer of the Spanish court; and "Brief Relation of the Destruction of the Indies," written by Spanish missionary and historian Fray Bartolome de las Casas, which recounts the cruelty of the Spanish conquest of the Indians. More than 15 million Native American men, women, and children were killed in a period of forty years. "Of Cannibals," in *The Complete Essays of Montaigne,* trans. Donald Frame (Palo Alto, CA: Stanford University Press, 1948), offers an account of how Indians were tortured on the pretext of piety and religious zeal.

3. NAFTA, the North American Free Trade Agreement, took effect in 1994 and aims to phase out all tariffs and quotas between and among the United

States, Canada, and Mexico. GATT, the General Agreement on Tariffs and Trade, is a worldwide trade agreement among more than 100 nations seeking to reduce trade barriers and increase world trade.

4. Many foreign capitalists are heavily invested in the United States. See James Bennet, "Mercedes Selects Alabama Site," *New York Times,* 30 September 1993; Susan Dentzer, "The Coming Global Boom," *U.S. News & World Report,* 16 July 1990, 22-7; and Rob Norton, "Strategies for the New Export Boom," *Fortune,* 22 August 1994, 67-83.

5. Read the article by John Barnett, Rita Weathersby, and John Aram, "American Cultural Values: Shedding Cowboy Ways for Global Thinking," *Business Forum* (Winter/Spring 1995): 9-13.

6. The quote was attributed to Federico Mayor Zaragoza, Director General of UNESCO, in a special issue of *Time* magazine (Fall 1993).

7. The chess-playing computer, Deep Blue, possesses a brute-force computing speed capable of examining 200 million playing positions per second, or 50 billion positions in three minutes.

8. According to "Gary Kasparov's Toughest Match," an article in *Asian Week* (21 May 1996), both Tan and Hsu and Chinese Americans, one from Taiwan and the other from China.

9. See chap. 5, "Sitting in Two Chairs at Once: The Second Generation."

10. Ronald Takaki, *Strangers from a Different Shore* (Boston: Little, Brown, 1989).

11. The Regent Beverly Wilshire Hotel and others in the U.S. are now managed and financed by conglomerates of Asian investor groups. For interesting accounts of how some leading-edge, wealthy Asians are internationalizing, read Mitchell Pacelle, "Going Global: Asian Investors Buy up Hotels in U.S., Europe, But Move Cautiously," *Wall Street Journal* 19 February 1997 (http://wsj.com).

12. The degree of difficulty in adjusting varies considerably among Southeast Asian refugees. For a good account, see Ngoan Le, "The Case of the Southeast Asian Refugees," in *The State of Asian Pacific Americans* (Los Angeles: LEAP Publications, 1993).

13. Recommended reading for more information: B. B. Dunning, "Vietnamese in America: The Adaptation of the 1975-1979 Arrivals," in *Refugees as Immigrants,* ed. D. W. Haines (Totowa, NJ: Rowman and Littlefield, 1989); N. Caplan, J. K. Whitmore, and M. H. Choy, *The Boat People and Their Achievement in America* (Ann Arbor: University of Michigan Press, 1989).

14. Diana T. L. Wu, "Immigrant Women in Professional Occupations: Inherent Abilities or Focused Energy?" (Working paper, Saint Mary's College of California, 1981).

15. Margaret Blenkner, *Social Work and Family Relationships in Latin Life* (Englewood Cliffs, NJ: Prentice Hall, 1965); J. W. Whiting and B. B. Whiting, "Contributions of Anthropology to the Methods of Studying Child Rearing," in *Handbook of Research in Child Development* (New York: John Wiley, 1980).

16. Robert W. White, *The Enterprise of Living: Growth and Organization in Personality* (New York: Holt, Rinehart & Winston, 1972), chap. 4.

17. Ibid., chap. 9.

18. Ibid., chap. 12.

19. The sentence is taken from President Clinton's Chinese New Year greetings, 19 February 1996.

20. Robert B. Reich, *The Work of Nations: Preparing Ourselves for 21st Century Capitalism* (New York: Knopf, 1991).

21. Among the companies that actively promote the commitment are Apple Computer, Avon, Corning, DuPont, Hewlett-Packard, Honeywell, Pacific Bell, Procter & Gamble, U.S. West, and Xerox. See "12 Companies That Do the Right Thing," *Working Woman* (January 1991): 82.

22. Thomas McCarrol, "It's a Mass Market No More," *Time* special issue (Fall 1993): 60-5.

23. The long-distance telephone companies' ad campaigns are not limited just to television. To target specific Asian Pacific American customers, AT&T, Sprint, and MCI have each recruited an aggressive group of Asian Pacific American operators with native language abilities. They match Asian Pacific American personnel with potential customers according to country of origin. Local telephone companies also compile Yellow Pages directories in many Asian languages for their customers.

24. Cognac is a congratulatory drink used for celebrations and festivities in Chinese tradition. One might equate cognac in China with champagne in Western functions.

25. The entire preconvention workshop of the 1993 Academy of Management annual meeting was devoted to research on diversity in organizations. Many of the conference participants expressing this sentiment in regard to current diversity programs.

26. See Sara Ryne and Benson Rosen, "What Makes Diversity Programs Work?" *Human Resources* (October 1994): 67-75.

27. According to "Challenges of Retaining a Diverse Workforce," an article in "Working Together" (*Boston Globe,* 7 March 1994), diversity

training for managers is currently the most popular cultural awareness program. It is offered by 63 percent of U.S. companies, and an additional 16 percent are planning to implement similar programs soon.

28. Compiled by Diana T. L. Wu during years of management consulting work and further influenced by an article by Anthony Carnevale and Susan Stone, "Diversity—Beyond the Gold Rule," *Training and Development* (October 1994): 44.

29. Derived from the management consultancy, research, and teaching experience of the author.

30. The pioneering work in this area was done by Charles Walker and Robert Guest, *The Man on the Assembly Line* (Cambridge, MA: Harvard University Press, 1952).

# Bibliography

Agbayani-Siewert, Pauline. 1990. Filipino American families. Paper presented at the thirty-sixth annual meeting of the Council of Social Work Education, New Orleans.

Agbayani-Siewert, Pauline, and Linda Revilla. 1995. Filipino Americans. In *Asian Americans: Contemporary Trends and Issues,* ed. Ruben G. Rumbaut. Thousand Oaks, CA: Sage.

Alderfer, Clayton P. 1963. Job attitudes in management: Perceived deficiencies in need fulfillment as a function of size of the company. *Journal of Applied Psychology* (October): 386-97.

———. 1972. *Existence, relatedness, and growth: Human needs in organizational settings.* New York: Free Press.

Allport, G. W. 1954. *The nature of prejudice.* Reading, MA: Addison-Wesley.

Almirol, E. B. 1988. *Reflections on shattered windows: Promises and prospects for Asian American studies.* Seattle: Washington State University Press.

Andrews, Gerald. 1993. Mistrust, the hidden obstacle to empowerment. *HR* Magazine (November): 66-74.

Avolio, Brice J., and Bernard M. Bass. 1988. Transformational leadership, charisma, and beyond. In *Emerging Leadership Vistas,* ed. James G. Hunt, B. Hajaram Baliga, H. Peter Dachler, and Chester Schriesheim. Lexington, MA: Lexington Books.

Baker, R. P., and D. S. North. 1984. *The 1975 refugees.* Washington, DC: New Trans Century Foundation.

Bandura, Albert. 1982. Self-efficacy mechanism in human behavior. *American Psychologist* (February): 122-47.

Barnett, John, Rita Weathersby, and John Aram. 1995. American cultural values: Shedding cowboy ways for global thinking. *Business Forum* (Winter): 9-13.

Bass, Bernard M. 1985. *Leadership and performance beyond expectations.* New York: Free Press.

———. 1990. *Handbook of leadership.* New York: Free Press.

Bateman, Thomas, and C. Zeithaind. 1990. *Management: Function and strategy.* Homewood, IL: Irwin.

Bennet, James. 1993, September 30. Mercedes selects Alabama site. *New York Times.*

Bennett, Claudette E. 1994. The Asian and Pacific Islander population in the United States. Washington, DC: Racial Statistics Branch, Population Division, U.S. Bureau of the Census.

Blenkner, Margaret. 1965. *Social work and family relationships in Latin life.* Englewood Cliffs, NJ: Prentice Hall.

Bonacich, E. 1973. *A theory of middleman minority.* New York: John Wiley.

Bond, Michael Harrison. 1994. *Beyond the Chinese face: Insights from psychology.* Hong Kong: Oxford University Press.

Bull, R., and N. Rumsey. 1988. *The social psychology of facial appearance.* London: Springer-Verlag.

Burke, R. J., and C. A. McKeen. 1990. Mentoring in organizations. *Journal of Business Ethics* 9:317-22.

Burns, T., and G. H. Stalker. 1966. *The management of innovation.* London: Tavistock.

Cabezas, A., L. Shinagawa, and G. Kawaguchi. 1986-1987. New inquiries into the socioeconomic status of Pilipino Americans in California. *Amerasia Journal* 13:1-22.

Campbell, John P., Marvin D. Dunnette, Edward E. Lawler III, and Karl E. Weick. 1970. *Managerial behavior performance and effectiveness.* New York: McGraw-Hill.

Caplan, N., J. K. Whitmore, and M. H. Choy. 1989. *The boat people and their achievement in America.* Ann Arbor: University of Michigan Press.

Carnevale, Anthony, and Susan Stone. 1994. Diversity—Beyond the Gold Rule. *Training and Development* (October): 44.

———. 1995. *The American mosaic.* (New York: McGraw-Hill.

Carter, Deborah, and Reginald Wilson. 1992. *Minorities in higher education.* A report prepared for the American Council on Education, Washington, DC.

Caudill, William, and George De Vos. 1972. Achievement, culture, and personality: The case of the Japanese Americans. In *Socialization for Achievement: The Cultural Psychology of the Japanese,* ed. George A. De Vos. Berkeley: University of California Press.

Chai, Chu, and Winberg Chai. 1973. Confucianism. *Barons.* Hauppauge, NY:

Chan, Sucheng. 1991a. *Asian Americans: An interpretive history.* Boston: Twayne.

———. 1991b. *The exclusion of Chinese women.* Philadelphia: Temple University Press.

Chang, Stephen. 1986. *The integral management of Tao.* San Francisco: Tao Publishing.

Chen, J. 1980. *The Chinese of America.* New York: Harper & Row.

Chen, Nina. 1995, July 7. Spotlight on Pacific Islanders. *Asian Week.*

Cho Sung-Nam, and Herbert Barringer. 1989. *Koreans in the United States.* Honolulu: Center for Korean Studies.

Choy, B. Y. 1979. *Koreans in America.* Chicago: Nelson-Hall.

Chung, R. L. 1988. People's Republic of China. In *Comparative Management: A Regional View,* ed. R. Nath. Cambridge, MA: Ballinger.

Clinton, Hilary Rodham. 1996. *It takes a village.* New York: Simon & Schuster.

Clinton, William J. 1997. Asian Pacific American Heritage Month 1997: A proclamation. Speech given on 5 May in Washington, DC.

Conroy, Hillary E. 1953. *The Japanese frontier in Hawaii 1868-1898.* Berkeley: University of California Press.

Copeland, L. 1988. Valuing workplace diversity. *Personnel* (June): 52-60.

Cordova, F. 1983. *Filipinos: Forgotten Asian Americans.* Dubuque, IA: Kendall/Hunt.

Cox, Taylor H. 1991. The multicultural organization. *Academy of Management Executive* 34:34-7.

———. 1994. *Cultural diversity in organizations.* San Francisco: Berrett-Koehler.

Cox, Taylor H., S. Lobel, and P. McLeod. 1991. Effects of ethnic group culture differences on cooperative and competitive behavior on a group task. *Academy of Management Journal* 34:827-47.

Daft, Richard L. 1994. *Management.* Chicago: Dryden.

Daniels, Roger. 1971. *Concentration Camps USA: Japanese Americans and World War II.* New York: New York University Press.

De Vos, George A. 1973. *Socialization for achievement: The cultural psychology of the Japanese.* Berkeley: University of California Press.

———. 1995. Ethnic pluralism: Conflict and accommodations. In *Ethnic Identity,* ed. Lola Romanucci-Ross and George A. De Vos. Walnut Creek, CA: AltaMira.

De Vos, George A., and Hiroshi Wagatsuma. 1995. Culture identity in Japan. In *Ethnic Identity,* ed. Lola Romanucci-Ross and George A. De Vos. Walnut Creek, CA: AltaMira.

Dentzer, Susan. 1990. The coming global boom. *U.S. News & World Report,* 16 July, 22-7.

Der, Henry, and Howard Ting. 1992. *The broken ladder: Asian Americans in city government.* San Francisco: CAA.

Dickey-Bryant, L., J. L. Mendoza, and L. Lautenschlager. 1986. Facial attractiveness and its relation to occupational success. *Journal of Applied Psychology* 21:16-29.

DuBrin, Andrew. 1995. *Leadership: Research findings, practice, and skills.* Boston: Houghton Mifflin.

Dumaine, Brian. 1993. Payoff from the new management. *Fortune,* 13 December, 5-9.

Dunning, B. B. 1989. Vietnamese in America: The adaptation of the 1975-1979 arrivals. In *Refugees as Immigrants,* ed. D. W. Haines. Totowa, NJ: Rowman and Littlefield.

Earley, Christopher. 1994. Self or group? Cultural effects on training on self-efficacy and performance. *Administrative Science Quarterly* (March): 89-117.

Escueta, Eugenia, and Eileen O'Brien. 1991. *Asian Americans in higher education: Trends and issues.* A report prepared for the American Council on Education, Washington, DC.

Espiritu, Yen Le. 1992. *Asian American panethnicity: Bridging institutions and identities.* Philadelphia: Temple University Press.

Ester, G., and Joel M. Maring. 1977. *Historical and cultural dictionary of the Philippines.* New York: Harper & Row.

Fawcett, James T., and Ben V. Cavino. Eds. 1987. *Pacific bridges: The new immigration from Asia and the Pacific Islands.* New York: Center for Migration Studies.

Fein, D. J. 1990. Racial and ethnic differences in U.S. Census omission rates. *Demography* (March): 285-301.

Fernandez, John P. 1993. *The diversity advantage.* New York: Lexington Books.

Finnan, C. R., and R. A. Cooperstein. 1983. *Southeast Asian refugee resettlement at the local level.* Menlo Park, CA: SRI International.

Fischer, B. 1988. Whiz kid image masks problems of Asian Americans. *NEA Today* (June): 14-5.

Fong, Pauline, and Amado Cabezas. 1980. Economic and employment status of Asian Pacific women. U.S. Department of Education Conference on the Educational and Occupational Needs of Asian Pacific American Women, October.

Forsythe, S. M. 1990. Effect of applicants' clothing on interviewers' decision to hire. *Journal of Applied Social Psychology* 20:1579-95.

Foster, B., G. Jackson, W. Cross, B. Jackson, and R. Hardiman. 1988. Workforce diversity and business. *Training and Development Journal* (April): 38-42.

Fottler, M. D., and T. Bain. 1980. Sex differences in occupational aspirations. *Academy of Management Journal* 23:144-9.

Frame, Donald. Trans. 1948. *The complete essays of Montaigne*. Palo Alto, CA: Stanford University Press.

French, John, and Bertram Raven. 1960. *The bases of social power*. Ann Arbor: University of Michigan Press.

Frese, Michael, Wolfgang Kring, Andrea Soose, and Jeannette Zempel. 1966. Personal initiative at work: Differences between East and West Germany. *Academy of Management Journal* 9:37-63.

Garn, Stanley M. 1971. *Human races*. 3d ed. Springfield, IL: Charles C Thomas.

Gibson, James L., John H. Ivancevich, and James H. Donnelly. 1997. *Organizations: Behavior, structure, and processes*. 9th ed. Homewood, IL: Irwin.

Gist, Marilyn E. 1987. Self-efficacy: Implications for organization behavior and human resources management. *Academy of Management Review* 12:472-85.

Glass Ceiling Commission. 1995. *Good for business: Making full use of the nation's human capital*. Washington, DC: U.S. Government Printing Office.

Glaser, Barney, and Anselm L. Strauss. 1973. *Grounded theory: Strategies for qualitative research*. Chicago: Aldine.

Glazer, Nathan, and Daniel Moynihan. 1963. *Beyond the melting pot*. Cambridge: MIT Press.

Gold, S. 1992. *Refugee communities: A comparative field study*. Newbury Park, CA: Sage.

Goldsby, Richard A. 1977. *Race and races*. 2d ed. New York: Macmillan.

Goleman, Daniel. 1996. *Emotional intelligence*. New York: Bantam.

Greenhaus, Jeffrey H., and Nicholas J. Beutell. 1985. Sources of conflict between work and family roles. *Academy of Management Review* 10:76-88.

Groves, Ross. 1991. *The Disney touch*. New York: Irwin.

Hampden-Turner, Charles. 1989. *Corporate culture and leadership effectiveness*. New York: McGraw-Hill.

———. 1990. *Charting the corporate mind*. London: Macmillan.

Hampden-Turner, Charles, and Alfons Trompenaars. 1993. *The seven cultures of capitalism*. New York: Doubleday.

Handy, Charles B. 1976. *On roles and interactions*. London: Hazall Watson & Viney.

———. 1986. On the motivation to work. In *Understanding Organizations*. Hammondsworth, Middlesex, UK: Penguin.

Harrison, Roger. 1972. How to describe your organization. *Harvard Business Review*, September/October, 77-85.

Heilbroner, Robert L., and Lester Thurow. 1987. *Economics explained*. New York: Simon & Schuster.

Helweg, A., and U. Helweg. 1990. *The immigrant success story: East Indians.* Pittsburgh: University of Pennsylvania Press.

Henderson, Lucius S., III, et al. 1995. *Report on six focus groups with Asian, Black and Hispanic executives in three cities on issues related to the glass ceiling in corporate America.* A report prepared for the U.S. Department of Labor, Washington, DC.

Hennig, Margaret, and Anne Jardin. 1978. *Managerial women.* New York: Simon & Schuster.

Hensley, Wayne. 1987. Height and occupational success. *Psychological Reports* (June): 163.

Herrnstein, Richard, and Charles Murray. 1994. *The bell curve: Intelligence and class structure in American life.* New York: Free Press.

Herzberg, Frederick, B. Mausner, and B. Syndman. 1959. *The motivation to work.* New York: John Wiley.

Hewstone, M., and C. Ward. 1985. Ethnocentrism and causal attribution in Southeast Asia. *Journal of Personality and Social Psychology* 48:614-23.

Hofstede, Geert. 1984. The cultural relativity of the quality of life concept. *Academy of Management Review* 9:389-98.

———. 1991. *Cultures and organizations: Software of the mind.* London: McGraw-Hill.

———. 1992. Cultural constraints in management theories. Paper presented at the annual meeting of the National Academy of Management, 11 August.

Hofstede, Geert, and Michael H. Bond. 1988. The Confucius connection: From cultural roots to economic growth. *Organizational Dynamics* (Spring): 4-21.

Holt, David H. 1995. *Management: Principles and practices.* 3d ed. Englewood Cliffs, NJ: Prentice Hall.

House, Robert J. 1977. The path-goal theory of leadership effectiveness. *Administrative Science Quarterly* (September): 321-39.

House, Robert J., and Terence R. Mitchell. 1974. A path-goal theory of leadership. *Journal of Contemporary Business* (Autumn): 81-98.

Hsia, Jayzia. 1988. *Asian Americans in higher education and at work.* Hillsdale, NJ: Lawrence Erlbaum.

Hurh, W. M., and K. C. Kim. 1990. Religious participation of Korean immigrants in the U.S. *Journal of the Scientific Study of Religion* 19:19-34.

Ivancevich, John. 1969. Perceived need satisfaction of domestic versus overseas managers. *Journal of Applied Psychology* (August): 274-8.

Iwata, Edward. Ed. 1993. *Qualified, but . . . : A report on the glass ceiling issues facing Asian Pacific Americans in Silicon Valley.* A report prepared by Asian Americans for Community Involvement, San Jose, CA.

Iyer, Pico. 1993, Fall. The global village finally arrives. In a special issue of *Time* magazine, "The new face of America: How immigrants are shaping the world's first multinational society."

Jasper, C. R. 1990. Perceptions of salespersons' appearance and evaluation of job performance. *Perceptual and Motor Skills* 71:563-6.

Jenkins, M. C., and T. V. Atkins. 1990. Perceptions of acceptable dress by corporate and noncorporate recruiters. *Journal of Human Behavior and Learning* 7:38-46.

Jensen, J. M. 1988. *Passage from India: Asian Indian immigrants in North America.* New Haven, CT: Yale University Press.

Keller, Robert T. 1989. A test of the path-goal theory of leadership with need for clarity as a moderator in research and development organizations. *Journal of Applied Psychology* (April): 208-12.

Kim, I. S. 1981. *New urban immigrants: The Korean community.* Princeton, NJ: Princeton University Press.

Kim, K. C., and W. M. Hurh. 1985. Ethnic resources utilization of Korean immigrant entrepreneurs in the Chicago minority area. *International Migration Review* 19:82-111.

Kingston, Maxine Hong. 1976. *The woman warrior.* New York: Knopf.

Kinlaw, Dennis C. 1991. *Developing superior work teams.* Lexington, MA: Lexington Books.

Kitano, Harry, and Roger Daniels. 1988. *Asian Americans: Emerging minorities.* Englewood Cliffs, NJ: Prentice Hall.

Klass, Morton, and Hal Hellman. 1981. *The kind of mankind: An introduction to race and racism.* New York: Harper & Row.

Klassen, Michael L. 1990. Stereotypical beliefs about appearance: Implications for retailing and consumer issues. *Perceptual and Motor Skills* 71:519-28.

Klassen, Michael L., Cynthia R. Jasper, and Richard J. Harris. 1993. The role of physical appearance in managerial decisions. *Journal of Business and Psychology* 8:181-98.

Korn, P. 1991. Agent Orange in Vietnam: The persisting poison. *The Nation,* 8 April, 440-6.

Kouzes, James M., and Barry Posner. 1995. *The leadership challenge.* San Francisco: Jossey-Bass.

Kram, Kathy E. 1985. *Mentoring at work: Developmental relationships in organization life.* Glenview, IL: Scott, Foresman.

———. 1993. Phases of the mentor relationship. *Academy of Management Journal* 36:608-25.

Krech, D., R. S. Crutchfield, and E. L. Ballachey. 1962. *Individual and society.* New York: McGraw-Hill.

Labich, Kenneth. 1991. Take control of your career. *Fortune,* 18 November, 87-96.

Lawler, Edward, and J. L. Suttle. 1972. A casual correction test of the need hierarchy concept. *Organization Behavior and Human Performance* (April): 265-87.

Lawrence, P. R., and J. W. Lorsch. 1967. *Organization and environment.* Cambridge, MA: Harvard University Press.

Le, Ngoan. 1993. The case of the Southeast Asian refugees. In *The State of Asian Pacific Americans: Policy Issues to the Year 2000.* Los Angeles: LEAP Publications.

Lee, Robert G. 1976. *The origins of Chinese immigration to the United States, 1848-1882.* San Francisco: Chinese Historical Society of America.

Lee, Rose Hum. 1952. *Chinese in the U.S.: The war has changed their lives.* San Francisco: Chinese Press.

Lee, S. M., and K. Yamanaka. 1990. Patterns of Asian American intermarriage and marital assimilation. *Journal of Comparative Family Studies* 21:287-305.

Light, Ivan, and P. Bhachu. 1993. *Immigration and entrepreneurship.* New York: Transaction Books.

Light, Ivan, and Edna Bonacich. 1988. *Immigrant entrpreneurs: Koreans in L.A.* Berkeley: University of California Press.

Liu, J., P. Ong, and C. Rosenstein. 1991. Filipino immigration to the United States. *International Migration Review* 25:487-517.

Locke, Edwin. 1991. *The essence of leadership.* New York: Macmillan.

Locke, Gary. 1997. One mile, one hundred years. Gubernatorial inaugural address given in January in Olympia, Washington.

Lopez, Julie Amparano. 1992, August 5. Firms elevate heads of diversity programs. *Wall Street Journal.*

Maslow, Abraham. 1954. *Motivation and personality.* New York: Harper & Row.

Matloff, Norman. 1995, December 1. When it comes to African Americans, why do so many Asian Americans tolerate intolerance? *Asian Week.*

Maznevski, Martha. 1994. Understanding our differences: Performance in decision-making groups with diverse members. *Human Relations* (May): 531-2.

McCarrol, Thomas. 1993, Fall. It's a mass market no more. In a special issue of *Time* magazine, "The new face of America: How immigrants are shaping the world's first multinational society," 60-5.

McClelland, David C. 1962. Business drive and national achievement. *Harvard Business Review* (July/ August): 99-112.

———. 1965. Toward a theory of motive acquisition. *American Psychologist* (May): 321-33.

———. 1988. *Human motivation.* Cambridge, UK: Cambridge University Press.

McKissack, Patricia, and Frederick McKissack. 1994. *African American scientists.* Brookfield, CT: Milbrook Press.

McManns, James. Ed. 1993, Fall. The new face of America: How immigrants are shaping the world's first multinational society. Special issue of *Time* magazine.

Miceli, Marcia P., and Janet P. Near. 1989. The incidence of wrongdoing, whistle-blowing, and retaliation. *Employee Responsibilities and Rights Journal* (June): 91-108.

Min, Pyong Gap. 1989. Korean immigrant entrepreneurship: A mulitvariate analysis. *Journal of Urban Affairs* 10:197-212.

————. 1991. Cultural and economic boundaries of Korean ethnicity. *Ethnic and Racial Studies* 14:225-41.

————. 1995. Korean Americans. In *Asian Americans: Contemporary Trends and Issues,* ed. R. G. Rumbaut. Thousand Oaks, CA: Sage.

————. Ed. 1995. *Asian Americans: Contemporary trends and issues.* Thousand Oaks, CA: Sage.

Mintzberg, Henry. 1995. The five basic parts of the organization. In *Classics of Organization Theory,* ed. J. M. Shafritz and T. S. Ott. Belmont, CA: Wadsworth.

Mitchell, T. T., C. M. Smyser, and S. E. Weed. 1975. Locus of control: Supervision and work satisfaction. *Academy of Management Journal* 18:623-31.

Morrill, C., and C. K. Thomas. 1992. Organizational conflict management as disputing process: The problem of social escalation. *Human Communication Research* (March): 400-28.

Morrison, A. M., K. P. White, and E. Van Velsor. 1987. *Breaking the glass ceiling.* Reading, MA: Addison-Wesley.

Morrow, P. C. 1990. Physical attractiveness and selective decision making. *Journal of Management* 16:46-60.

Narayanan, V. K., and Raghu Nath. 1994. *Organization theory: A strategic approach.* Boston: Irwin.

Nord, Walter R. Ed. 1976. *Concepts and controversy in organizational behavior.* Santa Monica, CA: Goodyear.

Norton, Rob. 1994. Strategies for the new export boom. *Fortune,* 22 August, 67-83.

Omi, Michael, and Howard Winant. 1994. *Racial formation in the United States: From 1960s to the 1990s.* 2d ed. New York: Routledge.

Ong, Paul. Ed. 1994. *The state of Asian Pacific American economic diversity, issues and policies.* Los Angeles: LEAP Asian Pacific American Public Policy Institute.

Onishi, Normitsu. 1996, May 30. New sense of race arises among Asian Americans. *New York Times.*

Pacelle, Mitchell. 1997, February 19. Going global: Asian investors buy up hotels in U.S., Europe, but move cautiously. *Wall Street Journal.*

Patterson, W. 1988. *The Korean frontier in America: Immigration to Hawaii, 1896-1910.* Honolulu: University of Hawaii Press.

Peretz, Martin. Ed. 1994, October 31. A class thing. In Race and I.Q.—An apologia: Murray and Herrnstein. *The New Republic,* 11-2.

Peterson, J. 1989, August 6. Asian entrepreneurs. *Los Angeles Times.*

Peterson, Mark F., Jyuji Misumi, and Charlene Herreid. 1994. Adapting Japanese PM leadership field research for use in Western organizations. *Applied Psychology* (January): 49-74.

Phegan, Barry. 1995. *Developing your company culture.* Berkeley, CA: Context Press.

Pido, L. L. 1986. *The Pilipinos in America: Macro/micro dimensions of immigration and integration.* New York: Center for Migration Studies.

Porter, Lyman. 1961. A study of perceived need satisfaction in bottom and middle management jobs. *Journal of Applied Psychology* (February): 1-10.

————. 1963. Job attitudes in management: Perceived deficiencies in need fulfillment as a function of size of the company. *Journal of Applied Psychology* (December): 386-97.

Rachman, David, Michael Mescon, Courtland Bovee, and John Thill. 1996. *Business today.* 8th ed. San Francisco: McGraw-Hill.

Reich, Robert B. 1991. *The work of nations: Preparing ourselves for 21st century capitalism.* New York: Knopf.

Reid, Barbara A. 1994. Mentorships ensure equal opportunity. *Personnel* (November): 122-3.

Reimers, David M. 1985. *Still the golden door: The Third World comes to America.* New York: Columbia University Press.

Reiss, Paula, and Delores Thurgood. 1993. *Summary report of doctorate recipients from United States universities.* Washington, DC: National Academy Press.

Robbins, Stephen P. 1974. *Managing organizational conflict.* Englewood Cliffs, NJ: Prentice Hall.

Rosen, Jeffrey, and Charles Lane. 1994, October 31. Neo-Nazis! Scouring the bell curve's footnotes. *New Republic,* 14-5.

Rotter, Julian B. 1966. Generalized expectancies for internal vs. external control of reinforcement. *Psychological Monographs* 1 (609): 80.

Rumbaut, Ruben G. 1995. Vietnamese, Laotian, and Cambodian Americans. In *Asian Americans: Contemporary Trends and Issues.* Thousand Oaks, CA: Sage.

Ryne, Sara, and Benson Rosen. 1994. What makes diversity programs work? *Human Resources* (October): 67-75.

Sanford, Nevitt. 1964. *Family impact on personality: The point of view of a psycho-analyst.* Champaign: University of Illinois Press.

————. 1967. *Self and society: Social change and individual development.* New York: Atherton.

Schein, Edgar H. 1985. *Organizational culture and leadership.* San Francisco: Jossey-Bass.

Schwartz, F. 1989. Management women and the new facts of life. *Harvard Business Review,* January/ February, 65-76.

Shaver, Kathy G. 1995. The entrepreneurial personality myth. *Business and Economic Review* (June): 20-3.

Shinagawa, Larry Hajime. 1994. Racial classification of Asian Americans. Paper presented at the Office of Management and Budget hearing, San Francisco, 15 July.

————. 1996. The impact of immigration on the demography of Asian Pacific Americans. In *Reframing the Immigration Debate,* ed. Bill Ong Hing and Ronald Lee. Los Angeles: LEAP Publications.

Shinagawa, Larry Hajime, and Gin Yong Pang. 1996. Asian American Pan-Ethnicity and Intermarriage. *Amerasia Journal* 22:3, 32.

Simon, Herbert. 1960. *The new science of management decision.* New York: Harper & Row.

Skinner, B. F. 1971. *Beyond freedom and dignity.* New York: Knopf.

Steward, Kim A. 1997. Notes on transformational leadership. In supplemental sourcebook to J. Gibson, J. Ivancevich, and J. Donnelly, *Organizations.* Homewood, IL: Irwin.

Strand, Paul J., and Woodrow Jones, Jr. 1985. *Indochinese refugees in America.* Raleigh, NC: Duke University Press.

Sue, Francis. 1991. *Confucians.* Newbury Park, CA: Sage.

Sue, Stanley, and Harry Kitano. 1973. Stereotypes as a measure of success. *Journal of Social Issues* 29 (2): 83-98.

Sue, S., N. Zane, and D. Sue. 1985. Where are the Asian American leaders and executives? *Research Review* 9:13-5.

Tagaki, C., and T. Ishisaka. 1982. *Cultural awareness in the human services.* Englewood Cliffs, NJ: Prentice Hall.

Takagi, Dana. 1992. *The retreat from race: Asian American admissions and racial politics.* New Brunswick, NJ: Rutgers University Press.

Takaki, Ron. 1987. *From different shores: Perspectives on race and ethnicity in America.* New York: Oxford University Press.

————. 1989. *Strangers from a different shore: A history of Asian Americans.* Boston: Little, Brown.

Tan, Amy. 1989. *The joy luck club.* New York: Putnam.

Tannen, D. 1990. *You just don't understand: Men and women in conversation.* New York: William Morrow.

Then, Deborah. 1986. *The impact of physical attraction.* Palo Alto, CA: Stanford University Press.

Tresemer, David. Ed. 1976. Current trends in research on fear of success. *Sex Roles* special issue, Spring.

Tse, D. K., K. Lee, I. Vertinsky, and D. A. Wehrung. 1988. Does culture matter? A cross-cultural study of exectives' choice, decisiveness, and risk adjustment in interational marketing. *Journal of Marketing* 52: 81-95.

Unterberger, Amy. Ed. 1995. *Who's who among Asian Americans.* Detroit, MI: Gale Research.

U.S. Bureau of the Census. 1993. 1990 census of the population, Asian and Pacific Islanders in the U.S. Washington, DC: U.S. Government Printing Office.

———. 1993b. We the Americans: Asians. Washington, DC: U.S. Government Printing Office.

———. 1993c. We the Americans: Pacific Islanders in the United States. Washington, DC: U.S. Government Printing Office.

———. 1994a. Household income by ethnicity. Washington, DC: U.S. Government Printing Office.

———. 1994b. 1990 census of the population, general social and economic characteristics in the United States. Washington, DC: U.S. Government Printing Office.

———. 1996a. The Asian & Pacific Island population in the United States. Washington, DC: Racial Statistics Branch, Population Division, U.S. Bureau of the Census (http://www.census.gov).

———. 1996b. Current population survey conducted by the U.S. Bureau of the Census, Statistical Branch (http://www.census.gov).

U.S. Commission on Civil Rights. 1992. Civil rights issues facing Asian Pacific Americans in the 1990s. Washington, DC: U.S. Government Printing Office.

Van Maanen, John. 1978. People processing: Strategies for organizational socialization. *Organizational Dynamics* (Summer): 18-36.

Vandushaf, Sarah. 1987. The prejudice of height. *Psychology Today* (March): 110.

Vroom, Victor, and Arthur Jago. 1988. *The new leadership: Managing participation in organizations.* Englewood Cliffs, NJ: Prentice Hall.

Wain, Barry. 1981. *The refused: The agony of the Indochinese refugees.* New York: Simon & Schuster.

Wakatsuki, Yasui. 1979. Japanese emigration to the United States, 1866-1924. *Perspectives in American History* 12:389-516.

Walker, Charles, and Robert Guest. 1952. *The man on the assembly line.* Cambridge, MA: Harvard University Press.

Wang, Sing-Wu. 1976. *The organization of Chinese emigration, 1848-1888.* San Francisco: Chinese Material Center.

White, Joseph, and Carol Hymowitz. 1997, February 10. Broken glass: Watershed generation of women executives is rising to the top. *Wall Street Journal.*

White, Robert W. 1972. *The enterprise of living: Growth and organization in personality.* New York: Holt, Rinehart & Winston.

Whiting, J. W., and B. B. Whiting. 1980. Contributions of anthropology to the methods of studying child rearing. In *Handbook of Research in Child Development.* New York: John Wiley.

Williams, R. B. 1988. *Religions of immigrants from India and Pakistan: New threads in the American tapestry.* Cambridge, UK: Cambridge University Press.

Wolcott, Harry F. 1995. *The art of fieldwork.* Walnut Creek, CA: AltaMira.

Wong, M. G. 1986. Post-1965 immigrants: Where do they come from, where are they now, and where are they going? *Annals of the American Academy of Political and Social Science* 487: 150-68.

Woo, Deborah. 1990. The overrepresentation of Asian Americans: Red herrings and yellow perils. *Sage Race Relations Abstract* 142 (2).

————. 1994. The glass ceiling and Asian Americans. A report prepared by the Glass Ceiling Commission, U.S. Department of Labor.

Woodward, Joan. 1965. *Industrial organization: Theory and practice.* London: Oxford University Press.

Wu, Diana Ting Liu. 1981. Immigrant women in professional occupations: Inherent abilities or focused energy? Working paper, Saint Mary's College of California.

————. 1992. *A short history and overview of organization theory.* Moraga: Saint Mary's College of California.

Yang, Jeff. 1995. A national Asian American sex survey. *A. Magazine: Inside Asian America,* August/ September.

Yankelovich, D., and J. Immerivoki. 1983. *Putting the work ethic to work.* New York: Public Agenda Foundation.

Yip, Althea. 1997, January 3. The big picture. *Asian Week.*

————. 1997, March 7. Careers on the fast track. *Asian Week.*

Yu, E., and W. T. Liu. 1980. *Fertility and kinship in the Philippines.* Notre Dame, IN: University of Notre Dame Press.

Zenner, W. 1991. *Minorities in the middle: A cross-cultural analysis.* Albany: State University of New York Press.

# About the Author

DIANA TING LIU WU, Ph.D., has been a Professor at Saint Mary's College of California since 1981. She is a former chairperson of the Business Administration Department there and has conducted research and published numerous articles on Asian Pacific Americans and women and organizations. She has been a guest lecturer on the subject of organizational psychology on Hong Kong radio and television stations and was invited by the Chinese Academy of Science to tour and lecture about American business in the cities of the People's Republic of China. She has also given lectures to the World Affairs Council, World Trade Center, Rotary Clubs, Soroptomists Clubs, and various community groups and scholarly conferences. Last year, she was interviewed by KTSF Channel 26 in connection with her ongoing research into Asian Pacific Americans in the workplace.

Dr. Wu, an eleventh-generation descendent of a large Chinese family, was born in Shanghai, China, and left that country in 1948 with her parents, going first to Hong Kong. She traveled extensively in Southeast Asia and came to the United States in 1958 after her father lost his business ventures in Saigon,

Vietnam. She studied accounting in her undergraduate work and received an M.B.A. degree from New York University. In 1976, after years of being an accountant and business woman, wife and mother, she joined the graduate program of the Wright Institute in Berkeley, California, under Dr. R. Nevitt Sanford and received her Ph.D. in organizational psychology in 1980.

# Index